The Unfractured Faith
of Erik Routley

The Unfractured Faith of Erik Routley

From Brighton to Princeton

Nancy L. Graham

LEXINGTON BOOKS/FORTRESS ACADEMIC
Lanham • Boulder • New York • London

Published by Lexington Books/Fortress Academic
Lexington Books is an imprint of The Rowman & Littlefield Publishing Group, Inc.
4501 Forbes Boulevard, Suite 200, Lanham, Maryland 20706
www.rowman.com

86-90 Paul Street, London EC2A 4NE, United Kingdom

Copyright © 2024 by The Rowman & Littlefield Publishing Group, Inc.

The article "Books that Shaped My Life," copyright © 1977 by the Christian Century. Reprinted by permission from the September 2, 1977, issue of the *Christian Century*. www.christiancentury.org.

All rights reserved. No part of this book may be reproduced in any form or by any electronic or mechanical means, including information storage and retrieval systems, without written permission from the publisher, except by a reviewer who may quote passages in a review.

British Library Cataloguing in Publication Information Available

Library of Congress Cataloging-in-Publication Data

Names: Graham, Nancy L., author.
Title: The unfractured faith of Erik Routley : from Brighton to Princeton / Nancy L. Graham.
Description: Lanham : Lexington Books/Fortress Academic, 2024. | Includes bibliographical references and index. | Summary: "Nancy L. Graham unveils the extraordinary life of the churchman and musician, Erik Routley, the most significant hymnologist of the twentieth century. Using anecdotes from his personal correspondence, the foundations of his faith, scholarship, and pastoral relationships are made public"— Provided by publisher.
Identifiers: LCCN 2023034511 (print) | LCCN 2023034512 (ebook) | ISBN 9781978714045 (cloth) | ISBN 9781978714052 (epub)
Subjects: LCSH: Routley, Erik. | Composers—England—Biography. | Hymn writers—England—Biography. | Church musicians—England—Biography.
Classification: LCC ML410.R8807 G73 2024 (print) | LCC ML410.R8807 (ebook) | DDC 780.92 [B]—dc23/eng/20230815
LC record available at https://lccn.loc.gov/2023034511
LC ebook record available at https://lccn.loc.gov/2023034512

∞™ The paper used in this publication meets the minimum requirements of American National Standard for Information Sciences—Permanence of Paper for Printed Library Materials, ANSI/NISO Z39.48-1992.

*"Speak to one another in psalms and hymns and spiritual songs,
Singing to the Lord and making melody in your heart,
Giving thanks always for all things unto God,
In the name of our Lord Jesus Christ."
Ephesians 5:19–20*

To Robin A. Leaver

*In memoriam
Carlton R. Young (1926–2023)*

Contents

Foreword	ix
by Nicholas Routley	
Preface	xi
Introduction	xiii
Abbreviations	xv
Author's Notes	xvii
Chapter 1: Beginnings	1
Chapter 2: Magdalen and Mansfield, 1936–1943	21
Chapter 3: Wednesbury and Dartford, 1943–1948	41
Chapter 4: Mansfield College, 1948–1959	49
Chapter 5: Edinburgh, 1959–1967	79
Chapter 6: Newcastle upon Tyne, 1967–1974	105
Chapter 7: Princeton, 1975–1982	127
Epilogue	171
Acknowledgments	177
Appendix A: Book Dedications	181
Appendix B: "The Books That Shaped My Life"	185
by Erik Routley	
Appendix C: Statement from Sir Ronald Johnson	187
Appendix D: Letter to Friends	189

Appendix E: Letter to John Wilson about *Ecumenical Praise*	191
Appendix F: Prophetic Article from the *Church Times*	193
Bibliography	199
Index	207
About the Author	217

Foreword

When my father died at the age of sixty-four in 1982, a half-finished mathematical crossword he was composing was found in one of his jacket pockets and a detective novel was lying on his bedside table. At his funeral in Princeton, more than four hundred people filled the small chapel at Westminster Choir College. Each person there felt a special connection with him; he was known so well, by so many. However, I think it is fair to say that no one, apart perhaps from my mother, Margaret, knew him in all the disparate facets of his life.

Erik Routley wrote thirty-nine books and more than one thousand articles in which he expounded his thoughts about theology, hymnology, church music, and detective fiction (though not, I think, mathematical crosswords). At least one compendium of tributes, *Duty and Delight*, brings together some of these heterogeneous subjects; yet what is lacking among all this writing is a biography.

It is this lacuna that Nancy Graham has addressed in the present book. It is the first biography of Erik Routley, a man with so much excess brain power that he had to burn some of it up writing mathematical crosswords, but still not enough to ever give up smoking his pipe. Drawing much from Erik's prolific corpus of letters, and the gathered material from Nancy Wicklund Gray, Graham presents his life through the lens of both his daily and professional lives. She shows not only that his work was his life but also, convincingly and much more unusually, that his life was his work.

As with any such enterprise, one of the most important skills is knowing what to leave out. What Graham has included will contain surprises even for those who thought they knew him well, and yet she presents a picture they will instantly recognize.

Nicholas Routley
Georgica, New South Wales, Australia
January 12, 2023

Preface

Erik Routley made important contributions in so many areas, and writing this book has required a constant refocusing to keep this his biography and not a summation of his legacy. The story here is about the life of Erik Routley. It is not about Oxford, Westminster Choir College, the United Reformed Church, music and theology, hymnals, or even detective novels. He, like most of us, was a product of his upbringing and education. Erik was happily married and fathered three children. He had a dog and a cat. He put up with car problems, housing repairs, financial worries, and was concerned about the well-being of his wife, Margaret, and the futures of Nicholas, Patrick, and Priscilla. Erik wasn't raised a Calvinist, but he learned the *Shorter Catechism* and knew that his duty and delight were to glorify God and enjoy Him forever.

The intensely private Dr. Routley was enigmatic and beyond labels. He could not even be defined by nationality; he happily lived in Great Britain for nearly fifty-eight years and never gave up his citizenship, yet he led a rich life in Princeton for his last seven. His colleagues in the UK saw a Reformed churchman, preacher, and writer with a deep understanding of hymns. Though he was a Fellow of the Royal School of Church Music (RSCM), an organist, and a composer, those pursuits always took place outside of his ministerial and tutorial obligations. In the United States, his grateful audiences understood him as a superb and remarkable musician and hymnologist who happened to be an ordained minister. Princeton Theological Seminary and Westminster Choir College gave Routley the chance to work in an academic environment, supporting students who wanted to learn what he wanted to teach: hymnody and liturgy, as well as his theological assertion that musicians and preachers are collaborative artists in service to the Gospel. In both countries his self-deprecating ebullient optimism, ready wit, distain of lazy mediocrity, subtle compassion, and profound faith made people listen. But his straightforward and pragmatic approach to life, his biting criticism, and his casual editing prompted many in Britain to begrudge his move to the United States, and Americans to resent what they saw as an arrogant judgment of their culture. This book will attempt to reconcile these perceptions into one unique figure—flawed, yes, but extraordinarily important.

Erik largely tells his own story here. Routley easily shared his thoughts in correspondence, and he famously typed an immediate response to every letter he received. In the foreword to the revised *A Panorama of Christian Hymnody*, Alan Luff ponders the existence of these letters and, in the case of those with John Wilson, their relevance to twentieth-century hymnody. Finding those letters was where I started, and fortunately they were not difficult to uncover. Routley saved few personal documents, but thankfully his close friends John Wilson, Geoffrey Beck, and Caryl Micklem did. Palace Green Library at Durham University holds over four hundred letters to John W. Wilson in the Fred Pratt Green Collection. Micklem and Beck letters are with the Routley papers at Talbott Library, as well as in private collections. The voices of many colleagues provide anecdotal details in interviews collected in the United States and England by Nancy Wicklund Gray from 1997 to 2004.

Routley's Mansfield has disappeared, and so has his Westminster Choir College; Congregationalism is barely recognizable, and the United Reformed Church (URC) is a struggling denomination. Yet Routley's assessment of the music of theology and the theology of music was developed through whatever these institutions had to offer, and his conclusions are prophetic and timeless. I don't think Routley would be dispirited or discouraged by these changes but instead excited and energized to see what great things come next.

Nancy L. Graham
Mobile, Alabama
April 2023

Introduction

Nancy Graham has produced a complete, detailed, and accurate account of the life and witness of the enigmatic, inscrutable, bigger-than-life Erik Routley as parent, educator, author, musician, and scholar, and how he was able bring it all together.

The author accomplishes this by carefully integrating her reader-friendly, inviting commentary, with Routley and others speaking for themselves via excerpts from their correspondence, conversations, and publications—a process enhanced with copious endnotes.

Salient features of Graham's account include a glimpse into church and secular educational systems in his time in the UK; his early childhood and youthful attraction to hymns and their singing, especially in Anglican school worship; as well as his aversion to the sounds of Reformed preachers preaching.

It is the first complete account of Routley's roles in developing the hymn explosion in the UK (late 1960s–mid-1980s) and importing it to North America, where a number of the hymns with their tunes found their way into a wide range of North American hymnals and their supplements, prompting Robin Leaver (b. 1939) to comment, "The British hymn explosion was more like a hymnal explosion in the United States."

In all this activity, Erik was not above controversy; indeed, he may have relished it, as seen in his widely published views, including "The Billy Graham Song Book" (1955), "Amen and Christian Hymnody" (1979), and "Sexist Language from a Distance" (1980).

A unique feature of this study chronicles Routley's spouse, Margaret, who sustained a relationship with family and friends in the UK with correspondence and extended visits—always with a view of their retiring in England following Erik's sabbatical leave in 1983 and one year of teaching. Margaret was an excellent author-writer and proofreader of words and music, as I learned firsthand in my interaction with her in producing a collection of

Erik's hymn tunes, carols, and texts: *Our Lives Be Praise: The Hymn Tunes, Carols and Texts of Erik Routley* (Hope Pub. Co., Carol Stream, IL, 1960).

The author sets straight two often-blemished self-serving accounts, one regarding who prompted and facilitated Routley's move in 1975 to the United States—the details of his transition from a church pastor to his brief time as a faculty member and director of the chapel at Princeton Theological Seminary and, later that year, becoming a professor of music at Westminster Choir College. Simultaneously, Routley conducted sojourns throughout North America as an itinerate preacher, lecturer, and conductor of hymn festivals.

The second is an accurate account of Routley's final days—October 6–8, 1982—that began in Princeton then moved to New Brunswick and his lecturing on the Reformed hymnal, *Rejoice in the Lord* (1985). Later in the day, he traveled to Nashville, where he presented lectures at the Scarritt Graduate School before dying suddenly from a heart attack in his motel room. Graham then recounts the funeral services in Trinity Episcopal Church, Princeton, and Bristol Chapel, Westminster Choir College, and the memorial at Westminster Abbey.

The enduring quality of this volume, in the author's words, is "Routley's assessment of the music of theology and the theology of music, and his conclusions are prophetic and timeless."

Carlton R. Young
Professor of Church Music, emeritus
Candler School of Theology
Emory University
Atlanta, Georgia
April 2023

Abbreviations

ABC	Augustine-Bristo Church
ABS	Alexander Brent Smith
BBC	British Broadcasting Company
BW	*British Weekly*
CD	*Cantate Domino*
CDH	*Canterbury Dictionary of Hymnology*
CCEW	Congregational Churches of England and Wales
CP	*Congregational Praise*
CUEW	Congregational Union of England and Wales
DD	*Duty and Delight*
DNB	*Dictionary of National Biography*
EP	*Ecumenical Praise*
ER	Erik Routley
FPG	Fred Pratt Green
GB	Geoffrey Beck
HPC	Hope Publishing Company
HSGBI	Hymn Society of Great Britain and Ireland
HSUSC	Hymn Society of the United States and Canada
JCR	Junior Commons Room
JWW	John Whittredge Wilson
LHB	Lee Hastings Bristol
MR	Margaret Routley
NWG	Nancy Wicklund Gray
NBTS	New Brunswick Theological Seminary
OLBP	*Our Lives Be Praise*
OUP	Oxford University Press
PTS	Princeton Theological Seminary
RCA	Reformed Church in America
RCM	Royal College of Music

RSCM	Royal School of Church Music
RIL	*Rejoice in the Lord*
SCR	Senior Commons Room
TCM	Thomas Caryl Micklem
URC	United Reformed Church
WCC*	Westminster Choir College
	World Council of Churches

Depends on context

Author's Notes

Nomenclature:

"Erik" is used when Erik Routley is in a personal or informal situation.
"Routley" is used when he is in a professional role.

Letters are identified by the receiver; e.g., "JWW" means a letter from Routley to John Wilson.

Journals are listed in the bibliography. Specific issues are in the endnotes.

Spelling, vocabulary, and structure used in the letters appear as the sender wrote them. In the body of the text, American spellings are used; e.g., "humourous" (letter, UK), "humorous" (text, US).

Dates are month/day/year in all contexts.

Chapter 1

Beginnings

BRIGHTON

The county of Somerset lies in the southwest corner of England. There are only two small cities within its borders: Bath and Wells. Though the nineteenth century experienced an industrial boom, the area's definitive strength is its agricultural reputation. The bitter apples of the Somerset orchards are the core of cider making, authorizing the area as cider's spiritual home.[1] In the nineteenth century, Congregationalism and its corresponding solid moral foundation ran through the heart of the region; Somerset people took life seriously, with a respect for learning, a strong work ethic, and an expectation that religious beliefs should lead to action. The arts were to be practiced as well as enjoyed, and helping people was a duty not to be outweighed by other commitments. On Monday morning, December 8, 1884, John Routley (1884–1966) was born in the hamlet of Brompton Ralph to William and Emma Routley, the sixth of seven children. William died in 1887, and Emma and her son John moved to the coastal city of Brighton in Sussex. She died there in 1903, leaving John to find his niche.

Without an advantageous family background or education, John relied on his fondness for numbers for steady employment as an accountant and financial manager.[2] Known personally as the quietest and most unassuming of men, over the years John's sound judgment, concern for others, polished speaking gifts, and idealistic outlook confirmed him as one of Brighton's most honored citizens.[3] As chair of the Brighton Council Finance Committee, he presented budgets and monetary concerns year after year without notes, relying on his astonishing memory.[4] In 1936 the Brighton City Council appointed John as mayor of Brighton for the customary one-year term.[5]

In April 1913, John married Eleanor Clark (1884–1963), a schoolteacher; their only child, Erik Reginald Routley, was born on October 31, 1917, the quatercentenary of Martin Luther's legendary public defiance of church policy.[6] Routley had this to say about his name:

> What a singularly complex thing a name is; a name is a precious possession. Modern life demands that I have at least two names, an epitome of my history. My surname tells you that I come from Somerset, and the meanings of my Christian names are easily furnished.[7] Christian names are given at the child's baptism and have some pleasant or noble association for the parents. No name is an accident.[8] The power of a name is the most primitive and universal association. A name identifies a human being and is a part of the person, inseparable.[9] Accuracy is important. Ministers are difficult [people]—the one appalling thing that sends me right through the roof is being addressed in speech or writing as "Reverend Routley"! The title is only written, never spoken. And when used it has to be written with the Chistian name, or if that isn't known then the title (Mr. or Dr.), never with the surname alone. And call me Erik, NEVER Eric![10]

The Routleys lived in an unremarkable, semidetached house in residential Brighton. Time and again, in future lectures and writing, Erik refers to his amiable childhood and pleasant school days. He concludes that he couldn't possibly write an autobiography because, unlike others, he enjoyed these early years. For better or for worse, Erik had the full attention of his parents, or as full as could be with their involvement in the everyday demands of their local obligations. Yielding to the importance of the arts, Eleanor saw to it that her son had music lessons at home and at the newly founded Brighton Music Academy. An amusing bit of family lore, corroborated by Erik's visiting school friends, involves a long-haired sheepdog named Marcus.[11] This remarkable member of the family had been trained to stand on his hind legs and play and sing at the piano. Schoolmate Geoffrey Bush (1920–1998) says "Marcus just slapped the keys and howled but did keep some kind of rhythm." Even more noteworthy, Marcus frequently enjoyed a dip in the Channel. Unaccompanied by a human being, he got to the sea nearly every day by bus—identifying the correct one and leaping on by himself and, assumably with the driver's help, knowing when to get off. He had to cross several main streets in this journey, and then repeat the process to get back to Surrenden Crescent![12]

The family elected to worship and serve at the Queen Square (Union) Congregational Church. This congregation was known by many names from its inception as the Union Street Congregational Chapel in 1698. Through mergers and denominational changes, the final name, Brighton Central Free Church,[13] held until it disappeared in the twenty-first century, when the building was sold and refitted as flats. Erik's participation in the Union church Sunday School, youth group, choir, and two worship services every Sunday was of prime importance. John served as the secretary of the Brighton congregation for more than twenty years, and long before his son showed any talent for the instrument, John raised funds for a new Walker organ.[14] Forty years later, when the congregation engaged organ builders Hill, Norman, & Beard to renovate the instrument, the church secretary, Frank Fowler, remembered the old instrument fondly as a "real Rolls Royce." As soon as he was able, Erik often played this same magnificent instrument. Eleanor sang in the choir and gave witness to the public in various educational and civic matters.

> From about six years old I went to church with my parents and sat through 40-minute sermons, and I am probably unusual in not holding this against anybody. But although I didn't understand anything much of what was being said, I remember this very vividly: During a time when there was no minister in this church with a packed congregation, a different minster appeared in our pulpit again and again, I found myself saying, while he was reading the Bible or saying prayers, "I wonder whether he'll go on all through the service using that voice?" We must have been much afflicted with the peculiarly British ideas of "parson's voice" in those days, for these men of God again and again impressed me by the very peculiar, almost unbelievable, sounds they made when they were at prayer in public. They looked odd enough, but they sounded odder. It was always the same: When they really got warmed up in the sermon, they sounded quite human; they had one voice for talking to God and another for talking to me. I was thankful that I wasn't God.[15]

John and Eleanor demanded the best education possible for their son, as well as a wide range of friends. In their eyes, regardless of sectarian differences, the only fulfillment of this goal lay in the academics and influence found in Anglican schools. From age eight to age fourteen, Erik boarded during the week at nearby Fonthill Preparatory Academy. Here, and later at Lancing College, Erik was completely captivated by the drama and music of the Anglo-Catholic liturgy that prevailed at both schools. Returning to the Queen Square church on weekends and holidays, he rebelled at Sunday School, but he usually accompanied his parents to the services. Erik was blatantly inattentive during these dull, sermon-centered occasions, but he noticed a sharp and distinct contrast in doctrine and its manifestation between the Anglicans and the Congregationalists. Routley was already experimenting with composing hymn tunes, and often scribbled one out during those stuffy sermons because he just liked hymns.[16] When Routley's career began to take shape, he writes in the introduction to *Hymns and Human Life*:

> I love to think of the church where I was brought up and the hymns that my mother and father taught me before I even went [to worship services]. I love to hear over again "Ye holy angels bright"[17] as sung by the shrill, unbroken voices

of the boys in the chapel [at Fonthill], or "Come, O Thou Traveller"[18] in the more august setting at Lancing.[19]

His solid fascination with hymn tunes was further bolstered through bold, untrained, and responsive singing at the daily chapel services in both schools.

> I knew, intimately, by the age of eighteen, four hymnbooks, and was fascinated by the differences between them. By a stroke of good fortune, these were: *Worship Song*, which we used at home—a book of literary distinction and musical mediocrity; the old *Hymns A & M* (1889), which I learned at Fonthill; and *Hymns A & M* (1904)[20] and *The English Hymnal* (1906), which we used at Lancing.[21]

The music teacher at Fonthill was Winifred Barbara Wrightson (1895–1970). At age twelve, after many ghastly tries, Erik plunked out a hymn tune in the remote, romantic, and rather arrogant key of B major.[22] One day, Ms. Wrightson found Erik's manuscript of this tune left behind in the classroom. To his surprise, she transposed it into C major and handed it out at the next rehearsal as the tune for "Now the daylight fills the sky."[23] Routley reveals, "She at once took me in hand and gave me a single lesson in the principles of harmony, which is the only lesson I ever had in that subject, and taught me what little I know of it."[24] Somewhat later, Routley reworked his initial efforts into FONTHILL (2) using the harmonies provided by Ms. Wrightson, including it in *Congregational Praise*, with Isaac Watts's text: "Wide as His vast dominion lies."

LANCING COLLEGE

In September 1931, Routley matriculated from Fonthill to another school in Sussex, Lancing College. Contemporary Lancing is an independent, coeducational institution and the flagship school of the Woodard Corporation, the largest group of Church of England schools in the UK. Today, Lancing is coeducational for boarding and day students, though in pre-war Britain it was quite different.

> An English public school of the 1930s was a curious preparation for life. After a very tough beginning of servitude and humility, conditions gradually softened and the opportunities to live more freely and to pursue one's own interest slowly increased. The effect of all this is that these personal interests get caught up with one's progress within the school so that no other life seems to exist.[25]

In Erik's memory, Lancing combined the best of a system of unchallengeable authority with a civilized tolerance of dissent.[26] At one point, he was one of only two boys who were not card-carrying Anglicans, the other being John Horder (1919–2012).[27] According to Erik's friend Peter Self (1919–1998), Lancing shared the contemporary muscular, philistine attitudes of public schools.[28]

> There was a worship of sport, an official respect for scholastic achievement, but little encouragement of music and the arts, in which instruction and guidance did not extend beyond the more obviously talented boys.[29]

This sour assessment was not echoed by Erik, Horder, or Geoffrey Bush. Their recollections are that Lancing had a good, if casual, reputation for music. It must be noted, however, that Horder, Bush, and Routley were among "the more obviously talented" in Self's memory. Bush grew into a composer of some renown who referred to Horder as "far and away the best pianist of our generation." Horder's path turned to medicine, but he remained an accomplished organist. Routley's reputation as an organist preceded him to Lancing, where he quickly became well-respected. During the tenure of chapel director Alexander Brent Smith (1889–1950), these young men were the only students at Lancing allowed to play for the twice-daily, required services.[30]

Within their first two years at Lancing, Horder, Bush, and Routley were recognized as a united and lively threesome. As time passed, other boys joined or left the group, among them Peter Self, Bartle Frere (1919–2002), and John C. Hugill (1917–1981). Geoffrey Bush, just up from the Salisbury Cathedral school at age twelve, recounts his first evening meal at Lancing:[31]

> When one is 13, boarding school is a formidable place to arrive. [At Lancing], as you come up and cross the downs to the chapel, it's pretty staggering; suddenly this huge cathedral is upon you. As we trooped into supper, everyone was in a pretty crushed state. A few places down the table, there was one small gathering that was not crushed. A group of boys were actually enjoying themselves. They were chattering away and laughing together. Gazing enviously at them, I observed that the source of their enjoyment was the boy sitting in the middle of them—sort of squashed, stocky, rather older than myself, and with a slight squint. He was making everybody happy. Since different student years tended to be carefully segregated until the sixth form was reached, I didn't dare speak to him. I did not get to know Erik Routley for a considerable time, but when I did, I found that my first impression of him as the life and soul of the party was absolutely correct."[32]

Peter Self,[33] closer to Bush than to Routley, tells of walking the downs one beautiful evening with Erik as they experimented with pipe smoking.[34] In those days, all the best people smoked, especially forward-looking nonconformists.[35] What undoubtably began as an affectation between two teenage boys stuck with Erik for life. Caryl Micklem recalls:

> One sometimes had the impression with Erik's pipe that the lighting was more important than the smoking. From the moment he felt in his pocket for his tobacco-pouch he seemed to settle into a kind of concavity around his pipe—hunched, almost as if, even when he was indoors and no wind threatened the operation, he must guard, like Neolithic Man, the precious gift, the central yet vulnerable fire which he carried with him everywhere.[36]

These boys turned in to men of influence and reputation in music, medicine, and economic and foreign affairs. Though they remained in touch, Erik traveled the farthest.

PATHWAY TO ACADEMIA

Routley studied the classics, working toward a scholarship at Oxford. In his typically self-effacing manner, Erik declared his position at top of the academic list in Olds as an accident. Nonetheless, this success is revealed through his accrued awards and certificates. He was the first student to win the Higher Certificate in Greek, and the music director, Jasper Rooper (1898–1981), created the first Higher Certificate in music just for his talented student. Every achievement added the coveted "with distinction" to Erik's efforts. The Debate Society accommodated his passion for oratory, and he and his friends were members and officers during all four years at Lancing. Topics ranged from interpreting driving safety laws to the wages of war. In this discussion, Erik, the budding pacifist, claimed that modern civilization demanded peace, against his friend Horder, who took a more hawkish approach.

Between the two world wars, British schools provided mandatory Officers Training Corps. Most students obliged, as the alternative exercise was an extra course in physical training, and although sports and games were very popular, PT was not. Routley remarks:

> I was the only child of rather intellectual parents, and I had no aptitude for what they called "games," and I myself called "disciplines and mortifications," with no ear for football or boxing.[37]

When it came to interaction with his companions, Erik was hardly an independent thinker, so he initially took on this OTC. But ultimately, the nonconformist sentiments of his parents were provoked, and they informed the Lancing administration that their son would exercise his right to opt out of OTC and into PT. Most of Erik's peers were secretly envious as they watched Erik and four others of the over three hundred Lancing students split off every Friday to attend their alternative instruction. While the Corps band played on the lower quad and other boys changed into army dress, five young pacifists met with a navy man, Chief Petty Officer Knight, a perceptive coach. Instead of the more tiresome PT, he invented games for these dissenters. After a while, Knight took Erik aside and said, "Look here. You don't want to mess about with this. Why don't you take this time to practice?"[38] The grateful fledgling organist flew up to the loft.

FIRST MENTORS

In Anglican schools, music studies were three-quarters church music, with chapel as the center of it all, and for Erik this was a perfect match. Routley's career trajectory was set by the three men who oversaw Lancing music for the second quarter of the twentieth century: Alexander Brent Smith (1889–1950), Jasper B. Rooper (1898–1981), and the Reverend W. M. Howitt (1886–1977). There never was such an improbable trio: Brent Smith, a composer and brilliant organist who hated the organ; Rooper, a genius at getting music out of other people; and Howitt, who cherished the liturgy with a great and simple love.[39]

Alexander Brent Smith

Brent Smith[40] arrived at Lancing in 1912 from Worcester Cathedral, where he served as assistant organist. He was the only musician on the staff, aside from adjuncts who lived in Sussex communities, with neither degree nor diploma. ABS made up for that with a striking appearance and a truly patrician manner. He was a very good organist yet despised the instrument, but he loved the violin and, like his champion, Edward Elgar (1857–1934), was a militant romantic.[41] Basil Handford (1900–1991), a friend and Lancing historian, remarks:

> He [ABS] was an exceptionally able executant of the piano, organ, and choir master, as well as a composer of great facility . . . he was essentially a shy, modest person who shunned the limelight and never received the recognition from the world of music and letters which he deserved.[42]

Erik's friends had their specific and somewhat diverse interpretations of the man and his impact. Self was predictably critical: "Encouragement of the arts and music did not extend past the more obviously talented boys. I had been learning the piano [in Brighton] and no one ever considered the idea that I might continue."[43] Geoffrey Bush was just as indignant and sharp:

> Some of his earlier pupils have assured me that they found him an inspiring teacher, but as far as I was concerned, he was worse than useless. He seemed neither to know nor care that the training of a potential composer had been placed in his hands. My piano playing deteriorated due to his lack of interest. Nothing, apart from the occasional Sunday organ recital,[44] was done to foster music appreciation.[45]

John Horder, on the other hand, thought ABS a supportive teacher who strongly encouraged his (Horder) own development of the dexterity he needed on both piano and organ.[46] Erik's summation is a little kinder and less personal:

> [He was] a composer with a special gift of composition for what our generation could enjoy, whether it was something to sing in Chapel, or the music for the beautiful and memorable *Drama of the Incarnation*,[47] or the masterly comic operas with which he occasionally diverted us at the end of term. He wrote several violin concertos and at least one symphony. He had an Olympian contempt for any kind of nonconformity—religious or social—and at the same time, a sure grasp for the kind of music which would edify and give pleasure in that [college] environment.[48]

Still, there was also a critical side to Erik's appraisal:

> He was certainly not a born teacher unless you were really good. I don't think he did anything to repair my always deficient piano technique, and as for starting me on the organ? Those hours spent in the loft must have been some of the most grievous he ever spent. But I only met one other person who, in piano music, had such keen and assured insight into what the music was about.[49] "All down the page; it's <u>that</u> note he's leading to," he would say, and he was never wrong.[50]

Routley's organ lessons always included a hymn. One day he was playing "All Hail the Power of Jesus' Name"[51] and ABS was down in the nave. From there, Brent Smith bellowed, "STOP THAT! STOP THAT AT ONCE!" Bounding up to the loft, he continued, "I can just hear you singing it in that Tabernacle[52] of yours!"[53] But Brent Smith left his mark.

> A spectacular fellow he was, picturesque and immensely gifted in ways which neither his age nor ours really appreciated. He had a streak of holy vulgarity which made him able to sing what unmusical people can sing, and to write what

a school could enjoy.[54] I gave him no satisfaction. He gave me, at many points, huge pleasure, and treasurable memories.[55]

Jasper B. Rooper

During the early 1930s, Lancing at large, and music in particular, did not enjoy a healthy reputation. Public embarrassment from the acrimonious head of school disturbed the faculty and administration, with ABS leading the "more-or-less civil war among the place."[56] Eventually, the head of school-[57]was sacked, but not before he dismissed ABS in retribution for his atypical position as the prominent voice of the faculty dissidence. Somewhat later, Erik and his friends recognized that ABS's aloof and distant demeanor was likely due to preoccupation with this power struggle.[58]

> So, they needed a new music master, and rather than advertise and go into all earth kerfuffle, they looked around and they saw, crawling out of the woodwork, a totally insignificant man who was, apparently, the sub-warden's assistant. He was a pupil of Vaughan Williams, but Brent Smith would not allow him to do anything. Though anybody hardly knew him, he was appointed to his [ABS's] vacancy. And he just transformed the whole of music at the school.[59]

There could have been no greater contrast with Brent Smith had the governors searched all of Europe.[60] Jasper Rooper had studied at Lancing as a boy, followed by acceptance to the Royal College of Music under Ralph Vaughan Williams (1872–1958). Rooper was a strange combination of personal diffidence and musical integrity. One of the first things he tackled at Lancing was the organ in the chapel. "At that time the instrument was placed half a block away from the singers."[61] ABS had used full and overwhelming accompaniments for every hymn and anthem, even plainsong. He led the choir with this same registration, and when the choir sang, all one could hear was the organ. Rooper thought it was thoroughly unprofessional to make the choir sing accompanied anthems with this dismal instrument, so he changed the choir's repertoire to works of "Byrd, Tallis, Palestrina and anybody else who wrote unaccompanied music, making the music education gained by singing in the [Lancing] choir as good as that in any cathedral."[62] Once, on a visit, even John and Eleanor Routley commented on the transformation, for the better, of the congregational singing.

Rooper formed a conducting class and added a contest for the student compositions—with a prize of £5![63] He was the architect for Lancing's outstanding music reputation into the twenty-first century. He constructed the requirements for the first Higher Certificate in music[64] and built up the orchestra with Lancing students, no longer relying on instrumentalists from

West Sussex inhabitants for larger works. Instead of the sea chanties and operetta solos favored by ABS,[65] Rooper stretched the limits of what was appropriate. Concerts and term programs became venues for classical repertoire as well as student-conducted and student-organized madrigals. Under Rooper's eye, Erik's compositional work expanded from hymn tunes to include full piano sonatas and romantic rhapsodies written for his friends.[66]

Rooper required his organ students—Routley, Horder, Bush, and a younger student, Peter J. Gould (1922–1993)[67]—to accompany full chapel services, including voluntaries and recessionals, and they were encouraged to experiment with improvisations on the hymns. "He threw you in at the deep end and would remonstrate later."[68] Rooper wanted to know about his students' compositions. His Socratic style was based on his conviction that student and teacher were all learning from each other. "Brent Smith went up the mountain and called you to follow; Jasper always threw you a rope and waited for you."[69]

The Reverend W. M. Howitt

William Howitt, the chaplain, worked successfully with the exceptionally contrasting tastes of ABS and Rooper, and was remembered by Routley as the ideal man to do so. Neither the flamboyantly Victorian Brent Smith nor Rooper's devotion to the clean music of the Tudors gave Howitt pause.

In the early years of the twentieth century, Howitt served as a priest for the Community of the Resurrection at Mirfield, founded as an offshoot of the Oxford Movement.

> Mirfield, one supposes, nourished in him an equal love of liturgy according to the best Tractarian principles and the popular taste and warm-hearted "missionary" music. Temperamentally, he was neither eloquent not ambitious. Howitt's sermons were personal and expository but, from the point of view of most of us, remote.[70]

This Anglican community for men is still vibrant and utilizes the Benedictine routine of work and prayer along with community involvement in social issues and hospitality. In the late 1920s, one of the other resident priests was advised that Howitt's health was quite frail, and the only treatment would be to move south by the sea for what little time he had left. Thus, Howitt was shoved off to Lancing. "In that case, it did him some good. He lived to be 92. And, I say, in passing, that few places in the country could have been as fiercely disciplinary as the cloisters and Chapel at Lancing in January."[71]

At opening chapel on Routley's initial term at Lancing,[72] Brent Smith was the first presider to enter Erik's awareness; Howitt was the second, two or three minutes later.

> The thing I first noticed about him was his voice. He sang a very musical countertenor in the choir, but I mean his speaking voice. In that vast chapel, without benefit of a public address system, he made himself heard in every corner. His was a gentle voice and his articulation was perfect.[73]

Religion was central to the Lancing ethos of the 1930s, and Howitt presented it as something relaxed and colorful. With twice-daily services every week, the school could explore all the assorted treasures of the *English Hymnal* and *Hymns Ancient and Modern*.

> Both organists [ABS and Rooper] had to take the rough with the smooth. Neither man enjoyed playing everything Howitt chose, as Howitt's streak of evangelism was a little hard to swallow.[74]

Moffatt, as the boys called him, was a devoted minister and a natural musician—except, Routley notes, when he was playing the organ.

> [He played] with a sort of ghastliness that at once told you how he loved the instrument as well as how appalling his ideas were. Howitt was the force that bound Brent and Rooper together; he admired both, supported both, and was loved by both. It was fascinating to see how his choice of hymns (at which he was an artist) subtly varied when the transition took place to Rooper. He disciplined us with Gibbons and Lawes, then hurled at us "Thou didst leave thy throne and thy kingly crown," and even "Beneath the cross of Jesus."[75] When [Rooper] allowed him to play the organ for certain services, he [Rooper] always put down the corniest hymns. That way, everybody was happy.[76]

Years later, in a letter to the hymnist John W. Wilson (1905–1992), Routley recalled:

> [Howitt] was a man of uncompromising taste who used the *English Hymnal* in an almost monkish fashion. In consequence, he taught the school a great deal of music which was not immediately attractive, but which had a cathartic effect . . . he didn't think it necessary that the roof always be raised . . . a great soul if ever there was one, passionately musical, solitary, cultured and respected by all.[77] You went to chapel as a boy with the knowledge that whatever happened, there was something nobody could interfere with, and, what's more, nobody interfered with you.[78]

12   Chapter 1

With Rooper's instruction, Routley discovered *Beati mundo corde*, a seventeenth-century motet by William Byrd (1538–1623). The text segment translated as "blessed are the pure in heart; blessed are the meek; blessed are the poor in spirit" relays Routley's affectionate and predictably romantic perception of these men. Their influence marked his life for keeps.[79]

> The attempt to make a civilized community out of the unbelievably heterogeneous aggregation of boys that was Lancing was successful. ("One class school"? Rubbish!) And, if the place was unusual in being one which could accommodate an archetypal misfit like me, a Congregationalist, a non-corps man, an athletic non-story, inarticulate, provincial, and socially stupid, then its unusualness had something to do with the place it gave to the three unusual men I have recalled to memory. The two members of the teaching staff who were neither Oxford nor Cambridge men, and the gentle monk from Mirfield may well have had their moments when they felt as incongruous as I did. But a system which not only accepted them but enabled each to give of what was best in him and made them memorable is a system to be reckoned with.[80]

THE CALL

Routley never publicly disclosed a personal conversion. Congregationalists, with their orthodox Reformed theology, felt that a specific conversion experience was rarely definitive. They tended to agree that true faith involved an inward obedient preparation and would manifest itself in an individual covenant with God.[81] As a response to the personal testimonies related in the popular Billy Graham crusades, Routley wrote *The Gift of Conversion*,[82] in which he asserts that there is no correct moment of conversion, and that the famous experiences of John Wesley, Saul of Tarsus, and Augustine cannot be used as a comparison to any other person's reality.

> There was neither in the puritans nor in the children of John Knox any lack of zeal for souls; but the characteristic manner of winning them was rather by persuasion and lengthy instruction than by dramatic conversion through prophetic eloquence . . . you must pursue faith, but you must not be made to believe, not by Pope or by preacher, by artist or by law.[83]

Routley does give regular glimpses of his youthful experiences that offer clues to a transformation, or, as he calls it, freedom. The story he relates on many occasions happened in the spring of 1929 at Fonthill.

> I can remember vividly how I felt about arithmetic, algebra, and more especially geometry before that day in my twelfth year. They were subjects which I hated

and feared. The whole climate of the subject was terrible to me. I inherited a rather good mind for figures from my father, who has a prodigious memory for them and is a born mathematician. I was able to bluff my preceptors and found myself in advance of my contemporaries in the subject. Nonetheless, I hated and distrusted it because I just could not *do* it. I quaked with fear of the master's tongue, a powerful weapon, and I hated the thought of always getting so many answers wrong and made to feel like a fool and blunderer. "Maths," I said to myself, "stinks." That morning, we were sitting there in class and the matter under review was Euclid's Theorem 41. The forty that preceded it I had learned by rote and were all double-Dutch to me. The master drew the relevant diagram on the blackboard and turned to us and asked, "Now, who can tell me why this is so?" My hand shot up into the air and the master responded. I went on to tell him that the angle in the semi-circle must obviously be a right angle since the angle at the centre was a straight line, 180 degrees, and the angle at the circumference, the Theorem 34 (or whatever) must be half 180 degrees, that is, a right angle. The master dropped his chalk and stared in bewilderment and said, "Good Lord! You've started at last!" I had thought for myself and advanced along Euclid's way under my own power. I enjoyed geometry from that time forward, and I believe that nothing in the world will ever take away the realization that maths no longer stink. Nothing in the world will ever take away from me that freedom of the subject which began on that day. After all credit is given all around, [this event] credit belongs to no one. The thing remains as something that was given to me.[84]

This gift of freedom contains all the ingredients for a proper conversion in Routley's outline in *The Gift of Conversion*, containing both the diagramming of the thesis and the preparation involved for the divining moment. While on sabbatical in the 1960s, the hymnologist and musician Mary Oyer (b. 1923) studied with Routley in Edinburgh. This concept of freedom shaped her career.

[Routley] spoke of the parabolic quality in a work of art which moved me away from my very realistic and simplistic interpretation of things. I felt a great freedom, enabling me to withstand the pressures of people who said [things like], "Why are you working on a hymnal instead of playing the cello?" Routley said, "Of course, why not?"[85]

In *Hymns of the Faith*, a more mature Routley remarks:

No Christian who knows himself to be in any way "free of" the Faith can say there was no time when he remembers being delivered from bondage. It is no use looking for some occasion in the past when you suddenly found you knew all about life. What most of us must be content with is to discern in our lives many moments which mark turnings in the road.[86]

Douglas W. Langridge

For the young Routley, a more direct discernment came close to home. The Union (Queen Square) Church had a long, rich history of ministers known for their passionate sermons, intellectual and tinged with social and political responsibility. Until Erik left for school, the minister at the Brighton church was Thomas Rhondda Williams (1860–1945), a Welsh minister who came to the Union Church in 1909 after his reputation as a progressive—almost heretical—pastor at a congregation in Bradford led him to a more sympathetic congregation that appreciated his powerful sermons.[87] Williams served as chair of the Congregational Church of England and Wales toward the end of his Union appointment, which ended with his retirement in 1931. The flat and pedantic nature of the subsequent supply preaching drove Routley to exasperation, though many of these men were famous throughout England at the time. After most weekends, Routley fled in relief back to Lancing, where the plain, functional building that housed the Congregationalists in Brighton faded next to the impressive and awe-inspiring Gothic chapel at Lancing.

> I consider it fortunate that my godly parents sent me off to two Anglican boarding schools, from ages eight to eighteen, where the emphasis wasn't on rousing sermons but on liturgy and the kind of worship in which youngsters could really participate, and by the age of fourteen I had become an Anglican snob. I was spending two thirds of my life observing the delightful routine of Anglican worship and one third being opposed to the stimulating and athletic worship of the Reformed tradition. My parents were musical, hence so was I, and that's where the Anglicans really got to me. By the spring of 1934, I was enjoying the aesthetics of the church more than its dogma. The Anglicans were winning.[88]

One Sunday in the early spring of 1934, the Routleys were at breakfast before church; the conversation concerned the morning's visiting pastor at Union. John, who served as secretary, remarked, "I don't know anything about this man who is coming this morning. Never heard of him, myself, but Berry[89] recommends him. Comes from Colchester, or somewhere else in the north."[90] Erik had a cavalier attitude toward preachers and was not impressed.

> I was brought up in my early years to regard preaching as primarily a performance. A good preacher was one who, at a high intellectual level, entertained and stimulated the congregation. Looking back, I now think that there was no very deep difference between the goodness of Bernard Shaw and what we judged as the goodness of the "best" preachers. Everything turned on whether it had been a "good" sermon.[91]

After the service at lunch, at the same family table, Erik announced to his surprised parents, "I'm coming again this evening. I must hear that man again!"[92] When he became a fruitful Congregational minister, he observed:

> This was the first one [preacher] I listened to; the first one who wouldn't let my mind wander; the first one who said what I was longing to hear. I am never out of sympathy with youngsters who are critical of our kind church. THIS was something. The sermon that morning was on the "Unknown Disciple," and he brought Jesus Christ right into the room. The evening one was "Hosea," a masterpiece of pathos and appeal. Within a few weeks I was saying, "That's the job I'd like to do!"[93]

John Routley was correct. The new and permanent minister, Douglas Walter Langridge (1887–1973), came to Brighton from the Lions Walk Congregational Church in Colchester, and Langridge was immediately both controversial and compelling.[94] He made a church out of what had been known as a preaching house. He made it his business, without lowering the high standard of sermons, to inject a spirit of comradeship into that massive congregation. From their first meeting, he endeared himself to the large segment of younger members, and the Young People's Society was always the most exciting thing about the church.[95] Yet it was his preaching that made Langridge famous and, at the same time, drew him into controversial dilemmas.

> He was in no sense a lyric preacher. He came of a tradition which looked at the Bible much as the contemporary preacher does, and not at all as I was to be taught at Mansfield. It wasn't expository preaching: it was explosive, inimitable, individual, and pure art. There was wit, there was warning, and it pierced and changed the listener. The real explanation of his ministry was this: he was a great lover of life and of people as God made them, but he had an incredible hatred of pomp and pretension. If you said what you didn't believe, you had lost him. Though driven by this insistent integrity, he was gentle and courteous. But he couldn't say what didn't mean anything. This is what got him into trouble; he was loved by many but not popular with all. Those who sought for pastoral trivia sought in vain. So, I was launched into a ministry that has given me many surprises and a normal quota of heartaches.[96]

NOTES

1. Richard Hood, "10 Best Somerset Ciders," *The Independent*, May 25, 2017, https://www.independent.co.uk/extras/indybest/food-drink/beer-cider-perry/best-somerset-cider-a7338021.html, viewed August 29, 2020.

2. John's first job was with the Sussex timber company owned by John Eede Butt, now a real estate firm.

3. *West Sussex Gazette*, September 15, 1936, 4.

4. It is an interesting fact that whether genetic or environmental, this characteristic was enjoyed by Erik, much to the amazement of friends and family. Upon Erik's death in 1982, his wife, Margaret, remarked that she had to buy an address book, as all necessary private and professional phone numbers and the like garnered throughout their marriage were kept, precisely, in his head!

5. After his highly effective term, John and Eleanor moved to Kent and became members of the Congregational Church in Dartford, which, like Union in Brighton, has undergone many changes in the last eighty years and is now the United Reformed Church in Bexley.

6. This date is noted, with appropriate irony, by many throughout the years as fitting and even foretelling, considering his strong responsibility to the Reformed church.

7. "Erik" is Old Norse for "eternal ruler"; "Reginald" means "wise counsel/ruler." https://www.behindthename.com/name/eric, https://www.behindthename.com/name/reginald, accessed September 11, 2020.

8. *Hymns and the Faith*, 187.

9. Ibid., 188.

10. *Encounter with Erik Routley*, 227. In the late 1970s, a colleague in Edinburgh explained the etymology of "Routley" as probably Norman, from the word "roitelet," meaning "wren." Erik was delighted by this connection to prominent hymn writer and fellow Congregationalist Brian Wren.

11. Over the years, the Routleys had three dogs bearing the name Marcus.

12. Correspondence with John Horder by Nancy Wicklund, March 27, 2002.

13. In October 1983 the church, colloquially called "Central," held a celebration of the many different shapes of this congregation and included a memorial to their favorite son, Erik Reginald Routley.

14. Installed in 1921.

15. "Three Lectures on Preaching," delivered at Perkins School of Theology, Dallas, Texas, February 1970.

16. OLBP, x.

17. Richard Baxter (1615–1691), 1681.

18. Charles Wesley (1707–1788), 1742.

19. *Hymns and Human Life*, 2.

20. OLBP, xii.

21. OLBP, xii.

22. Ibid. The tune is the original FONTHILL.

23. St. Ambrose of Milan, translated by John M. Neale, *Hymns Ancient and Modern*, 1906, 1.

24. OLBP, op. cit.

25. "Lancing: Expanding Horizons," *Through a Glass Brightly*, unfinished memoirs of Peter Self, archive of Will Self, the British Library.

26. Ibid.

27. NWG, interview with John Horder, April 16, 2002. John Horder inherited a strong Congregational legacy through his grandfather, William Garrett Horder (1841–1922), a Congregational minister who was a voluminous writer of pastoral concerns and a pioneer in the study of hymns. He had a special interest in American hymns and introduced several to Great Britain. He was the publisher of two hymnals, *Congregational Hymns* (1884) and *Worship-Song* (1905), which had a strong influence on Routley's own studies ("William Garrett Horder" by J. R. Watson, CDH). John Horder initially wanted to follow in his grandfather's Congregational footsteps as well as become a concert pianist. Like many young men, he changed his mind.

28. "Lancing: Expanding Horizons."

29. Ibid.

30. Ibid.

31. Bush and Routley were both assigned to Olds House.

32. NWG, interview, April 22, 1997.

33. Peter had strong Brighton and Lancing connections. His maternal grandfather, Sir John Otter, also served as mayor of Brighton—twenty years prior to the term of John Routley. His maternal great-grandfather, Nathaniel Woodard, an Anglican priest, founded eleven middle-class boarding schools throughout England, the basis of today's Woodard Group. Woodard is entombed in the Lancing College Chapel, which must have served as a daily reminder to Peter and his brother, Hugh, of the weight of ancestry—and of scholarly expectation.

34. *Through a Glass Brightly*.

35. Ruth Micklem, "Music and the Pastoral Ministry: A Personal View," DD.

36. Caryl Micklem, "Erik Routley, 1917–1982," DD, 6.

37. "Music at Lancing 50 Years Ago," lecture at Lancing, 1982, Routley Collection.

38. Ibid.

39. Ibid.

40. Lancing had six houses in 1931; Erik was assigned to Olds, and the housemaster was ABS. "Brent Smith was [also] in charge of music when I arrived at Lancing. Formidable and authoritative, aristocratic, and sensitive, I was terrified of him—which he hated.

41. "Music at Lancing."

42. Basil W. T. Handford, "*Requiescat in Pace*: Alexander Brent Smith," *Lancing College Magazine*, Summer 1950, 62–64.

43. *Through a Glass Brightly*.

44. Lancing records indicate that Routley was often a featured organist as well as John Horder. Brent Smith did allow Routley to present his [Routley's] own compositions at Music Society events. Geoffrey Bush was a vocal soloist from time to time.

45. Geoffrey Bush, *An Unsentimental Education* (Thames Publishing: London, 1990), 92.

46. NWG. Interview with John Horder, April 16, 2002.

47. Libretto by Basil Handford, 1932. Routley remembers "a memorable nativity play that only got one performance, and the libretto was masterful, the music heraldic. I am told that this has entirely disappeared."

48. "Lancing and Its Music Fifty Years Ago," 1982.

49. Peter Scott (1918–1978).
50. Ibid.
51. "Lancing and Its Music Fifty Years Ago," 1982.
52. Metropolitan Tabernacle, London.
53. "Lancing and Its Music."
54. Ibid. Two of ABS's tunes written for use at Lancing, COTSWOLD and COME MY WAY, have endured as active tune choices included in hymnals of the twenty-first century. COTSWOLD appears at #512 in *Rejoice in the Lord* (Wm. B. Eerdmans Publishing, 1985). COME MY WAY was first published in *The Clarendon Hymn Book* (Oxford University Press, 1936); Routley included this tune in each hymnal he edited.
55. Ibid.
56. NWG, Bush interview.
57. Cuthbert H. Blackiston (1879–1949), https://timesmachine.nytimes.com/timesmachine/1932/07/31/100781991.html?pageNumber=25.
58. Basil Handford, *Lancing College: A History and Memoir* (Phillimore Book Publishing: Bognor Regis, 1986), 175.
59. NWG, Bush letters.
60. "Lancing and Its Music."
61. Ibid.
62. Ibid.
63. As the winner of one such contest, Erik used his prize money to buy two hymnals.
64. Routley being the first winner.
65. The first such offering was the *Sanctus* from Bach's Mass in B minor.
66. These thirty-two compositions include meditations, preludes, and ballades plus two suites, one titled, simply, "221." Another is the *Lakeland Suite*, inspired by visits to the Borrowdale valley in the Lake District.
67. Later, he was organ scholar at Queen's, Cambridge.
68. "Lancing and Its Music."
69. Ibid.
70. Ibid.
71. Ibid.
72. Friday, September 18, 1931. Fifty years later, Routley still remembered the music of the liturgy, "Psalm 93, Magnificat chant 1, Hymn 523 part 1. Correct me if I am wrong.."
73. Lancing and Its Music."
74. Ibid.
75. Ibid. "Thou didst leave thy throne" by Brighton's own Emily Elizabeth Steele Elliott (1836–1897), A&M #776; "Beneath the cross of Jesus" by Elizabeth Cecilia Douglas Clephane (1830–1869), A&M #667.
76. JWW, October 5,1959.
77. Ibid.
78. Ibid.
79. "Lancing and Its Music."
80. Ibid.

81. S. E. Ahlstrom, *A Religious History of the American People* (Yale University: New Haven, 1972), 130–32.

82. In an email to NWG in April 2015, Nicholas Routley comments: "*The Gift of Conversion* is, in large part, a polemic against Billy Graham. The vigour with which he defends a gradual growth of what he calls conversion might well lead us to suppose that this was his own story."

83. Routley, "The United Reformed Church," occasional paper, 1972, private collection.

84. Ibid., 37–39, abridged.

85. NWG, July 3, 2003

86. *Hymns and the Faith*, 134.

87. Obituary, *Manchester Guardian*, London edition, November 22, 1945.

88. Erik Routley, "Something New Every Day," *What Faith Has Meant to Me*, Claude Frazier, ed. (Westminster Press: Philadelphia, 1975), 128.

89. Local minister and friend, the Reverend G. W. Berry (1846–1938).

90. Erik Routley, "Douglas Walter Langridge."

91. Erik Routley, "In Those Days There Was No King in Israel," *British Weekly*, December 6, 1956.

92. Ibid.

93. Ibid.

94. "The minister who shoved me into the ministry—a preacher of superb originality and fascinatingness—once gave a sermon on the Phariasism of the Publican. He often did things like that! Not quite kosher, I suppose, but it did remind us that if the publican knew the Pharisee was there, he might have been making a parade of humility. Isn't life difficult?" Letter to Adrienne Tindall, July 8, 1981.

95. Ibid.

96. Ibid.

Chapter 2

Magdalen and Mansfield, 1936–1943

Erik earned Higher Certificates *with distinction* in Latin and Greek for all but the first year of his time at Lancing, and in July 1936 he was granted a Classical Exhibition and State scholarship to Magdalen College, Oxford. With the blessing of his Brighton and Lancing communities, and proud encouragement of his parents, up he went. For a sixth form student in the United Kingdom, the anticipation of university, with the release from parental rules and school behavior codes, hovers as a sort of guardian angel—life in the way it is meant to be lived. As this perception fades from a dream to reality, confidence often falters, and old insecurities and doubts can cloud even the most optimistic temperament. Routley refers to his early years at Madgalen as "those awful years when war was imminent, and it was no fun being nineteen."[1]

THE WAR

Magdalen College

Oxford in 1936 was preparing for war. By 1933, Britain had already set up the Air Raid Precautions department to enact what was termed "passive air defense." This included instructions for gas masks, blackouts, and shelters; and by early 1939 the Home Office had issued pamphlets to the residents of Oxford with instructions on how to protect themselves from an air war with Germany. As Erik was becoming adjusted to a new life at Magdalen, British government offices began moving into the Oxford colleges, conscripting their use for the probable wartime period. St. John's housed the director of Fish Supplies; Balliol was the location for the Royal Institute of International Affairs. The RAF Maintenance Command relocated to Magdalen, and Mansfield accommodated the Cyphers Branch of the Foreign

Service. London University medical students took over Keble, Wadham, and St. Peter's Hall. Trinity College was the instruction site for the Officers' Training Corps.[2] Fixtures like books, furniture, artwork, and stained glass were moved all over Oxfordshire for the duration of the war.[3] Often, as in the case at Mansfield,[4] the government work was classified, and students, lectures, meals, and chapel services were moved elsewhere. Some wartime students never saw the dining room or common rooms in their own colleges.[5] In 1941 the JCR,[6] of which Erik was a part, dug up Mansfield's tennis courts for a Victory garden.[7] The constant and imperturbable Blackwell's bore a red-lettered sign reading, "The Emergency Blood Transfusion Service."[8] Apprehension was a persistent companion.

In these pre-war years, the population of Oxford city swelled by thousands, though the student numbers, decimated by World War I, remained low. Undermined by uncertainty, entire families fled London's East End[9] and crowded the platforms at the Oxford train station with a grim stoicism and an eye toward survival.[10] Many of these displaced persons, especially unaccompanied children, were funneled into rural foster homes and farms. Assuming massive bombing was inevitable, more than five thousand evacuees came from Kent, home to all manner of military establishments.[11] Academics from Europe, particularly Germany, were absorbed into newly created university positions. There was an unaccustomed presence of single, intellectual women both in college and around the town. Military officers and their accompanying personnel flooded the cafés and pubs in The Cornmarket and the High Street. Everyone had their "war work," from tending to refugees and establishing garden plots for vegetables to equalizing manual labor and military service. Food, fabric, and petrol were rationed.

> It was clear from early on that this conflict would remake Britain in profound ways . . . the war would scramble living situations, pushing some people together, and dividing others.[12] The mass cultural and social experiment of evacuation produced a new science of child psychology; scientific advancements and novel ideas of socialized medicine and religion in a post-war society that looked toward a more ethical working environment than pre-war capitalism had done.[13]

Largely due to a shortage of newsprint, the BBC radio was a constant, universal presence in every home and office. During these years, the BBC[14] reduced its multiple regionalized radio channels to one unified source of information, entertainment, and inspiration. When the Germans, followed by the Soviets, invaded Poland on Friday, September 1, 1939, it was the BBC that relayed this message, marking the onset of World War II. On Sunday the 3rd, all of Britain was tuned to the radio at 11:15 to hear this announcement from Neville Chamberlain:

At nine a.m. on Sunday, the 3rd, Sir Nevile Meyrick Henderson, the British ambassador, went to the German Foreign Ministry Building in Berlin. He presented the ultimatum that unless the German government began the process of removing their troops from Poland by 11:00 am a state of war between Britain and Germany would exist. I have to tell you that no such undertaking has been received, and consequently, this country is at war with Germany.[15]

Though primed for this news, the listeners were overcome by grief and fear. In *Hymns and the Faith*, Routley remarks:

"Our God Our Help in Ages Past" is the gravest and most universal of all English hymns. It is always to be regarded by Englishmen as the indispensable hymn for the day of decision or the day of distress. Nobody who ever heard that last verse[16] sung, unaccompanied, by the BBC singers at an early morning broadcast on 3 September 1939,[17] will ever forget the penetrating impact of the hope and the sorrow which were there expressed.[18]

Stunned and shaken, the British people put their war preparations into place.

The most anxious people in the Second World War in Britain were neither the air-raid wardens nor the dwellers in Lewisham, Bermondsey, and Clydeside,[19] but the people who lived in Oxford, to whom nothing had happened but who were persuaded that at any moment it might.[20]

First Publication

In 1939, as England anticipated the war, Walter Matthews (1881–1973), then dean of St. Paul's, wrote an article for *The Spectator* entitled "War: The Christian Dilemma."[21] Bound by his oath to the King, Matthews claimed that the Church owed something to the national community, as it was protected by this and flavored by the characteristic tang of England.[22]

We have inherited a culture and tradition, a freedom and a way of living which are distinctive. Can it be maintained that the community has no right to call upon its members to defend it, or that there is no obligation on the individual to preserve the inheritance to which he owes so much?[23]

The next week, Routley's reaction, addressed to the editor, is widely noted as his first published article. The twenty-two-year-old Magdalen student showed both insightful maturity and his Congregationalist pacifism when he wrote:

I would respectfully reply that the source of our culture, freedom, and security is not the British government or community, but the accumulated knowledge of several scores of nations over about eight millennia. We owe our culture to

English poets, German musicians, Italian artists, and French Philosophers. The Greeks had democracy; the Romans had drains. Culture and Law are a composite heritage which is claimed as justifiably by Germans as by Englishmen. It is misleading to talk of defending so abstract a conception as culture or freedom. If we are indebted to mankind, are we to defend these privileges by slaughtering the very same?[24]

C. S. Lewis

The university's original mission in the twelfth century was to train clerics—first Roman Catholics and then, with the schism created by Henry VIII, only Anglicans. The late 1800s saw the inclusion of many nonconformist colleges. Divinity studies and ordination remained a strong academic component at the university colleges in the 1930s. In his memoirs, the poet John Wain (1925–1994) observed:

> It was impossible, at that time, to take in Oxford without taking, if not exactly the Christian faith, at least a very considerable respect for Christianity. Everybody with an imaginative and bookish youth naturally looked up [as] every figure who radiated intellectual glamour of any kind was in the Christian camp.[25]

Yet most undergraduates had only a vague idea of the magnitude of intellectual and theological thought swirling around them. The most prominent of these academics was C. S. Lewis (1898–1963), a don of Magdalen College. Erik hadn't a clue to the significance Lewis's presence and didn't lay eyes on Lewis until 1939.[26] On Sunday, October 22, Erik was intrigued with a college billing stating that Lewis would speak at St. Mary's, the university church.

> It was odd in those days to have a preacher there [St. Mary's] who wasn't a clergyman of the Church of England; I thought I'd go along. The service was held at 8 pm and I supposed that I should arrive about 10 minutes before eight. The church was quite dim as only minimal lighting was allowed and there was hardly a seat to be had. The one I got was right under the pulpit. I could see this preacher only when he went up the steps—and I said to myself, "So *that's* Lewis!" Lewis gave us the sermon called "Learning in Wartime"[27] which was his debut as a preacher.[28]

Lewis spoke to the condition of students and scholars who, with the outbreak of war, were forced to question their vocation. He gave a second sermon at the university church in June 1941, after Erik had become a divinity student at Mansfield College.

This time it was a summer evening, so lighting was no problem. The place was packed solid long before the service began. The delivery took three quarters of an hour; its stunning effect is something one can hardly communicate. Here was a man who had been laid hold of [by] Christ and enjoyed it. Lewis had a superbly unaffected delivery—a deep voice that went well with his cheerful and bucolic appearance. It was a voice that really did vindicate the saying the medium is the message. No rhetorical tricks; he read every word. He used words as precision tools. The effortless rhythms of the sentences, the scholarship made friendly, the sternness made beautiful—these things all made it impossible for the listener to notice the passing of time.[29]

This notable sermon, "Weight of Glory," is considered one of Lewis's most profound.[30] It holds the premise that glory exists in the realization that God is delighted by humankind, as an artist delights in his work.[31] This concept is echoed in much of Routley's own writing as the necessary trajectory for Christian worship. Routley challenged every preacher or public speaker to study Lewis's poetic oral expression.

Most of these words are of one syllable and the startling contrast of the two syllable words is what makes Lewis's sermon so remarkable: "At present we are on the outside of the world, the wrong side of the door. We discern the freshness and purity of morning, but they do not make us fresh and pure. We cannot mingle with the splendours we see. But all the leaves of the New Testament are rustling with the rumour that it will not always be so."[32]

The draft and enlistments further reduced the Oxford student population; professors and other academics were encouraged to give their voices as their contribution to stabilizing and reassuring the British people. James W. Welch (1900–1967), the director of Religious Broadcasting at the BBC, was drawn to the power of Lewis's writing. Welch felt that messages from Lewis might recharge the courage of listeners who represented all sorts of ideological backgrounds. In February 1941 Welch wrote to Lewis, asking that he consider a weekly program, explaining:

The microphone is a limiting and often irritating instrument, but the quality of thinking and the depth of conviction which I find in your books ought surely to be shared with a great many other people.[33]

Lured by the promise of an intelligent audience of millions of listeners, Lewis responded affirmatively; the world tuned in for five years.

Pub owners were saying "quiet everybody, Mr. Lewis is on!" He talked in a way that they all understood, explaining his faith in the context of hardship and the war.[34]

Lewis was everywhere. He went about talking to packed audiences at student meetings and army camps.[35] One could always tell when he was lecturing at Magdalen by the bicycles stacked seven deep all along the wall.[36] He preached often at the chapel of Mansfield College,[37] as well as occasions at St. Mary's. He founded the Socratic Club as an academic venue for religious debate. He took on some of the leading sceptics in the university and demolished them with cheers from his student audience. Yet it all stopped abruptly at the war's end when Lewis went back to his study and got on with his work.[38]

Dorothy L. Sayers and Charles Williams

This Lewis phenomenon initiated a brief, yet remarkable, period of public Christian rhetoric;[39] prominent voices sprouted throughout academia. One notable contributor was Dorothy L. Sayers (1893–1957). Her Lord Peter Wimsey novels brought global acclaim, and Routley deemed her "the *English Hymnal* of the detection novel: high-toned, high-church, slightly intense, intellectual, scholarly, and business-like; she took the world very much as she found it."[40] As a poet and writer, Sayers had a busy professional life and was sought after by the BBC as a lay theologian, though foremost, Sayers considered herself a dramatist.[41] In 1942 she wrote *The Man Born to Be King*, a twelve-part play cycle. It was broadcast weekly and, though controversial, was considered the most powerful piece of Christian apologia for the next ten years.[42] Routley refers to this work as a beginning of the recovery of religious drama through the new technological developments of radio, television, and film, naming it the Church's greatest achievement of the twentieth century.

> The principle was that if you really understood that the Gospel is a story acted out by real people, the right ideas would generate themselves. Nowadays, the trouble often is that we start with the ideas and not with the people.[43]

The third force was Charles Williams (1886–1945), a wild and explosive poet and playwright who worked for the Oxford University Press. He spent most of his life in London until the evacuation when OUP relocated the entire publishing firm to Oxford. Though he never finished any formal degree, the University affirmed Williams as an honorary Master of Oxford. Williams developed the concept of Co-inherence[44] and a theology of the arts in which an artwork can provide truth of which the artist is not aware.[45] Both Lewis and Williams credit the other for most of their respective theological thought, and, until Williams's untimely death, the two took charge of Oxford, with Lewis acting as the mediator between Williams and the world.[46]

As I look back on those student days of mine, the one thing that I am profoundly thankful for is that they were the years when C. S. Lewis and Charles Williams were doing their astounding double act in Oxford.[47]

Both men were the arbiters of responsible lay thinking about religions.[48] Routley lists Williams's *He Came Down from Heaven* as the book that influenced his life second only to Lewis's *The Pilgrim's Regress*.[49]

Routley and Lewis

There were definitive differences between Lewis and Routley in their spiritual journeys. Lewis became a Christian well into adulthood, after he began teaching at Magdalen, while Routley was raised in an unabashed Christian household and sort of grew into his faith. In 1946 the Hymn Society of Great Britain and Ireland created a review panel for new hymns. Routley, a young member of the Society and already known as a collector of hymns, was asked to approach Lewis and inquire to his willingness to be a contributor to this discussion. With near distain, Lewis replied, "The truth is that I'm not in sufficient sympathy with the project to help you . . . the hymns are mostly the dead wood of the service."[50] When Routley responded, tactfully asking for further explanation of "dead wood," Lewis expanded his thoughts, a little less abruptly, saying that as they were not bad in principle, hymns must be included in worship in charity for those who like them, but "a humble acquiescence to anything that may edify their [priests] uneducated brethren is the first lesson they must learn."[51] In response to this exchange, Lewis wrote the essay "On Church Music,"[52] where he gives detail to his contrary opinion.

> We must define rather carefully the way, or ways, in which music can glorify God. All our offerings, whether of music or martyrdom, are like the intrinsically worthless present of a child, which a father values indeed, but values only for the intention. What we want to know is whether untrained communal singing is in itself any more edifying than other popular pleasures. And of this, I, for one, am still wholly unconvinced. I have often heard this noise; I have sometimes contributed to it. I do not yet seem to have found any evidence that the physical and emotional exhilaration which it produces is necessarily, or often, of any religious relevance.[53]

Routley outlived Lewis by twenty years, and he never let this subject rest. Always respectful and thoughtfully explanatory concerning Lewis's essay, many of Routley's writings contain references to Lewis's comments. Routley never declares Lewis wrong, but at least two books, *Music and Theology*[54] and its revision, *Church Music and the Christian Faith*,[55] devote chapters to Routley's subtle rebuttal. Even his posthumously published book,

The Divine Formula, contains a dissection of Lewis's remarks. In the spring of 1975, when Routley was teaching at the Princeton Theological Seminary, his library finally arrived *in toto* from England. In this, he reconnected with a book of poems by Lewis and discovered "Evensong."

> I got my copy of C. S. Lewis poems and found among them one which is undeniably a hymn. That prince of hymn-haters, I thought, has for once been caught napping! I do not know from what period in his life this exquisite poem came, but I thought it worth a tune, and I wrote KILNS, named after Lewis's house in Oxford. This tune in F minor certainly complements the text relaying prayerful, nocturnal images.[56]

Routley got the last word. Yet from his Oxford days until his death, Routley was disturbed that Lewis, Williams, and Sayers were not appropriately respected, were often criticized and, at worst, ignored. Routley feared that the world had become increasingly more uncomfortable with these three and their literary contributions and theological perceptions. He mourned that appreciation of their writing had deteriorated to a cultish level. Looking back nearly a century later, and considering the weight these writers still carry, Routley needn't have worried.

The Music and Worship of Oxford

In the early days of the war, university students were exempt from the conscription orders[57] and thus often adopted a casual attitude to the fighting on the continent. The many musical and theatrical societies in Oxford beckoned to fill in the nonacademic hours. Student governing roles and opportunities for political discourse were also popular. Unfortunately, the university imposed two weekly essays on each student, straining one's free time.[58] One way Erik ignored his own academic requirements was singing with the Oxford Bach Choir. In existence for over two hundred years and still thriving in the twenty-first century, this mixed-voice chorus consists of university and community citizens who usually present three or four concerts a year in either the Sheldonian Theater[59] or St. John the Evangelist Anglican Church.[60] When Routley's friend Geoffrey Bush came up to Balliol from Lancing in 1938, he, too, auditioned for the choir.

> The great thing was to join the Oxford Bach Choir. The audition was not too exacting but I was faced with a dilemma. My voice had broken into a thousand fragments and I was neither tenor nor bass. I was passed as a bass, but I arrived at my first rehearsal still undecided where I would fit in. I saw Erik sitting among the tenors and said, "that's for me!" I elbowed my way in and preempted the place next to him.[61]

Often in the company of other friends, Geoffrey and Erik regularly attended the professional chamber music at the Holywell Music Room.

> If the offering was not to Erik's liking, he would doodle away the time by writing out hymn tunes and ribald versions of hymn texts. He would often translate these into a sort of Greek alliteration and thought himself quite clever.[62]

If any of these impromptu compositions went any further, no one knows, but Erik wrote several tunes in his undergraduate years. A favorite hymn for Routley at that time was the last one in *Worship Song*, "Lord for the things we see," set there to AMESBURY.[63] Routley felt that the tune did not do justice to the words, and in his first term at Oxford, he wrote LULLINGTON for that text. It remains unpublished, however, and likely unfinished.[64] Tune writers often name their compositions after places of their residence or some other familiar distinction, and Lullington is a town in Somerset near his father's family home.

Erik was always part of the regular lively debate and discourse in the JCR, but despite his popularity, Erik was never comfortable at Magdalen. His Congregational roots made assimilation into the Anglican culture difficult, despite his years at Lancing. However, he gladly participated in daily chapel services and enjoyed the regular singing of the Psalms for the day, using settings that he had learned from Rooper and ABS. Like other Oxford Congregationalists, he attended Sunday services at Mansfield. Erik became an associate member of Mansfield in 1937 while studying at Magdalen,[65] which came with chapel and dining privileges. When the Mansfield Chapel organist, Trevor Harvey (1911–1989), graduated in 1938, Erik assumed Harvey's role and properly began his lifelong recognition as a church musician.

Peter Scott

One evening at Magdalen, another miserable student entered the JCR and observed a provocative discussion across the room. Three or four fellow undergraduates were strongly criticizing Erik about his Christian beliefs. The newcomer watched this uncomfortable exchange for a while and finally heard Routley react, "Do try to stop being so stupid." One of his tormentors responded, "Oh? I thought you Christians were supposed to suffer fools gladly!" Erik, characteristically, retorted, "Fools, yes! Congenital bloody idiots? NO."[66] The witness to the conversation decided immediately that this was someone he wanted to get to know. And that's how Peter Scott (1918–1978), the outsider, met Erik Routley. Scott read law at Magdalen and finished a year ahead of Erik. They shared lodging out of college for several years, as both went on to Mansfield, though Scott converted to Roman

Catholicism before ordination. In his chapter in *C. S. Lewis at the Breakfast Table*, Routley comments:

> My final memory of those otherwise dim Oxford days is [Peter and I] sitting up to the wee small hours with *Pilgrim's Regress*,[67] working it all about: getting inside his [Lewis's] "north-south" pattern and understanding all the allegorical references on every page. We took some satisfaction, when the explained edition came out, in finding that we had pretty well got it right. That and the *Summa Theologica*[68] more or less kept us sane.[69]

Peter and Erik were each accomplished musicians, Erik as an organist and Peter on the piano. At various Oxford functions, they joined their gifts and played four-hand piano to entertain each other and their friends, usually with no encouragement, and often included Erik's own silly and scurrilous songs of college life.[70] In *Duty and Delight*, Caryl Micklem (1925–2003) relays that "those who were their contemporaries at Mansfield cherish the recollection of their duo performances, both straight and not-so-straight."[71]

Though Routley excelled academically at Lancing, at Magdalen he did not.

> My studies there were in classics and theology. Well, in Classics I made a marvelous mess, but then the final examinations came in June of 1940 (anyone who didn't make a mess of final examinations in 1940 wasn't human). What I actually did was write a rather long piece for two pianos . . . I'm still quite fond of it.[72]

The composition, written as an ultimatum to his degree, is a four-hand, two-piano suite, "Hunsdon House," an English dance tune. Erik and Peter presented this work at one of the well-regarded Balliol concerts in 1941, and it was forever connected to the two men.[73] Public performance of this piece from other artists would not be heard for forty years.[74]

MANSFIELD COLLEGE

Foundations

The Elizabethan Religious Settlement, drawn in 1558–59,[75] was an attempt to assuage the deadly and calamitous religious turmoil that erupted with the decision of Henry VIII (1491–1547) to withdraw from the Roman Catholic Church. His daughter Mary I (1515–1558) reinstituted the Roman church, but when Elizabeth I (1533–1603) took the throne, she proclaimed the English Protestant church as the established church, amidst a perceived Catholic threat.[76] The accompanying protestant *Book of Common Prayer* fell in and out of favor until 1662, when, after the Restoration, the Cavalier Parliament[77] passed a new Act of Uniformity, restoring the Church of England as the established religious structure of the land. This action returned the BCP to public use, thereby permanently carving the shape of English culture. Yet, with this legislature, dissidents, Jews, and Roman Catholics became alternate citizens; and the provisions of this new legislation were binding, keeping non-Anglicans from holding office, ordaining clergy, and attending university. By the late 1660s, more than two thousand Puritan clergy were expelled from their positions, creating the concept of nonconformism. Presbyterians, Baptists, Quakers, Congregationalists, and other denominations fell into a wide berth of dissenters, which lasted more than 150 years. Banned from Oxford and Cambridge, non-Anglicans studied and often received degrees at the universities in Scotland, and London University[78] was founded in 1826 as a secular alternative. After years of rejection, in 1836 Parliament finally passed a reform allowing Oxbridge colleges to confer degrees on non-Anglicans.

In Birmingham around the same time, in planning his estate, George Storer Mansfield (1764–1837)—Anglican by history, dissenter by conviction—consulted with Timothy East (1783–1871), minister of the Congregational Ebenezer Chapel. East suggested founding a college for training men for the Congregational ministry. The unmarried Mansfield discussed the ideas with his sisters, Elizabeth (1772–1847) and Sarah (1767–1853). With no heirs among them, founding a school of this type in the Midlands[79] seemed the perfect solution for distribution of their funds and properties. Sarah's husband, George Glover, owned Spring Hill, an estate on the outskirts of the city.[80] He died in 1821, leaving the property to his widow, who, after consulting George and Sarah, decided that this site should house the new seminary. By 1826, a board of trustees was formed, headed by the Reverend East, which consisted of twenty Congregational ministers and laymen from the Birmingham area. The Mansfields were allowed to live at Spring Hill until their deaths. After George Mansfield died in 1837, the sisters turned over their lease to the trustees and moved to a smaller house nearby.[81]

The school opened for students in 1838, offering a course of general and theological education. Most of the first students had not attended university due to the restrictions against non-Anglicans.[82] To maintain the high standards of a university imagined by the founders, Spring Hill initially devised a demanding six-year course. All students originally prepared for the Congregational ministry, but in 1845 the trustees began to accept those with other plans.[83]

> Lay students [should] be admitted only on the condition of a blameless moral character, and subjected, after their entrance, to the ordinary rules of the

Institution, as the Theological Students can be injured by the association; but, on the contrary it is much more probable that they [theology students] will impart spiritual good to their lay-brethren than that they will derive any moral injury from them [lay students].[84]

As one might expect, discipline gradually slackened. The minutes of the JCR from December 10, 1862, reveal that one of the three principals, Thomas Barker (1799 1870), learned there existed in the house, "a fearful amount of crime, immorality, vice and profanity."[85] The next day five young men were charged with "Irreverence at Evening Prayers," "Habits of Loose Conversation," and "Insubordination within the House." Three of the five were expelled, but after a huge outcry they were reinstated due to "lack of pastoral oversight."[86] By 1871, almost all religious entry requirements at Oxford and Cambridge had been abolished, allowing a nonconformist presence at the universities. Nevertheless, the nonconformist and Roman Catholic communities were reluctant to send their young and immature men to an atmosphere where Anglicanism dominated. Every university college held regular Anglican chapel services, and though the Oxford Movement was strongly influential, non-Anglicans had to produce a written exemption. However:

There was a growing conviction among Congregationalists that theology was being neglected among them; something was amiss with the education and training of their ministers; and that their ministers should, without abandoning Dissenting principles, enter the mainstream of English cultural and intellectual life.[87]

With the adoption of the Universities Tests Acts of 1871, persons of all faiths and sects were permitted to obtain professorships, fellowships, and undergraduate and advanced degrees at all British universities, most particularly Oxford and Cambridge. As the sons, and even a few daughters, of Congregational families gained places at the universities, the local ministers could not afford to lag behind their congregations in intellectual attainment.[88] For several years the Congregational Union had been debating the aspects and implications of the new academic opportunities and the possibility of obtaining land at either Oxford or Cambridge for establishing a college. These meetings were steeped in drama and heated disagreement concerning whether ministerial educational qualifications should be made a prerequisite for Congregational positions. The locale of this training was also emphatically debated. New matriculation requirements demanded four years at Spring Hill and then the last two at New College in London.[89] New College liked the idea, but wanted this to lead eventually to the relocation of Spring Hill in London. Talk stopped.

Throughout the 1870s and early 1880s, the dispute and anxiety waxed and waned. From 1869, David Worthington Simon (1830–1909) was the theological tutor—in effect, principal—of Spring Hill. Simon strongly supported a move to one of the ancient universities to give authority and rigor to the proposed theological degree. Colleagues alternately supported and derided Simon through the years. Tensions became unsurmountable until, finally, Simon decided he needed to leave and accepted the position of principal at the Theological Hall of Scottish Congregational churches in Edinburgh. And although two Spring Hill colleagues, John Brown Paton (1830–1911)[90] and Robert William Dale (1829–1895),[91] tried to discourage this, Simon moved on. A mere month later, Dale gave rebirth to the relocation possibilities; this time, the proposal was accepted by both Spring Hill and Oxford University.

Within English Congregationalism there existed an awe-inspiring Scottish theologian, Andrew Martin Fairbairn (1838–1912). In 1883 Spring Hill persuaded Fairbairn to leave Airedale College in Bradford[92] and become principal at Spring Hill, where Fairburn supported Dale's determination to relocate to Oxford as Mansfield College. In Fairbairn's report to the governors in December of 1886, he emphasized the cause:

> Mansfield is simply, in its own order, the greatest positive denominational enterprise on which our churches have entered since the *Act of Uniformity*. It is not an assertion of right, a performance of duty, but duty which rises out of conquered and conceded rights.[93]

In a sermon, Fairbairn condensed the move as "the greatest work done for and by Independency since 1662."[94] As the most vocal advocate on the development of the new college, he crisscrossed England with his message of imperative conclusion: "[The move] is an ornament of victory and a symbol of duty."[95]

By 1936 Mansfield was entirely cemented in Oxford and was highly regarded as a center for liberal theology. The ministerial students bound for Mansfield were proclaimed associates of Mansfield while they earned their BA at another college. More importantly:

> [Mansfield] provided a place for University Congregationalists to worship, and the services drew significant numbers of nonconformists and others from the University and surrounding districts. From early days, the College organised grand services with many important and attractive preachers, drawing large audiences. The chapel came to function as a *de facto* Congregational church,

even being listed in The Congregational Yearbook, but had no membership, Church Meeting, or anything to make a Congregational church in any real sense.[96]

Routley's Mansfield

Erik was headed to Mansfield before he even finished at Lancing. In 1936 the Brighton Union Church minister, D. W. Langridge, wrote to his Mansfield colleague C. J. Cadoux (1883–1947),[97] proclaiming, "he [Routley] really is brilliant—almost, if not quite, a genius."[98] Mansfield historian Elaine Kaye remarks that Routley's friends and admirers would have said that Routley's subsequent career bore this out.[99]

Erik was as happy at Mansfield as he had been miserable at Magdalen. As important as ministerial preparation was to him, Mansfield had another far-reaching influence. There, Erik met three members of an important Congregationalist family—Nathaniel Micklem; his brother, Edward Romilly Micklem (1892–1960); and the latter's son, Thomas Caryl Micklem (1925–2003), all of whom left a substantial imprint on the rest of his life. The twentieth-century Micklems were steeped into a heritage of nonconformity and public service. Many attended Congregational colleges, and in 1877 Nathaniel and Romilly's father, also Nathaniel, was one of the first nonconformists to attend Oxford as a full student. New College, a family tradition, was where all three earned their first degree before attending Mansfield; in time, all were ordained as Congregationalist ministers.

Following his time as a student at Mansfield, Nathaniel served a short time as college chaplain at the end of World War I. His first academic position was at Selby Oaks, and after six years he took up a professorship at Queens College in Ontario, Canada, until he was appointed principal at Mansfield in 1930—a position he held until he turned sixty-five in 1953. It's easy to see the attraction between him and Erik Routley, as in many ways their personalities and sensibilities were mirror images. Micklem's Mansfield colleagues described him as "mercurial and puckish,"[100] "the best after-dinner speaker of his day,"[101] and "a man whose wit, charm, and intellect made him a most acceptable representative of Mansfield."[102] And, from Routley, a foreshadowing of his own professional reputation:

> [Nathaniel was] the most reliable and trustworthy friend, who was also formidable when he chose. Surely nobody has ever mastered so effectively the technique of administering a rebuke with a grace that directed your attention to the truth and not to your own grievances.[103]

During the war years, Micklem resided with his family in the only building left strictly to the college—a drafty and deteriorating four-story house, but a setting that Micklem warmly opened to the JCR. There were only thirteen or fewer members during Erik's years at Mansfield, yet many were destined to be among the most visible Congregationalists for the next fifty years.[104] Upon his retirement Micklem stated, fondly:

> Never before had so many men of such various and remarkable abilities been present at the same time in the Junior Common Room. Their affectionate kindness to me was boundless. My wife and I kept open house on Saturday evenings, where I introduced them to C. S. Calverley and other great poets, while they provided the music in the persons of Peter Scott and Erik Routley. Their [the JCR] intellectual gifts were balanced by a remarkable spiritual maturity. Their prayers and their preaching in the College Chapel were my wonder and joy. I often felt that my task was to stand aside, lest I should inadvertently hinder the manifest work of the holy Spirit in their hearts.[105]

NOTES

1. OLBP, xiii.
2. Vera Brittain, *England's Hour*, common reader edition (Arkadine Press: Pleasantville, NY, 2002), 159.
3. Christ Koenig, "The Day Oxford was the Bombers' Target," *Oxford Mail*, August 30, 2007, www.oxfordmail.co.uk/news/1653048.day-oxford-bombers-target /, accessed October 31, 2020.
4. All college events, including meals, were moved to Regents College. The only offices remaining at Mansfield were the principal's residence and the JCR.
5. Elaine Kaye, *Mansfield College Oxford: Its Origin, History and Significance* (Oxford University Press: Oxford, 1997), 211.
6. Junior Commons Room. This is an undergraduate term for both a place and a comradery.
7. Nathanial Micklem, *The Box and the Puppets* (Geoffrey Bles: London, 1957), 128.
8. Brittain,152.
9. The East End of London contains some of the city's most important dockland areas. At the time, it was a hub for imports and was used to store vital goods for the war effort, making this a prime target for German bombing raids. The East End was densely populated with families and daily laborers who settled here because of their jobs. Bombed every night for fifty-seven days, residents that did not evacuate spent their nights in the tube stations. Notably, when Buckingham Palace was bombed in 1940, the Queen is reported to have said that she was pleased they had been bombed, as this meant, "Now I can look the East End in the face." *Eastlondonhistory.co.uk*, accessed November 4, 2020.

10. Brittain, 158.

11. The most devasting and deadly attack came on March 24, 1943, the Southern Railway Works being the primary target. Much of the area's residential neighborhoods fell victim as well. *Kentonline.co.uk*, accessed November 4, 2020.

12. Mo Moulton, *The Mutual Admiration Society* (Basic Books, New York, 2019), 215.

13. Ibid., 246.

14. A noncommercial company, the BBC serves the British people under a royal charter and includes a substantial religious dimension, as Great Britain is, by law, a Christian nation. During the years of World War II, the BBC leadership took that description more seriously than did most of the British public. Sunday programming included church services and religious programs that had to be tasteful, and include no jazz or comedy shows. The BBC, with its monopoly on broadcasting, relaxed those rules a bit during the war for the sake of the troops.

15. Peter Neville, "The Man Who Shouted at Hitler," *History Review*, issue 45, March 2003, https://www.historytoday.com/archive/man-who-shouted-hitler-sir-nevile-henderson-berlin, accessed November 12, 2020.

16. "Our God, our help in ages past, our hope for years to come, be Thou our guard while troubles last, and our eternal home," written in 1719 by Isaac Watts (1674–1748).

17. Broadcast from Bristol Cathedral and conducted by Nathaniel Micklem.

18. *Hymns and the Faith* (J. J. Murray Press: London, 1955; Seabury Press: Greenwich, CT, 1956), 34.

19. All these locations were bombed heavily during the Blitz, 1939–1941.

20. *The Puritan Pleasures of the Detective Story* (Gollancz: London, 1972), 221. In terms of bombing, nothing ever did happen. In 1940 a German bombing squadron, headed for the Morris Radiator factories up the Woodstock Road and nearby Crowley, was intercepted by the RAF, thwarting the raid.

21. Walter Matthews, "War: The Christian Dilemma," *The Spectator*, February 10, 1939, 210.

22. Matthews, 210.

23. Matthews, 210.

24. Erik Routley, "Letter to the Editor of THE SPECTATOR," February 24, 1939, 305.

25. John Wain, *Sprightly Running* (MacMillan: London, 1965), 142.

26. The two men met briefly only two or three times at social functions in Oxford.

27. Ibid.

28. Using his renowned memory, Routley recalls that the text was Deuteronomy 26. This sermon can be found in Lewis's *The Weight of Glory* (HarperOne: New York, 2001), 47–63.

29. James T. Como, ed., *C. S. Lewis at the Breakfast Table* (Macmillan: New York, 1979), 34.

30. Nearly forty years later, Routley remembers the final hymn, "Bright the Vision that Delighted," written by Richard Mant (1776–1848) and #372 in *The English Hymnal*.

31. *Weight of Glory*, 43.
32. *Breakfast Table*, 34.
33. Justin Taylor, *The Gospel Coalition* blog, "75 Years ago: C. S. Lewis Speaks to Britain about Christianity on the BBC," August 5, 2016, https://www.thegospelcoalition.org/blogs/evangelical-history/wayne-grudem-evangelicals-and-the-trump-option/, accessed November 8, 2020.
34. Dalya Alberge, "Quiet, C. S. Lewis is on!" *The Guardian*, February 15, 2021, https://www.theguardian.com/books/2021/feb/15/quiet-cs-lewis-is-on-why-subject-of-new-film-could-be-right-for-now. Though few of these broadcasts survive in their original audio format, Lewis's notes and addresses do. They can be found in many written and online sources.
35. "C. S. Lewis: Scholar, Artist, Apologist," CC blogs, *Christianity Today*, November 24, 2020, https://www.christianitytoday.com/history/people/musiciansartistsandwriters/g-k-chesterton.html.
36. NWG interview with Anne Renwick Scott (1919–1997), April 23, 1997.
37. Nathaniel Micklem relied on Lewis, W. Russell Maultby (1866–1951), Terrot Glover (1869–1943), and George MacLeod (1895–1991) to serve the pulpit at Mansfield Chapel during his years as principal.
38. "C. S. Lewis: Scholar, Artist, Apologist."
39. Ibid.
40. *Puritan Pleasures of the Detective Story*, 134.
41. Ibid., 138.
42. *The Man Born to Be King* is a radio drama produced by the BBC and initially broadcast in 1941–42. It's in twelve segments depicting periods in the life of Jesus. Sayers brought a dramatic immediacy to the stories that conservative Christians strongly criticized, but the program was praised by the general public. The characters emit real human emotions and speak using colloquial English vocabulary and phrasing. https://en.wikipedia.org/wiki/The_Man_Born_to_Be_King, accessed November 24, 2020.
43. Richard Proulx, *The Pilgrim: A Liturgical Music-Drama in the Manner of a Medieval Matins Drama for Eastertide* (GIA Publications: Chicago, 1980), foreword by Erik Routley.
44. "The Oddest Inkling," CC blogs, *The Christian Century*, June 5, 2013, accessed November 24, 2020. "This signature doctrine is an odd blend of the natural and the supernatural. It is the idea that Christ's risen life inhabits believers and all share the divine interrelationship of the Trinity and live as members of one another. From this theological viewpoint, all human love and co-operation are made possible."
45. For a time, Williams was both tutor and intimate friend to Anne Renwick, who later married Peter Scott.
46. Erik Routley, "A Prophet," *C. S. Lewis at the Breakfast Table*, James T. Como, ed. (Macmillan Publishing: New York, 1979), 37.
47. *Breakfast Table*, 33.
48. Ibid., 144.
49. Appendix C.
50. *The Presbyter*, vol. VI, no.2, June 25, 1946, 15–20.

51. Ibid., September 21, 1946.

52. C. S. Lewis, *Christian Reflections*, Walter Hooper, ed. (Wm. B. Eerdmans: Grand Rapids, MI, 1967), 94–99.

53. Ibid.

54. *Church Music and Theology* (SCM Press, 1959).

55. *Church Music and the Christian Faith* (Agape: Carol Stream, IL, 1978).

56. OLBP, xxvi. The hymn remains unpublished.

57. Divinity students were exempt for the entirety or the war.

58. These were assigned by one's tutor and presented orally in a group of three or four students. The topics were of the tutor's choosing and ranged from politics to the arts.

59. The Sheldonian Theater was built from 1664 to 1669 after a design by Christopher Wren for the university. The building is named for Gilbert Sheldon, chancellor of the university at the time and the project's main financial backer. It is used for music concerts, lectures, dramatic productions, and university ceremonies.

60. Now part of St. Stephen's House, a PPH and theology college for the Church of England.

61. NWG Geoffrey Bush, April 22, 1997.

62. Ibid.

63. Text by John Greenleaf Whittier (1807–1892), American Quaker; tune by Arthur Berridge (1855–1932), English Congregationalist.

64. It appears in OLBP with the Watts text: "There is a land of pure delight."

65. This was a customary practice for those committed to Congregational ministry.

66. Interview with Anne R. Scott by Nancy Wicklund, April 23, 1997.

67. C. S. Lewis, *Pilgrim's Regress* (J. M. Dent & Sons: London, 1933). This was Lewis's first prose fiction and the first book published after his conversion.

68. Best known work of Thomas Aquinas (1225–1274).

69. *Breakfast Table*, 34

70. *Duty and Delight: Routley Remembered*, Robin A. Leaver and James Litton, eds.; Carlton Young, exec. ed. (HPC: Carol Stream, IL, 1985), 3.

71. Ibid.

72. Harry Eskew, "An Interview with Erik Routley," *The Hymn* 32:4 (Hymn Society of America), 198.

73. Concert no. 1036 of the Balliol College Music Society, Sunday, February 23, 1941.

74. Westminster Choir College Faculty Recital, March 3, 1981, performed by William and Louise Cheadle.

75. The Settlement contained two parliamentary acts. The Act of Supremacy (1558) reconfirmed England's separation from the Roman church. The Act of Unity (1559) set forth specific religious guidelines.

76. Henry VIII was a practicing Roman Catholic, and this separation was a political move. The King wanted a male heir, and his marriage with Catherine of Aragon had only produced one child who lived past infancy (the future Mary I). He decided to take a new wife, as Catherine was past her fertility years, and requested that the pope annul their marriage, which the pope refused to do. The resulting upheaval had Henry

splitting from Rome, divorcing Catherine, and marrying the younger Anne Boleyn. Ironically, Anne only bore a daughter (the future Elizabeth I) before Henry had her beheaded for treason.

77. The first English Parliament after the Restoration of Charles II. May 8, 1661– January 24, 1679.

78. Now the University College London.

79. Kaye, 6. There were ten Congregationalist academies (colleges) at the time, but none in the Midlands. These were Homerton College, London (moved to Cambridge in 1894); Wymondley, became Coward College, London (closed in 1849); Western College, Tewksbury; Cheshunt, London (moved to Cambridge in 1905); Highbury, London (absorbed into New College London in 1854); Newport Pagnell, near Olney (absorbed into Cheshunt in 1850); Idle then Airedale in Bradford (merged with Rotherham); Bradford, which became Yorkshire United Independent (merged with Bradford University in 1963); Hackney, London (merged with New College London in 1900); and Blackburn, Manchester (closed in 1843).

80. Kaye, 8. Glover supervised the organization and building of the Ebenezer Chapel, beginning in 1816. This was the spiritual home of Sarah and Elizabeth for their entire adult life. In 1819 Glover, a loyal Anglican like Mansfield, became a "Dissenter by conviction" (as written in the Spring Hill College deed).

81. Kaye, 9.

82. Kaye, 11.

83. Kaye, 15.

84. Kaye, 16. *Report of the Committee of Management of Spring Hill College Birmingham for the Year 1847–48.*

85. Kaye, 21.

86. Kaye, 27.

87. Ibid.

88. Ibid.

89. New College description.

90. Simon and Paton had been classmates at the Yorkshire Independent College and Spring Hill.

91. Also educated at Spring Hill, and a highly regarded Congregationalist.

92. Eventually educated at the University of Edinburgh and the University of Berlin, Fairbairn was principal at Airedale from 1877 to 1886. Fairbairn was awarded Doctor of Divinity degrees from Yale and Edinburgh and was granted a D.Litt. from Oxford in 1903.

93. A. M. Fairbairn, "Our First Term and Its Moral," December 1886, Kaye, 70–71.

94. Kaye, 43.

95. Kaye, 69.

96. Michael Hopkins, *Congregationalism in Oxford*, MA thesis, University of Birmingham, January 2010.

97. Cadoux was a significant liberal theologian of the early twentieth century. He was appointed as the Mackennal Professor of Church History in 1933. As vice principal, his sparring with Nathaniel Micklem, principal of Mansfield, over Christian

dogma rattled the college for many years, though, ironically, this strengthened the public opinion of the nonconformist theologians at Mansfield.

98. Kaye, 207.

99. Ibid.

100. Norman Goodall, "Nathaniel Micklem, CH," *The Journal of the United Reformed Church History Society*, vol. 1, no. 10, October 1977, 286–95.

101. *Mansfield* magazine, July 1953, 164

102. Kaye, 190.

103. "The Principal of Mansfield," *British Weekly*, July 2, 1953.

104. Among these were Horton Davies, George Caird, Daniel Jenkins, and Erik Routley.

105. *Box and the Puppets*, 121.

Chapter 3

Wednesbury and Dartford, 1943–1948

Routley's favorite teaching tool was the community hymn sing. His inspiration for these much-loved events was planted by the visionary Sir Hugh Allen (1869–1946), who regularly held such gatherings in the Sheldonian Theater for the Oxford community—town and gown alike. Through the first half of the twentieth century, the British music world was overshadowed and subtly guided by Allen who, beginning in 1918, was associated with New College, Oxford. From his position as college organist and professor, he revitalized the musical life of the whole university. Concurrently, he directed the Oxford Bach Choir and served as director of the Royal School of Church Music. With the gifts of communication and imagination, Allen was a born teacher. "He did not get behind you and coax you along; he strode along ahead of you and made you enjoy trying to keep up with him."[1] Accordingly, it was Sir Hugh who, "with pugnacious courage, brought down Beethoven's *Mass in D* from the romantic region of inaccessible legend and showed that ordinary people could both sing it and listen to it."[2] Routley liked to relay this oft-told story:

> A student of his was a brilliant musician of the very first class.[3] While serving in World War I [this musician] lost his right arm. He wrote to Allen, his old tutor, in such grief and despair as may be imagined. Allen replied at once with what encouragement he could offer. Then, a week passed and he [Allen] wrote again. During that week, Allen had played the services in New College Chapel using only his left hand and two feet. The second letter was simply to tell his student that it could be done. This student went on to become a well-respected organist and music director.[4]

This and many similar anecdotes about Allen popped up often, and Erik absorbed them all. Rather like the words of C. S. Lewis, Allen's aura permeated Routley's musical opinions and experiences in his early, formative college years and accompanied his career as a churchman and musician. When Routley was working on his Mansfield thesis, he turned to Allen for guidance.

> Shivering with a shyness that was three parts vanity, and a diffidence that was mostly fear of rebuke, I knocked at the Great Man's door in New College. Invited to come in by a thin bark of a voice that I had so often heard but whose owner I was about to meet personally for the first time, I went in. "G'morning," said Sir Hugh. "You want to talk about writing a thesis? Look, you'd better know I'm a dead Protestant, myself. Well—not quite dead yet, I daresay!"[5]

This Mansfield thesis, "The Church and Music: An Enquiry into the Music, the Nature, and the Scope of Christian Judgment of Music," was well received in 1946, and would be published in 1950 by Duckworth Books. Duckworth republished a revised edition in 1967.

WEDNESBURY

In 1943, with this monograph well underway, Routley set out to his first pastoral position at Trinity Church in the ancient market town of Wednesbury[6] in the former Staffordshire Black Country—self-described as "one of our less notorious and more amiable industrial towns."[7] In medieval, pagan Saxon days, a temple to Woden sat on a prominent hill, now in the city park. A natural defense fortified with a deep ditch and high stockade, this place was known as *Woden's burh*, which eventually modified to Wednesbury. At the turn of the twentieth century, the manufacturing and mining companies south of Birmingham attracted sturdy laborers and their families, as well as their accompanying pleasures and vices. A local historian had this to say: "Wednesbury is not a fashionable watering place, nor can it boast anything in its immediate neighbourhood which is at all attractive to the average tourist."[8] Though long absorbed into suburban Birmingham, historic Wednesbury boasts its own Facebook page.

THE TOWN AND CONGREGATIONALISM

The roots of Trinity Church can be traced to the Toleration Act of 1689, when it became possible for nonconformists to have their own places of worship. In 1742, as the nonconformist presence was becoming accepted in Staffordshire, Dissenters were attracted to the traveling Methodists, most prominently John (1703–1791) and Charles Wesley (1707–1788). When the local vicar, Edward

Eggington (1650–1743), heard their message of strong moral measures and personal devotion, and saw how their work had resulted in ridding communities of "drunkenness, uncleanness, and idle diversions,"[9] he extended the Wesleys a warm invitation to come preach.[10] After two very successful revivals where John assured Eggington that "nothing should be done by him [Wesley] or his followers to alienate the Affections of the people from him [Eggington], or to withdraw them from the Church of England," Eggington eagerly encouraged Wesley to return in the spring of 1743.

In the meantime, an associate converted lay minister, Robert Williams, warned the citizens:

> Look upon your ministry: there are dicers and carders, some blind guides and cannot see, some dumb dogs and will not bark. It might be better if all dull ministers were hanged up in their church.[11]

When Wesley returned in April, he was immediately arrested and jailed by an enraged Eggington. At the urging of the vestry, Wesley was released the next day, and this chapter of Wednesbury life was forgotten when Eggington died in December. All manner of nonconformists flourished in the town from then on.

Several meeting places existed for Trinity from the certification of the gatherings in 1720 to 1750, when the church was properly constituted and organized as Congregationalist. Trinity Church developed and expanded until the devasting social consequences of two world wars took their toll. By 1943, membership had dwindled to about one hundred. This number remained steady during Routley's short term but declined from 1945 onward until it disappeared entirely with the formation of the United Reformed Church in 1972.

TRINITY CONGREGATIONAL CHURCH

But in 1943 that was yet to come, and on Saturday, 4th of September, Routley officially became ordained as a Congregational minister and was installed as pastor at Trinity Church. Among the presiding ministers were his mentors and old friends Nathaniel Micklem, who, as Mansfield principal, provided the congregational charge, and David Langridge, who delivered the charge to the new minister. Peter Scott gave the opening prayer. One thing delighting Routley in this otherwise dismal assignment was finding copies of the old *Congregational Church Hymnary* of 1887 stacked in a dark corner of the church. Reminiscent of his childhood, he put it into use immediately, and for his entire stay it was his hymnal of choice.

Routley versus Wednesbury was not a good fit. Opinions as to why range from his youthful idealism to his Oxford education. In a letter years later, Routley said it was his desire for orthodoxy and order that produced a "disobedient" congregation.[12] An ever-present factor to discontent was housing, for the church was not accompanied by the customary manse. Finding a room was not insurmountable for a single man, but in May 1944 Erik and Margaret were married.

T. CARYL MICKLEM

Family and friends remember that the next fourteen months saw the Routleys in at least four different dwellings, and many of these were far less than comfortable. The couple was not faultless, however. One story has them evicted due to their uncontrolled laughter over a rousing game of checkers! This housing situation was a frequent topic of gossip among the church members, varying from supportive, "A minister and his wife deserve a good house," to the absurd, "Lots of people have to do without housing." Routley himself says this was the real reason they moved on, though the position itself was quite satisfactory.[13] Caryl Micklem, a frequent visitor to Wednesbury, remarked candidly in retrospect:

> The town was at the heart of the Black Country, which had not yet been liberated from its pall by the Clean Air Acts. The church belonged to that tradition of "self-help," "I-know-what-I-like" Congregationalism which the commercial spirit of the Birmingham conurbation tended to nurture. It was hardly to be expected that the young Erik, full of the ideals of classical Puritanism, and unpersuaded of the musicianly virtues of Dr. John Bacchus Dykes, could minister in such a context for long without hackles being raised. On the other hand, for the members with whom [Routley's] style and content rang bells, his short stay was the gift of a lifetime.[14]

Caryl Micklem enjoyed a career as a well-respected minister, hymn writer, and editor and was secretary of the Hymn Society of Great Britain and Ireland from 1993 to 1999. But it almost didn't happen. Part of a long line of strong Congregational ministers of academic and political achievement, he was destined to attend New College, and then on to Mansfield for divinity training. Not unlike many in this right-of-passage predicament, this legacy contributed to an enormous emotional and intellectual struggle for the teenaged Caryl. In 1943 his father, Romilly, begging for confidential empathy, shoved his son off to Erik in Wednesbury. On many occasions, with typical patience and privacy, Erik listened as Caryl unloaded his doubts and questions. Caryl acclaimed,

"Speaking for myself, I can say that Wednesbury will for me always be the place where, thanks to Erik, I recovered my faith and vocation."[15] Despite what seemed then to be a huge age difference, the two men became lifelong close friends and colleagues.[16]

FIRST STEPS TO *CONGREGATIONAL PRAISE*

These two years in Wednesbury were not without other productive and bearable moments. The CUEW needed their own hymnal. In 1943 they reorganized their interrupted, pre-war attempt into a new committee, chaired by Eric Thiman (1900–1975).[17] Nathaniel Micklem was chairman of the Union for the 1944–45 term, and, respecting his former student's passion for hymns, enthusiastically recommended Routley as a contributor to this re-formed committee. According to George Caird (1917–1984):

> It was well known among the Mansfield community that Erik had a complete manuscript notebook of his favorite hymns from the hymnals he had used regularly for the first 25 years of his life. If he found the tune to a given text distasteful, he just wrote a new one! This kept the Mansfield Chapel on their toes. On the occasion of the hymnal committee's first meeting, Routley laid this book on the table and said, "Gentlemen, there is your hymnbook!"[18]

Thereupon he was made secretary to the Editorial Committee for the future *Congregational Praise*.[19]

> The book sought a revival of the classics and a fresh contemporary hymnody, a wide range of musical and theological vocabulary that would convey to the singing people a new sense of the greatness of the church to which, as Congregationalist, they belonged.[20]

COMPOSING

Routley's attention to composition continued. Margaret was an accomplished violinist, and her husband wrote a piece for them to play together, *Sonatina in A Minor*. He wrote another, *String Trio in G*, for her and her chamber music partners. Not surprisingly, writing hymn tunes was a priority in the "cracks" of his daily responsibilities.[21] While spending summers at the home and church of Romilly Micklem, Routley learned that Micklem favored the hymn text, "Eternal light! Eternal light!" by Thomas Binney (1798–1874).[22] The hymn was set to NEWCASTLE,[23] which Micklem felt too ordinary for the profundity of the text. So Routley wrote a new one, CHALFONT PARK,[24] which

Caryl Micklem claimed, "brought the words to life," sparking his own interest in tune writing. Though Routley minimizes the tune as too romantic, it is still often paired with the Binney text. The *Congregational Praise* committee rejected the new tune/text combination but accepted three other Routley tunes written in Wednesbury. One, SUTTON COURTNEY, was written for and sung successfully at the Trinity Wednesbury congregation.[25] Though Routley grew to dislike CLIFF TOWN, it appears with Routley's beloved text, "In praise of God meet duty and delight," in *Common Praise* (2000). ABINGDON is the most well-received tune from this era, and today is most often associated with "Lord God, your love has called us here," written in 1973 by Brian Wren (b. 1934).

MOVE TO DARTFORD

John and Eleanor Routley relocated to Dartford, Kent, south of London in 1938, and during his university years, the Dartford Congregational Church was Erik's home church. While at Mansfield he served as organist when needed, and his mother was often the choir director. The pulpit became vacant in 1945, and John Routley, a member of the church council, realized that his son might be interested in a temporary position; Routley was called to serve as interim, and he accepted. In a letter written to Geoffrey Beck, Routley says, again, it was the housing situation that drove him and Margaret from Wednesbury. Though he speaks of having made good friends in the church, he candidly continues:

> The moral is, I imagine, if you're in a jam don't expect any sympathy from a working-class congregation of that kind if you bear Oxford degrees after your name. The people are individually very good-hearted and kindly, but totally incapable of concerted action of any kind.[26]

Thinking about all this years later, Caryl had his own apologetic explanation of the unsuitable nature of the Wednesbury post:

> Polymaths are often tedious or self-important, or both. It was Routley's grace to be neither. To read him is not to be button-holed or hectored, pungent, even pugnacious, though his style often is. It is like going for a walk with a knowledgeable, entertaining, opinionated companion who will, if you encourage him, share his thoughts till the sun goes down, but who will also, disarmingly, stop talking and really listen if you venture a point yourself.[27]

Ironically, Erik and Margaret did not live in the provided manse in Dartford but with Erik's parents. As Routley was actively seeking a permanent position, he and Margaret did not expect to be in Dartford for any length of time, though in a few months the congregation extended a permanent invitation to the pulpit. Remembered for his friendliness, Routley's greatest legacy was helping the choir and congregation enjoy hymns and look forward to learning new ones from the anticipated *Congregational Praise*.[28] On Sundays, the older and younger Routleys opened their home to widely popular social evenings of music, games, puzzles, and reading aloud Sayers's *Man Born to Be King*.[29] Routley's enthusiasm spread to the Youth Club in particular, and under his direction the group began raising money to purchase an abandoned army hut for their activities.[30] In February 1946 the congregation extended a permanent call, and Routley accepted. In June of the next year, Margaret gave birth to their first child, Nicholas, and the couple delighted in watching him grow.[31]

Eleanor felt that her son's intellect was wasted in Dartford, but Routley himself showed no signs of discontent. The congregation was quite disappointed when he moved on, but, recognizing the suitability of the challenges in Oxford, they were not surprised and offered only encouragement, taking comfort that the church had experienced a minister like Erik Routley.[32]

NOTES

1. "I'm a Dead Protestant Myself," BW, March 15, 1956.

2. "Beethoven's Credo," BW, September 19, 1957.

3. Douglas G. A. Fox (1893–1978), student of Charles Villiers Stanford at Clifton College and organ scholar at Keble College from 1912 to 1915.

4. "I'm a Dead Protestant Myself."

5. Ibid.

6. A major urban reorganization in 1966 saw Wednesbury become part of an amalgamation that became Sandwell, a Birmingham suburb. In 1974 another reorganization combined several counties to the north and west of Birmingham, including Staffordshire, as a new metropolitan county, West Midlands. In the Industrial Revolution of the early 1800s, the area was known for its coal mines, coke furnaces, steel and iron foundries, brickworks, and glass factories. This term, officially recognized in the twenty-first century as the Black Country Consortium, is derived from the extreme pollution that had an adverse effect on the local air quality.

7. *I'll Praise My Maker*, preface (Independent Press: London, 1951).

8. F. W. Hackwood and Bev Parker, *Wednesbury Faces, Places and Industries*, preface.

9. Thomas Jackson, ed., *The Works of John Wesley*, vol. 13 (Wesleyan Conference Office: London, 1865), 164–65.

10. Ibid.

11. Ibid.

12. TCM, December 11, 1957.

13. GB, October 3, 1945.

14. Caryl Micklem, "Erik Routley, 1917–1982," *Duty and Delight: Routley Remembered*, Robin A. Leaver and James Litton, eds. (Hope Publishing: Carol Stream, 1985), 3–15.

15. DD, xii.

16. As adults, Routley and Micklem barely noticed their age difference, but an eight-year span at ages twenty-six and eighteen, respectively seemed generational.

17. A preliminary committee had been assembled in 1939, with A. G. Matthews (1881–1962) as editorial secretary.

18. Remarks by Caird at Routley's memorial service in Westminster Abbey, February 8, 1983.

19. Geoffrey Beck, "Our New President," *Congregational Monthly,* June 1970.

20. *The Story of Congregationalism* (Independent Press: London, 1962), 146.

21. Caird.

22. "Men of the Day Collection," *Vanity Fair*, October 12, 1872, 206. The magazine dubbed Binney "the Archbishop of Nonconformity."

23. Binney was from Newcastle, hence the name chosen by its composer, Henry Morley (1834–?).

24. Chalfont Park is a walking spot near Gerrards Cross.

25. Sutton Courtenay is a town outside of Oxford where Routley interned in his Mansfield days.

26. GB, October 3, 1945.

27. Thomas Caryl Micklem, "Erik R. Routley, 31 October 1917–8 October 1982," *Bulletin*, HSGBI.

28. Thirty years later, Routley returned to the church to introduce the new hymns in the URC's *New Church Praise*.

29. Carole Jones, church member, in an email to NWG, March 14, 2003. The church closed in 2000.

30. The appeal was successful, and Routley presided at the opening ceremony in 1950.

31. GB, September 28, 1947.

32. Christopher Gillham, *The Condensed History of Dartford Congregational Church*, Kent County Archives, www.kentarchives.org.uk.

Chapter 4

Mansfield College, 1948–1959

POSTWAR MANSFIELD

Everyday life in Oxford did not return to normal when the war ended in the summer of 1945. Operations in the university buildings that had been appropriated for war administration took at least a year to dismantle. Former and potential students were not released from the military for many months while they participated in the European recovery efforts, and food rationing continued well into the 1950s. Colleges saw this as a time to reassess their resources and direction. Though there was no shortage of intellectually and theologically capable students, Mansfield had unique considerations confronting their board of governors.

Financially, the college depended on the original Spring Hill endowment, some estate bequests, and contributions from Congregationalist churches and individuals. A slump in memberships and postwar secularism proved damaging to the demand for trained church professionals, so these once-reliable sources of revenue were drying up. The College Council tossed about several potential avenues for income. Some ideas included using the college for conferences off-term and inviting old students and their spouses to stay at Mansfield for a month as long as they remained in active ministry. Mansfield reconfigured the chapel and hallways to provide a makeshift hostel for unmarried ordination students, and it became a residential college, forcing the council to examine the rather ambiguous treatment of female students at Mansfield, although women had been part of it for fifty years.[1] The idea of becoming a permanent private hall of the university was raised and discussed,[2] as this would loosen some financial purse strings for the institution and its students, bring diversity into Mansfield, and allow matriculation within the university. But, again, this posed a problem for the Mansfield women.[3]

By 1937, only 17 women had been ordained and they faced a mountain of difficulty in persuading a local church to call them. Despite the indispensable role of women during the first half of the 20th century, the denomination was anchored in conservatism. Alice Platts, ordained in 1947, became Warden of St. Paul's House in Liverpool where women were trained for short-term ministries rather than confront male dominance head on.[4]

Nathaniel Micklem versus Cecil Cadoux

If the college was to survive, a reevaluation of purpose was crucial. By 1948, many names connected with the founding of the college and the powerhouse of Mansfield theologians[5] had scattered in different directions or retired. William B. Selbie, the most influential member of the SCR, died in 1944 at the age of eighty-two. In 1909 Selbie, a first-generation Mansfield student, became its second principal, following the Revered Andrew Fairbairn. By then, Mansfield was in a far more acceptable place among the other Oxford colleges. Selbie was given a place in the university theology faculty, and his lectures were shortly placed on the official lectures list. In 1920 Selbie was honored with a divinity doctorate, the first to be given to a Nonconformist since 1662, and the highest award the university could deliver. The next principal, Nathaniel Micklem, a Selbie student, remarked affectionately, "[Selbie] took hold of a congregation. Mansfield Chapel under Selbie was no retreat for spiritual invalids."[6]

Another Mansfield graduate, the strict Congregationalist theologian and firm pacifist Cecil John Cadoux (1883–1947), "represented those who saw the understanding of Scripture under the guidance of the Holy Spirit as more determinative of faith than dependence on historic doctrine."[7] A civil servant after college, Cadoux received a call to the ministry and entered Mansfield in 1911, having obtained a degree at London University. Following World War I,[8] he taught New Testament Criticism at Yorkshire United Independent College in Bradford. In 1933 he returned to Mansfield as the librarian and Alexander Mackennal Professor of Church History, and was soon appointed vice principal.[9] Cadoux and Principal Nathaniel Micklem were classmates and friends in their days as Mansfield students. Though they carried immense respect for each another, their opposite religious and political views led to disruptive conflict and turmoil throughout their tenure. Cadoux felt that each local congregation was the "Universal church in miniature,"[10] and he contested both "the increasing prominence to the denomination's Calvinist roots"[11] and the movement for a union with the English Presbyterians. Cadoux preferred mutual respect and cooperation between denominations rather than ecumenical consolidations.[12] Micklem, architect of the "New Genevans,"[13] saw ecumenism as the only way forward into a postwar world.

This discord was the climate at Mansfield for Routley's entire student years. In his postretirement memoir, Micklem remarks:

> In spite of our most painful differences and the resulting almost unbearable tensions, nothing broke our genuine friendship. He (Cadoux) was a man of decided opinions and an active and laborious conscience. Yet, in controversy, he was scrupulously fair. Theologically, we were, and always had been, far apart, but Cadoux never complained that I restricted his writing or teaching, but he felt that he had been appointed to Mansfield as a faithful watchdog to keep an eye on me and stop the rot in the churches. We nearly broke one another's hearts.[14]

ROUTLEY'S RETURN TO MANSFIELD

By the mid-1940s, this derisive friction found Cadoux progressively isolated from the churches and students. Physically, this took its toll. Cadoux fell into ill health and died in 1947. Finding a replacement was not an easy process. Three Mansfield names were proposed: Pennar Davies[15] (1911–1996), Geoffrey Nuttall (1911–2007), and Aubrey Vine (1900–1973). When approached, Davies declined, having only recently begun teaching history in Wales.[16] Vine and Nuttall were interviewed for the position, but both men carried strong Cadoux allegiances, and the council and principal could not come to any agreement for appointing either man. They began to consider a temporary appointment.[17] Micklem put Routley's name before the council, and, without interview, Routley was approached for an interim five-year lecturer position. Micklem announced, "After a careful survey of the field, it was ultimately decided that it would be best not to make any appointment to the Mackennal Chair at present, but to appoint Erik Routley as lecturer in Church History."[18]

Resentment shattered any affability in the SCR. Though Routley was already known as a person with many gifts, a prominent academic standing was not one of them. Because of postwar faculty compression, he was initially appointed as tutor in Church History, librarian, chaplain, and chapel organist. Tony Tucker (b. 1931) recollects:

> There were those who thought that a more significant church historian should have been appointed. Mind you, I don't think that there was any money to do it. Erik came cheap! But there is no question that Micklem saw Routley as a voice of the future.[19]

Nuthall's supporters were quite pointed and public in their dissatisfaction, and a year later, in the principal's column of *Mansfield*, the college magazine, Micklem wrote:

> We are very happy to have Routley here. He presides with enthusiasm over the Library and the organ quite apart from his necessary and extensive labours in Church History. I feel that he has never quite had a fair deal in Church History. It is not merely that the exigencies of the new hymn book have called him to a far wider service in the churches than a young man should normally anticipate; more than that, he is a minister and cannot willingly see ministerial work undone. The College can no longer afford to pay a chaplain, but the pastoral work of the chaplain must be done, and Erik Routley has done it. How he has managed at the same time to get his D.Phil. and to do the tuition and lecturing so successfully, I do not know. We have not yet given him time to elongate his erudition of his sentences to a quotable measure, but if we ask whether he has interested and stimulated students over the whole field of Church History, I should be happy about the answer.[20]

This call from Mansfield came as a surprise. Routley was comfortable in Dartford and had just been named permanent minister. In a letter to his friend Geoffrey Beck, he remarks:

> This appointment to Mansfield seems very extraordinary to me, but I shall love living there, and so will Margaret. I shall be spending most of my time in the library, reading about church history since I used to diligently cut the lectures of my revered predecessor. We will leave Dartford with real regret; it has been a very happy time here, and all too short. Nothing less than Mansfield would have got me away so soon.[21]

TUTORSHIP

As a lecturer, Routley bore responsibilities toward the primary purpose of Mansfield: to train ordinands for the ministry. The compulsory Sermon Class occurred weekly, and every student was required to lead the class once a year in their three-year course. David Goodall (1922–2014)[22] remembered this experience with exacting clarity.

> The proceedings began in the College chapel, where all the ordination students and the Principal and one theological Tutor formed the congregation. They spread themselves out around the chapel, pretending to make the room full of worshipers. The Principal and Tutor sat in the back row. There was no microphone, so the student "victim" in the pulpit was expected to audibly fill the room—or face severe criticism. There was no music, and therefore, no hymns. Apart from this a full preaching service was presented by the chosen student, using appropriate prayers, scripture, sermon, and connecting rubrics. This was a daunting task as all was received in total silence. In those days, it didn't occur to us to introduce spoken responses. At the end, we would file out to the Hall

for dinner—with no conversation about the class. After dinner we would head to the JCR, informally seated with the Principal and Tutor on either side of the fireplace. The student-victim sat in the center. Two previously selected ordinands led the criticism of any part of the service and incidental mannerisms. At length, the Principal would ask the Tutor to deliver a verdict followed by his own comments. We were then dismissed with an Archepiscopal blessing; we headed straight for the pub.[23]

At these classes, Routley was at his best, says Goodall. "His criticisms were always pertinent, though sometimes devastating; these were always accompanied with pure grace, so that we always felt that something positive had been served and that we were all capable of our task."[24]

In 1953 Routley's five-year contract had nearly expired. The new principal, John Marsh (1911–1978), created a joint Ecclesiastical History department with Regent's Park College. This new collaboration was headed by Horton Davies (1916–2005),[25] and the two instructors and tutors were W. Morris S. West (f. 1955) of Regent's and Routley of Mansfield.[26] Marsh also gave Routley the Mackennal Chair position and an additional title: Director of Chapel. Still a controversial choice, Marsh, like Micklem, also wrote a defense of Routley in the *Mansfield* magazine.

> I should like to pay a special tribute to Erik Routley, as the church historian who has had to make most adjustments. He has done it with his customary cheerfulness, courtesy, and goodwill, and we all have very much to thank him for.[27]

DIRECTOR OF CHAPEL

Chapel was central to the life of the college.[28] By 1940 it was the place of worship for all local Nonconformists and not just another confident and impressive architectural structure.[29] The Sunday-morning service and the assurance of a powerful sermon delivered by a respected academic attracted the Oxford community at large. As Director of Music, Routley was the organist, and he authoritatively emphasized strong hymn singing. He selected the hymns for the various weekly services throughout his chaplaincy, except for those on Wednesday nights. These services were led by students, who bore the hymn selection responsibility with Routley's encouragement and support. Over the years, the results were significant,

> The congregation is an alert one and many members bring their own tune books. The consequence is that they can sing almost anything. To hear the congregation take hold of some great hymn is a wonderful experience.[30]

Every day at 8:30 a.m. and 10:00 p.m., the college held morning prayers in the antechapel. As there were no liturgical or scriptural demands for these services, hymn choices enjoyed an unlimited variety. On Monday evenings there was a twenty-minute rehearsal session to learn the music for the week—four hymns for Sunday morning, two more and a psalm for the weekday-morning services, and one for the evenings.[31] Routley was accustomed to this structure from his days as an ordinand, so he wholeheartedly continued this preparation with his enthusiastic, witty, and historical style, subtly exploring the faithful elements of worship through the hymns. In his role as instructor, Routley asserted:

> It is part of a minister's education to know the hymnbook. In the course of three years any student may expect to have the chance of singing nearly everything that is in that book. There is much to be said for the creation of a fellowship of faithful praise in this practical fashion, in preference to the more obvious method of high-mindedly "educating" people in church music. Music is one of piety's handmaids, and what a joy it is to serve in such a household of faith.[32]

In 1953 Robert Courtney (b. 1931)[33] arrived at Mansfield by way of St. John's. He came to know Routley well.

> Indeed, he taught us almost every hymn in *Congregational Praise* (except the ones he didn't like) but I remember even more his informal Bible studies and his cogent and inspiring preaching..[34] Erik confidently maintained that reading good, exciting detective stories came next to Bible study for the competent preacher. He was utterly trustworthy, and all my confidences were completely secure. His humour, personal kindness and friendship deeply influenced my ministry and my life more than anyone else.[35]

CHAPLAINCY AND THE CONGREGATIONAL SOCIETY

Routley followed the trajectories established by the previous chaplains, Romilly Micklem and John Marsh, but it was during Routley's time as the music director that the institutional musical standard was fully established. In her history of Mansfield College, Elaine Kaye maintains that it was Routley who developed a theology to integrate music into the heartbeat of the college.[36]

> His lectures, his books, his work on *Congregational Praise*, and [role as] founder-president of the Congregational Organist's Guild flowed into the life of the churches of which Mansfield graduates were ministers and organists, and thence into the whole life of the denomination and beyond.[37]

Between the wars, universities in England supported intercollegiate social groups for various religions and Nonconformist denominations. These societies provided community within the generally unfamiliar Anglican atmosphere, but with the advance of secularism in the latter half of the twentieth century, these organizations nearly disappeared. Today there are more than four hundred student clubs and societies at Oxford, yet only a few are designated by religion.[38]

The concept of a society for Congregationalist students in Oxford began early in Mansfield's history. In May 1882, seventeen undergraduates gathered in the rooms of Robert F. Horton (1855–1934)[39] at New College, where he lectured in history. A stalwart dissenter, Horton saw the need for an association where students would be exposed to Nonconformist principles and in which new freshmen would feel secure. He organized recruitment teas in the rooms of various Oxford colleges at the beginning of each academic new year.[40] By 1947, this University-wide Congregational Society (CongSoc) met at Mansfield on Sunday afternoons during term. Well-known speakers were scheduled from all areas of the university and the Congregational Union of England and Wales;[41] Sunday evenings, the society met informally in Room 13 at the college. When Routley took over, he generously opened his home to these weekly gatherings, where Margaret added to the hospitality.

> On Sunday evenings he and Margaret would invite us to their home for coffee, chat, devotionals and—to crown the evening—Erik's reading from the collected stories of Damon Runyon. The 1930s New York underworld milieu was memorably rendered by Erik's crisp, educated English.[42]

Undergraduates involved during Routley's chaplaincy remember his leadership as an important part of their coming of age. Tony Tucker also recalls that Routley's influence was "very, very great indeed. He held everyone within the faith and in the Congregational tradition. People are grateful to this day."[43]

Margaret Ruth Monroe Micklem (1930–2018) joined CongSoc shortly after she went up to Oxford in 1951, and was soon won over by its chaplain with the peculiar stare.

> Through his unquestioning acceptance of the good faith of all the members of CongSoc, which nonetheless went with a healthy doubt about some of us, Erik earned our trust . . . he treated us with a respect we did not deserve. This curious reverence was typical of the whole of Erik's approach to life . . . and yet he was never intrusive, publicly or privately. He did not plunge into other people's affairs unless they had become unbearably idiotic. He simply enjoyed life.[44]

Ruth lived near the Routleys, who called on her often to babysit,[45] but despite this familiarity, she remained wary of the more structured elements of the Society.

> [Routley] appeared at the tea meetings on Sunday afternoons, but I often did not. I had a profound distrust for being told things about how I should behave. Erik was usually seen, but not heard. He would sit, smoking his pipe and watching. He was always inscrutable, and this impression was upheld by the fact that one was not always sure who he was looking at. It didn't take long to become aware that a keen intelligence and vigilance, bore up by an alarming memory and prophetic understanding of our natures, was working on our behalf. I did attend Sunday morning services and when Erik preached, the sermons were normally electrifying.[46]

THE LAKE DISTRICT

One particularly important and meaningful activity within CongSoc was the annual, weeklong Easter trip to the Lake District, and Ruth participated in a few of these. Typically, a group of thirty or so students would travel, with Routley and other chaperones, up to Seatoller House in Keswick at the head of Borrowdale. The participants wistfully mark the hiking, meals, storytelling, and singing as an important part of their education.[47] They are quick to add that though Routley and his pipe were always present, he did very little actual walking of the fells—but he was very happy to drive to the various gathering points along the way, providing supplies and humorous encouragement. Photographs of these gatherings portray laughing, exuberant young women and men enjoying comfortable companionship and the antics of their chaplain.

The days began and ended with a short prayer service, and evening's entertainment was usually talking—and more talking—as there were only oil lamps for light. Each night Routley read a Damon Runyon story aloud, continuing the practice that began the informal Sunday evening gatherings in Oxford.[48] These lively, contemporary stories of street people and their folk talk were decidedly popular within the Society, and members gave each other nicknames using the characters in the stories. Routley was "The Reverend Ambrose Hammer." Hammer appears in several Runyon stories as the autobiographical newspaper reporter, and sometime detective, who writes reviews for stage shows in New York City. In one story, "Broadway Complex,"[49] the omnipresent, unnamed narrator describes Hammer this way:

> This Ambrose Hammer, the newspaper scribe, is a short, chubby guy, with big, round, googly eyes, and a very innocent expression. To look at Ambrose

Hammer you will never suspect that he has sense enough to pound sand in a rat hole, but Ambrose is really a pretty slick guy. In fact, Ambrose is a great hand for thinking. . . . I will say one thing for Ambrose Hammer, and this is that he is at all times very gentlemanly.[50]

The year Caryl Micklem came along as chaplain, Ruth Monro met her future husband.

CONGSOC CHOIR

Routley's other role with the CongSoc members was the absolute opposite of the visible but silent chaplain.[51] As music director, from the organ bench Routley took control and formed a CongSoc choir, commanding them to sing—his way.

One Sunday evening in the tower room at Mansfield, Erik rose through the clouds of smoke and steam and announced: "I should be interested to see in the Chapel, at a time to be announced, all the following persons: excellent soprano singers, indispensable altos, either experienced or willing to have a try, and anyone who has ever dreamt that he might conceivably one day be able to sing tenor." We were being taken on by him in a joint enterprise in which we were all the instruments of praise. We were ready with as much obedience as we could possibly muster.[52]

In 1951 this first choir led an Advent lessons and carol service in the chapel, and this quickly became a beloved and much anticipated event into the 1970s. Routley got the ensemble singing new songs and old carols everywhere from Oxford to Scafell to London and back. When the BBC Third Programme featured the introduction of *Congregational Praise*, CongSoc members made up an octet to present the hymns. But, more importantly,

Erik Routley created the security that allowed us to work out our proper places through humour and high work. He laid open paths when we most needed them. The Congregational Society was the playground; here we could rehearse our lines without fear, and assume whatever character suited us at the moment. The high work was in the preaching groups and the choir. The friendships that all this generated have been profound, generous, and lasting."[53]

THE HYMN SOCIETY OF GREAT BRITAIN AND IRELAND

In 1943, while an ordinand, Routley saw an ad in a local church newsletter inviting new members to join the Hymn Society of Great Britain and Ireland. Membership was open to "scholars who had already published work in the field of hymnody and to 'ordinary members' with an interest in the subject."[54] In an interview with Harry Eskew (1936–2020),[55] Routley explained:

> I answered the advertisement and said, "well, it can't do any harm." The subscription was 2 shillings and 6 pence a year. I thought I could afford that, so I joined and started receiving the *Bulletin*.[56]

Another member, George Wallace Briggs (1875–1959), hymn writer and Anglican priest, convinced Erik to attend his first annual conference in 1945.

> Everybody in the Hymn Society knew who Canon Briggs was, and some of us were privileged to know him well. He was one of the founders of the Society and was always the most cheerful, energetic, and missionary-minded of its members. As the most distinguished hymn writer of the first half of this century [twentieth], he was also an influential hymn book editor.[57]

At the time, the Society's quarterly publication, the *Bulletin*, was edited by another founding member, Millar Patrick (1868–1951).[58] Patrick served in this role for ten years, and beginning with the July 1945 issue, Routley became assistant editor, though the two men never met. In December 1947, Routley received a letter from Patrick that began:

> It is time, I think that my name should disappear from the heading of the *Bulletin*. There is no point now in keeping it there, since the responsibilities of the Editorship have passed entirely into your hands . . . the Society is fortunate in having found in you an Editor so well equipped with knowledge of both the literary and musical fields of hymnody and with such magnificent enthusiasm with which to inspire others.[59]

Routley assumed the editorship with the January 1948 issue. At Patrick's suggestion, a new series was begun, Volume II. In the April 1948 issue, Routley honored Patrick:

> Under his guidance, the *Bulletin* has been started in a tradition of high scholarship, and the measure of that weight of learning has now passed into [my] hands. Furthermore, it was the *Bulletin* which held the Society together during the

years of war when Conferences were impossible and contact between members was very difficult. His spirit, more than any other, kept the Society alive.[60]

Routley held this editorship until he moved to the United States in 1974, a span of responsibility exceeded only by Bernard Massey (1927–2011).[61] Routley wrote at least one article for every issue and usually included a book review.[62] In the beginning, his typographical errors—and some factual ones—were notorious. This was usually kindly overlooked, but one person sent constant criticism to Routley.

JOHN W. WILSON

John Whitridge Wilson (1905–1992) was born of Congregationalist parents in Birmingham, England. He attended Sidney Sussex College at Cambridge, reading natural sciences, but realized when he graduated that music was his passion. Consequently, Wilson entered study with Ralph Vaughan Williams and became director of music at Charterhouse School in 1947, where he taught from 1932 to his retirement in 1965. Along with others in 1936, Wilson was a founding member of the Hymn Society. About this turn of interest, he says:

> I always had an instinct for music. But [after earning my Cambridge degree] the urge for music became too strong, so I gave up science, did a crash course at the Royal College of Music, and emerged as a rather raw young music master.[63]

In a centenary tribute to Wilson, Robin Leaver (b. 1939) refers to him as "a man whose energies, insight, and dogged persistence influenced many poets and composers of hymns, informed numerous hymnal editors and goaded hymnologists to get their facts straight."[64]

EDITORIAL CONTROVERSY AND *THE PUBLIC SCHOOL HYMN BOOK*

Just when Wilson began to upbraid Routley's work in the Hymn Society is unclear, but there are indications that it began early in Routley's editorial tenure. A pointed exchange between the two men centered on Routley's review of *The Public School Hymn Book* (1949).[65] In the July 1950 edition of the *Bulletin*, Routley, as editor, presents two contrasting articles on recently published hymnals. In the first, Routley gives high marks and laudatory comments on three new Methodist books. Though he points out editorial issues and decries the "outrageous price," he concludes with "Nobody who takes seriously any of the subjects with which [these books] deals can afford to be without it. It is a contribution to hymnology and an advancement of its study."[66] The very next article is a harsh and scorching non-review of the public school book. Using phrases like "[there are] elementary errors, on every fourth or fifth page, which decent proof-reading would have eliminated immediately," "inexcusable casualness," and "wooden and tedious harmonies," Routley declares that the *Bulletin* will not review "any book which treats its reader so cavalierly."[67] These observations were widely expressed elsewhere in the church music world, but none so sharply or openly.

Ironically, Routley's own writing frequently shows much of this same inattention to detail. Wilson contacted Routley often on this disparity and suggested that Routley send him (Wilson) the proofs before submitting copy to the printer.[68] By Routley's own admission, his uncorrected reviews and editorials in the *Bulletin* justified Wilson's criticism:

> I did it very badly; the thing was full of misprints. I was always forgetting to bring the issue out. Wilson wrote a rather acid letter saying [that] if I couldn't read proofs, he'd be glad to help.[69]

In 1955 the *Bulletin* contained a favorable and explanatory review of the same public school hymnal, written by organist A. V. Butcher (1907–1997).[70] An olive branch, perhaps, but Wilson didn't think that there was much improvement in Routley's unprofessional editing.

The Public School Hymn Book (1949) was very carefully corrected and reissued in 1959. When Routley's inconsistent habits prevented a review of the book in timely publication, Wilson wrote one more strident letter; Routley gave this reply:

> Yes, I know. I'm terribly sorry . . . the editor is impecunious and disastrously overworked—it being necessary to do at least two jobs in the time normally allotted for one in order to make ends meet, hence, [producing] appalling and indecent haste and the bad practice of sending stuff to the printer at the last minute and in a hurry. What you really want to do is to ask the Society to appoint a new printer and a new editor. I just can't keep it up much longer anyhow and shall soon offer a final resignation which I have already twice unsuccessfully offered to the Executive [*sic*]. Actually, the Executive will be meeting tomorrow at Cambridge, and I'll produce your letter there. I entirely agree. The thing is lamentable, and hopelessly organized. I apologize and will do so in print in the next issue.[71]

The Cambridge meeting came and went with no recorded mention of even a discussion of Routley's resignation. In a letter to Wilson following the session, Routley says:

> I raised your point at the Executive at Cambridge and was asked to have a look at some of the Edinburgh printers. Printing (as you'll know) is only succeeded by beer in the amount of employment it provides in this city. . . . I'm carrying on for a little longer. I hope there'll be some more John Wilson to print sometime soon.[72]

The next issue was Autumn 1960, and Wilson wrote a lengthy review of *The Public School Hymn Book* (1959). In his opening paragraph is a straightforward and strong reference to Routley's public criticism, but, surprisingly, it contains no resentment toward the earlier article or Routley himself.

RECONCILIATION

Wilson and Routley finally met face-to-face when, in 1962, the Headmasters Conference appointed a new committee to rethink and replan the public school hymn book, with Wilson as the secretary. The goals included omitting silly sentiment and feeble theology, enlightening editorial notes, mixing hymns from all periods of history, and lowering the keys for easier singing.[73] In 1964 a committee of four, including Wilson, felt the new edition needed a detailed inspection of the earliest hymn sources. This took the shape of a thirty-five-page, acclaimed introduction entitled "Hymns and Their Tunes: an historical survey, by Erik Routley." This was revised and printed for private circulation at the Joint Conference of members of the Hymn Society of Great Britain and Ireland, the International Fellowship for Research in Hymnology, and the Hymn Society of America, held at Oxford in August 1981.[74] Their rift was mended.

Harry Eskew conducted separate interviews with both men, and, concerning Wilson, Routley comments that after John started reading the proofs, the *Bulletin* became a respectable publication. He continues:

> He [John Wilson] is one of the people for whom I have the greatest possible respect. A promoter of hymns—he won't let us call him a hymnologist, but that's his modesty. He's done more for hymn singing in England than any other living person.[75]

Wilson's reflection of their rapport is warmer:

My acquaintance with Erik Routley, beginning in the 1950s, ripened into a close friendship, with a continuous sharing of ideas and discoveries that has become one of my greatest joys.[76]

When *A Panorama of Christian Hymnody* was revised and expanded by Paul A. Richardson (b. 1951) in 2004, Alan Luff (1928–2020) contributed a personal introduction.[77] Of the two men, Luff has this to say:

Erik would often be introduced as "the greatest hymnologist of our time." [Routley] would equally often demur, saying that accolade belonged to the English scholar, John Wilson. . . . Erik respected John for his meticulous scholarship, not always Erik's best side. [Erik] had a phenomenal memory, but he could forget things as well, assuming that the whole was in his grasp, and certainly details could go wrong. What John respected [Erik] for was his broad vision and his huge enthusiasm for what hymns have been and what they can be in the life of the Church and of the individual Christian.[78]

Wilson and Routley enjoyed similar full and paralleling careers, yet their schedules seldom permitted meeting in person. The RSCM set out to produce a supplement with no denominational emphasis in the early 1970s. They wanted Wilson to put it together, and Routley was called in as a consultant. But even then, they worked together to collect the hymns and make them suitable mostly by correspondence. For more than twenty years they exchanged letters at least monthly and usually more often. Revealing a mutual respect and familiarity, their candid interchange produced well over four hundred letters and lasted until Erik's abrupt death in 1982. Luff shares thoughts on this, as well.

When Erik moved to America, he and John enjoyed an almost weekly correspondence, largely on matters hymnological. John valued this hugely, and when Erik died, besides the personal loss, it was of great sadness to him that this exchange of letters had now come to an end.[79]

EARLY BOOKS AND PUBLICATIONS

Routley's Mansfield bachelor of divinity thesis was issued in book form in 1950 and entitled *The Church and Music*.[80] It bears a touching dedication to his parents.[81] A reviewer says, "This book is a lucid tracing of the development of music from the most primitive up through centuries of bondage to its modern autonomy."[82] Routley's intent is more specific:

I shall tell the story with as little technical language as possible, because I hope that this will be read by theologians and musicians whose sympathy with each other's subject may extend to good will. The relationship between music and theology should be one not of suspicion, contempt, or patronage, but of courtesy.[83]

The July 1950 issue of *Mansfield* college magazine features a review by Romilly Micklem, who observes that there is much on which to comment and discuss, especially Routley's argument on "the badness of music in the 19th century" and his [Routley's] "endearing vigor" that makes him extremely vulnerable to judgmental indignation.

Much unjust criticism will be avoided if it is remembered that he has essayed the hard task of writing for the theologian who moves unfamiliarly in the realm of music and for the musician to whom the realm of theology is similarly foreign . . . the next edition should pay attention to proof-reading, but a sequel to this story about Christian thought about music is essential.[84]

I'll Praise My Maker (1951)

An unfinished manuscript begun by Bernard Manning (1882–1941) on Moravian poet and hymn writer James Montgomery (1751–1854) is most often cited as the catalyst for Routley's extensive publishing career. While serving the congregation in Wednesbury, Erik read Manning's work. Using the momentum established to produce a thesis, Erik drew on this energy to write not only about Montgomery but also other hymn writers from the seventeenth and eighteenth centuries. The eventual result was *I'll Praise My Maker*, published by Independent Press in 1951.[85] Taking Romilly's advice, Routley turned to both Micklem and Arnold Gwynne Matthews (1881–1962) for proofreading and critical examination. A review in the *Bulletin* notes:

Mr. Routley's treatment is scholarly and authoritative, and never dull. In his analysis of character, he displays a rare insight into Protestant doctrine. Routley has done considerable service in bringing to our notice many hymns which have fallen into disuse or been undervalued. This book is a joy to read. He writes with gusto, and a touch of humor which will not be repressed.[86]

The book consists of literary, devotional, and historical comments on the Calvinistic hymns that came out of England in the eighteenth and early nineteenth centuries. Routley considers the hymns of Philip Doddridge (1702–1751), William Cowper (1731–1800), John Newton (1725–1807), James Montgomery (1771–1854), Josiah Conder (1789–1855), and a few others as the legacy of English Puritanism to Church history.

Dissertation and *Hymns and Human Life* (1952)

In 1903 the Queen's publisher, John Murray Ltd., released the well-known *Psalms in the Human Life* by Rowland Prothero (1851–1937).[87] After the war, the same printer approached C. S. Phillips (1883–1949) to write *Hymns in Human Life*.[88] Phillips agreed, but he became ill in the process. Recognizing that he would likely not finish, Phillips recommended that Routley be tapped to finish the work. Routley started from scratch, and his book *Hymns and Human Life*[89] is an examination of frequently sung hymns in Great Britain in the early 1950s and what they say about Christian faith. This is the first public manifestation of Routley's thoughts on the relationship between music and theology.

> Hymn singing is, as a matter of fact, the most insistent and clamorous of all the ways in which Christian faith and worship makes an impact on the world around it. . . . [Y]ou cannot close your ears. If a congregation is singing "How Firm a Foundation" in some rickety non-conformist chapel in industrial Yorkshire, the neighbors hear about it. Hymns are the folksong of the church militant.[90]

At the same time, Routley was finishing his doctor of philosophy dissertation.[91] The two works were published almost simultaneously.

Congregational Praise (1951) and Its *Companion* (1953)

Congregational Praise was finally released in 1951. By twenty-first-century standards, it appears cautious, but its adoption of texts and tunes from twentieth-century composers, and reintroducing some of the best hymns from pre-Victorian days, was bold and healthy.

> The book sought a revival of the classics and a fresh, contemporary hymnody, a wide range of musical and theological vocabulary that would convey to the singing people a new sense of the greatness of the church to which as Congregationalist they belong.[92]

To encourage appreciation of the new book, upon publication, Routley immediately began an intense campaign to provide support to the Congregational churches in England and Scotland using lectures, sermons, and his beloved hymn sings. It was largely due to his dogged devotion to this task that the denomination accepted, and eventually embraced, their new hymnal. In 1953, Kenneth L. Parry (1884–1962) and Routley produced a *Companion to Congregational Praise*.[93] In a letter addressed to Caryl Micklem in September 1949, Routley wryly expresses a common researcher's lament:

> My next large job is the musical part of the companion to *Congregational Praise*. We are trying to get that out fairly near the publication of the hymnbook. Parry is doing the hymns and authors, I the tunes, but the biographies will be quite a job. I have not yet evolved the technique of smoothly putting the question in writing, "Dear Sir, are you dead."[94]

Though companions had appeared alongside earlier hymnals, this one set the standard for future companions to hymnals of all denominations.

Hymns and the Faith (1955)

Routley felt that *Hymns and Human Life* "contributed nothing to the redress of what I believe to be a certain lack of balance in our interest in hymns,"[95] so he set out to present a commentary of popular hymns from a credal and scriptural view. In *Hymns and the Faith*, the representative hymns are those observed by Routley to be the most popular in the English churches, but not necessarily ones he liked.

> The rewarding thing about this present piece of work is that I have found that the popular hymns provide a much better balanced view of the Christian faith that you would have got from any collection of my own favorites.[96]

A review from an Episcopalian rector in New Brunswick, New Jersey, observes:

> [Routley] purposely avoids lengthy discussion of the sources or history of any of the hymns. Consequently, *Hymns and the Faith* is in no sense a book on hymnology, but rather a group of delightful sermonettes written for the layman, the clergy, and choirmasters.[97]

John Murray (1884–1967) was reluctant to publish the book, as "he didn't think it was quite their line."[98] The book was published at a reduced royalty, but, unexpectedly, an American book club picked it up, and Routley's first royalty check was an astonishing six hundred pounds![99] He was again surprised when Seabury Press republished it in the United States.[100] As a result, *Hymns and Human Life* and *Hymns of the Faith* were widely read and circulated in both English and North American seminaries and academic institutions. Routley became visible to the public in other ways as well.

The *British Weekly* and other Editorships

An editor at the venerable publishing house of Hodder & Stanton was responsible for the *British Weekly*, one of the most successful and progressive religious newspapers of its time. Founded in 1886 by one of the editors, William Nicoll (1851–1923), the paper was intended as a vehicle for liberal, Nonconformist opinion by introducing readers to the best in contemporary culture related to the purpose.[101] In 1955 Routley was asked to write a monthly feature on music and pen the occasional book review. His contributions stopped in 1970, when the ownership of *British Weekly* transferred to what is now the *Church of England Newspaper*.[102] Along with the Hymn Society's *Bulletin*, Routley contributed articles regularly to other journals. Among these were the *Congregational Monthly*,[103] in which his column "Sing Up" featured a new hymn from *Congregational Praise* in each issue. The fresh and clear treatment of the subject of music and theology in his books and articles led to his first invitations to lecture in Canada and the United States in the late autumn of 1955.

FIRST LECTURES IN NORTH AMERICA (1955)

Beginning with Andrew Fairbairn, Mansfield principals and tutors had academic posts in North America. Fairbairn and Selbie lectured at Yale; Nathaniel Micklem taught New Testament at Queen's College in Ontario. As professor of Christian Theology at Nottingham University, John Marsh was invited to teach and lecture at several places, including Union Theological Seminary in New York and Duke University. Contemporaries Daniel Jenkins (1914–2002) and George Caird (1917–1984) held roles at the University of Chicago and Princeton (Jenkins) and Caird at St. Stephen's College in Edmonton and McGill University in Montreal.

In October 1955 George P. Gilmour (1900–1963), president of McMaster University,[104] extended an invitation to Routley to come to Canada at the end of November and deliver three lectures based on *Hymns and Human Life*.[105] Routley accepted, and this was the impetus for a two-week whirlwind of additional speaking engagements at Emmanuel College[106] in Toronto, McGill University in Montreal, Harvard University, and the University of Chicago. He was well received.

> From his first lecture, the audience was keenly alive to the importance of worship; the interest kept mounting as one lecture followed another. Dr. Routley's visit was like a fresh breeze from another land. His naturalness and personal charm have made him many friends in Toronto.[107]

On his way to the Federated Theological School at the University of Chicago,[108] Routley was persuaded to fill the pulpit of the First Presbyterian Church of Crown Point, Indiana. The pastor was a Mansfield man and well-known minister, L. Humphrey Walz (1910–2003).[109] When Routley returned to Oxford, he received a letter from the president of Emmanuel College, the Reverend A. B. B. Moore (1924–2004), offering Routley a new position as professor of Liturgiology[110] and chair of the Department of Religion. Routley declined.

> I write this with a heavy heart. In so many ways, I should love to come, but I am as sure as one can be that I must not leave my work. Horton Davies has just left for Princeton, and that alone would be a strong point against my leaving. I feel real remorse at giving you this reply.[111]

John Marsh was openly relieved. In his yearly principal's report, Marsh wrote:

> Dr. Routley gave me reason for great concern during the year. As I predicted last June, he gave the St. Andrew's Lectures at Victoria University [Emmanuel College] in Toronto. He did this so well that, as I feared, the University invited him to become their first Professor of Liturgiology. For a day or so I was concerned lest we lose Dr. Routley but am glad to say he resisted the temptation and decided to remain here at Mansfield. We cannot speak too highly of his work in every capacity.[112]

FAMILY LIFE

Another likely reason to stay in Oxford was Erik's daily life as husband and father. The household had expanded to include two more children, Patrick (b. 1949) and Priscilla (b. 1953), and a cat, Orlando. Margaret's parents had moved to Oxford from Cheshire. Everyone enjoyed and endured the usual family activities, occasionally revealed in Erik's letters. In one to Caryl Micklem, there's an amusing description of developmental milestones:

> We are all well here. Patrick now weighs rather more than Nicholas did by Christmas; Nicholas himself is now talking with every appearance of intelligence; he can sing the first verse of "Once in Royal David's City" to a tune of his own composition which is strongly reminiscent of primitive plainsong. He has also begun to say his prayers but insists on substituting "Good Boy" for "Amen." Theologically this is reprehensible.[113]

While on most weekends Routley filled pulpits in and around Oxfordshire with occasional engagements across England, Margaret established herself as a violinist and kept a full studio of string students, independent of her husband's professional life. This remained the pattern until Erik's death in 1982. The couple recognized their different callings, and each deeply respected the other. Margaret supported Erik, and he likewise; they functioned in playful and loving tandem, not as a set. In later years, Margaret would occasionally join Erik at his conference locations, and a holiday to explore the United States and Canada often followed. In this spirit, Margaret and the kids gravitated to the Congregational Chapel in Summertown, a northern suburb of Oxford City. The minister there was Geoffrey Beck (1919–2019).

GEOFFREY BECK

The cohorts of JCR members during the war years were small but impressive. Many became important figures in academic circles and ecumenical efforts in the last half of the twentieth century.[114] Beck entered the JCR at Mansfield during Routley's last year, thus beginning a friendly collegial and family relationship until their deaths.

> On arrival in wartime, I had scarcely developed the usual annoyance at the unfamiliar hymns and tunes which the College organist insisted that we learn each week, when George Caird told me that the youthful Routley had a complete manuscript hymnbook, compiled from all hymnals and none—and that when no suitable tune existed, he wrote one![115]

Beck was both a Congregational minister[116] and first-class cricketer.[117] When Beck arrived at Summertown in 1950, Routley told Beck, unceremoniously, that he would be worshipping elsewhere, though he would endure the organ if an emergency arose to fill the pulpit.[118]

> After a year or so, circumstances brought both Routley and his precociously musical family to Summertown after all, becoming what Routley termed "bad" members. However, he got to a good many church meetings, asked to join a house group and gladly sat on a committee to plan church redecoration. In 1957, he agreed to baptize our club-footed daughter and thereby found himself leading a family worship festival, which he viewed with mixed feelings; but he brought his own wife, two sons and daughter in support. The result was a triumphant proclamation of the meaning of baptism which had everyone roaring with laughter. His children told him afterwards that this was *their* church from then on![119]

This same daughter required more than sixty weekly treatments in London, and Erik, with sharp insight, recognized the strain on the Beck family and quietly organized a rotation of drivers for these visits.

In 1965 Beck accepted a call to the new Coventry Cathedral as warden of the Chapel of Unity, an ecumenical chapel serving both the City of Coventry and all of Warwickshire. Beck wanted to devise a hymnal for this setting, and he and Routley worked several years, along with the Cathedral liturgist, Joseph Poole, toward this goal, but the project was eventually abandoned, primarily for other financial priorities.[120]

MORE HYMN TUNES

Somehow, amid all his family obligations, his administrative and teaching duties, pastoral responsibilities, publishing commitments, and launching the newly formed Congregational Organists' Guild,[121] Routley found time to compose an organ piece, "Wrestling Jacob," which defines one of his revered biblical events.[122] Through his connections in the Student Christian Movement, Routley came across the work of a Sinhalese poet, S. D. Karunaratne (*f.* 1948), which provided the texts for three tunes that Routley wrote as a set for children. He named the tunes after venerable Mansfield men: "Bartlet," "Selbie," and "Mackennal." These hymns appeared in a small collection of Karunaratne's work.[123]

The Congregationalist minister Albert Bayly (1901–1984) began writing hymns after World War II, interpreting central biblical teaching for the contemporary world.[124] Bayly received ministerial training at Mansfield and was ordained in 1929, serving various English congregations for forty years. As the forerunner of the hymn explosion of the second half of the twentieth century, Cyril Taylor (1907–1901)[125] describes Bayly as "the last of the old and the first of the new." Many of Bayly's hymns and poems were inspired by specific occasions and his interest in science and astronomy.[126] Bayly knew Routley through the Hymn Society, and in the late 1940s he approached Routley with a request for tunes to accompany several texts in irregular meter. "Sainthill," "Coleman's Hatch," and "Gravetye" are Routley's answer to Bayly's request.[127]

> His language is conservative, rather than self-consciously "with it"; he has never let himself be separated from good theology by the clamour of modernism.[128]

A fourth tune, named after a West Sussex[129] village, TYES CROSS, was composed for "What does the Lord require," one of Bayly's most loved texts.[130] In the late 1960s, *Hymns A & M* was preparing a supplement to fill in the gaps of *Hymns Ancient Modern, Revised*.[131] One of the music editors, John Dykes Bower (1905–1981)[132] contacted Routley about including "What Does the Lord Require" in the book.

> Sir John gently pointed out that I had duplicated a phrase in John Ireland's immortal tune LOVE UNKNOWN and asked whether I would consider altering it. My immediate answer was to write a new tune which will be seen as a paraphrase of [TYES CROSS] in a minor mode. [The original key] Eb was not the key for the prophet Micah.[133]

The new tune is "Sharpthorne"[134] and appears with the Bayly text in over thirty hymnals used in 2022. To date, both text and tune appear together.

A SUMMONS (1959)

About the time of that baptism at Summertown in 1957, Geoffrey Beck noticed that his friend seemed restless. The identity of Mansfield was rapidly changing. The new principal, John Marsh, had secured PPH status for the college, and students were admitted to Mansfield who did not study for the ministry. The first of these had been admitted to study geography.[135] By 1958 the college had doubled the population of the JCR from the lows of the 1940s, but though the students still came largely from Congregational backgrounds, those studying for the ministry dropped by half.[136] These circumstances and the increasing cultural secularity contributed to a subtle change in chapel services and the chaplaincy—the need for Routley's musical and pastoral contributions were not as imperative as when he had assumed his role ten years before. George Caird, by now a well-respected authority on the New Testament, was returning from Canada,[137] and David Goodall had been established as bursar. Though Routley considered Marsh, Caird, and Goodall as friends and esteemed colleagues, the college was clearly entering a new phase. Beck remembered:

> He told me how he had consulted our CUEW General Secretary, Howard Stanley (1901–1975), and was discouraged and dismayed to be told that there was no suitable church in England at that moment, but [Augustine-Bristo] in Edinburgh was vacant. Erik had just been made editor of the *Congregational Monthly*, a publication of the CUEW, and Howard told Erik that if he moved to Scotland, he must give up that position.[138]

Beck surmised that he may have been an unwitting pawn in Augustine-Bristo's decision to extend a call to Routley. The principal of the Scottish Congregational College was Charles Duthie (1911–1982) and a member of ABC. In Edinburgh on a cricket tour, Beck was surprised by an invitation for a coffee from Duthie. Beck recalled that the conversation was more like an interview, and in their discussion the empty pulpit came up, as did Routley's name and his desire to leave Mansfield. Beck assumed that the two were unrelated and forgot about their chat, but before long the Routleys had moved to Edinburgh.[139]

John Marsh taught a six-week course in the United States in the summer of 1958. Before he left, Routley confided that Augustine-Bristo Church in Edinburgh had approached him to become a candidate for their soon-to-be vacant pulpit.[140] Marsh carried this burden on his leave and was not surprised when he returned to find that Routley had accepted their invitation to preach before the congregation in November.

> He is not an easy man to replace. No Principal could have had a more willing, understanding, and co-operative colleague than he has been to me. We shall miss his penetrating judgement, his deep concern for preaching, his great gifts as musician and organist, his invaluable work as Chaplain, and his great honour in the denomination.[141]

Routley preached at Mansfield one last time just after his installment at Augustin-Bristo.[142] The scripture for the sermon was from II Kings, the story of Elisha's succession to Elijah.

> Because I have been given this terrifying responsibility [ABC], my mind will not detach itself from this story of traditions. Here, we have a college which lives, and has lived the past eleven years as I know, in a state of continuous crisis. Those of us who have served it over the past decade have known very well that we were serving it in a period of transition, and that means a period of crisis. But that's not all I feel today. I feel that if a theological college is to be alive and to serve its generation as it should, then it is bound to live in a constant state of crisis. It is bound to be especially alert to the fact that traditions [in the church] do not as a matter of fact change in abrupt and well-marked stages, but that they are constantly changing. The mercies of the Lord are new every morning, and as soon as you are a week out of date with those, you are losing the battle.[143]

NOTES

1. In a pamphlet on ecumenism written in 1951, Principal Micklem writes: "Few women have done useful and faithful and acceptable service in our ministry. On the other hand, I know only too well that there is in our Church little demand for women ministers. My view is that wherever there is a small group of ministers working together, there should be a woman." *Mansfield Ministry*, 83.

2. A PPH is an undergraduate educational unit within the university. The primary distinction between the PPH and a college is that the college is governed by a board within itself, whereas a PPH is associated with a given Christian denomination. Students of both have access to all university facilities and activities.

3. In *The Story of Congregationalism* (1962), Routley voiced doubts about the future of ministry of women in Congregationalism. Routley recommended that women receive practical training at St. Paul's House in Liverpool, in contrast to the more rigorous and intellectual training at Mansfield. It's easy to say that he was a man in his times, but it is unclear if this position is a sign of intellectual snobbery or of the situation within the current Congregationalist Church. Certainly, in his role as college chaplain, Routley supported and encouraged female students. Kirsty Thorpe, *Mansfield Ministry*, 82–83.

4. David Cornick and Robert Pope, eds., *Traditions and Transitions: Studies in the History and Theology of the URC* (United Reformed Church: London, 2022), 63–64.

5. These consisted most notably of Old Testament scholar George B. Gray (1865–1922) who upheld the college's intellectual reputation; champion of historic study James V. Bartlet (1863–1940); New Testament expert James Souter (1873–1949); biblical translator James Moffatt (1870–1944), and eschatologist Charles H. Dodd (1884–1973).

6. Elaine Kaye, *Dictionary of National Biography*, 154.

7. *Traditions and Transitions*, 56.

8. Cadoux was a registered conscientious objector during this war and served with the Friends Ambulance Unit. He worked on ambulance convoys for the British and French armies.

9. Mackennal (1835–1904) was a Congregational minister and church historian. He served as chair of the Congregational Union in 1887.

10. Cecil. J. Cadoux, *The Congregational Way* (Blackwell's: Oxford, 1945), 20–21

11. *Traditions and Transitions*, 56.

12. Kaye.

13. In 1939 three Mansfield theologians, Bernard Lord Manning (1892–1941), Nathaniel Micklem, and J. S. Whale (1896–1997), sent a manifesto to all Congregational ministers emphasizing the links between Congregationalism and other Reformed traditions, in line with John Calvin's ideas. Proponents were termed "New Genevans."

14. Nathaniel Micklem, *The Box and the Puppets* (Geoffrey Bles: London, 1957), 82–83.

15. Born William Thomas (Pennar) Davies.

16. Davies served both Bala-Bangor and Brecon Memorial theological colleges until 1950, when he became principal of the Brecon Congregational Memorial College, which closed in 1959.

17. Vine went on to the Yorkshire United Independent College; Nuttall remained at New College, London, until his retirement in 1977.

18. *Mansfield* magazine, January 1948.

19. NWG, Tony Tucker, May 6, 2003.

20. Nathaniel Micklem, "To the Brethren of Dispersion," *Mansfield* magazine, July 1952, 125–26.

21. GW, October 31,1947. By the spring of 1948, Margaret and Erik settled into a family routine at 17 Norham Road, adding Patrick and Priscilla by 1953. It was a busy place.

22. Goodall, a Routley student while at Mansfield, was ordained in the Congregational Church in 1951. He became bursar of Mansfield in 1957 and later chaplain and organist. He served on the editorial committee for the URC *Rejoice and Sing* (1991) and the editor of *Companion to Rejoice and Sing* (1999).

23. Goodall wrote a lengthy description of this sermon class and gave it to Nancy Wicklund Gray. It is dated October 27, 2003.

24. Ibid.

25. Routley contemporary in the Mansfield JCR, Davies was Congregationalist minister, theologian, editor, and writer; professor of Religion and emeritus at Princeton University, 1955–2005.

26. Unfortunately, when Davies moved to Princeton in 1955, the program didn't last much longer. Kaye, 238.

27. John Marsh, "To the Brethren of the Dispersion," *Mansfield* magazine, No. 144, January 1954, 228.

28. Anthony Tucker, *Mansfield's Ministry: A Celebration of Ordination Training at Mansfield College, Oxford, 1886–2009*, 88.

29. This was largely due to Nathaniel Micklem's theology and orthodox interpretation of Congregationalism. His first two chaplains, Romilly Micklem and John Marsh, played a big part toward the integration of word, sacrament, and music in public worship within the Oxford community.

30. *Mansfield* magazine, December 1954.

31. The Sunday morning service usually had four hymns but no psalmody.

32. *Mansfield* magazine, December 1954.

33. MA, Mansfield College, 1956. Courtney was both a student of Routley and the president of the Congregational Society. In 2022 Courtney is the last surviving member of the Joint Committee that facilitated the creation of the United Reformed Church in 1972.

34. *Mansfield's Ministry*, 86

35. Letter to the author, September 26, 2022.

36. Kaye, 244.

37. Ibid.

38. The Chabad Society, Islamic Society, Jewish Society, Newman Society, Orthodox Christian Society, Sikh Society, https://www.ox.ac.uk/students/life/clubs, February 5, 2022.

39. Horton was the first non-Anglican to have a teaching post at Oxford since the Reformation. https://en.wikipedia.org/wiki/Robert_Forman_Horton.

40. Tucker, 40.

41. The CUEW was an organization of independent Congregational churches from 1831 to 1966.

42. Brian Wren, "Erik Routley: Musician, Theologian, Mentor, Wit, and Friend," *The Hymn*, vol. 53, no. 4, October 2002 (the Hymn Society of North America), 9–10.

43. NWG, Tucker, April 4, 2003, Oxford.

44. *Duty and Delight: Routley Remembered*, Robin A. Leaver and James Litton, eds. (Hope Publishing: Carol Stream, 1985), 70.

45. CongSoc was a wellspring of babysitters for the Routley children. Another, Robert Courtney, also provided his fiancée, Rowena. Routley married the couple in 1956.

46. *Duty and Delight*, 69.

47. Over lunch at their home in 2022, Joanna and John Lumsden, both members of CongSoc in the mid-1950s, shared some of their memories and photos. The Lumsdens, members of St. James's United Reformed Church in Newcastle, were surprised and thrilled when Routley became their minister in 1968.

48. These stories were often read at any Routley gathering. Nathaniel Micklem read them to Mansfield students, and John and Eleanor read them at family and church social occasions. There are well over one hundred, many of which have become staged and filmed; arguably the most well-known is *Guys and Dolls*. They take place in Runyon's native Colorado, but more often in the seedy side of Broadway from 1920 to 1945. The peculiar style and folky street-talk make them quite entertaining, even in the twenty-first century.

49. Damon Runyon, *From First to Last*.

50. A. Damon Runyon, "What, No Butler?" *Ten Stories by Damon Runyon, Avon Modern Short Story Monthly*, no. 27 (New York: Avon, 1945). Alfred Damon Runyon (1880–1946) was an American newspaperman and writer.

51. DD, 72.

52. Ibid.

53. *Mansfield's Ministry*, 42.

54. Ian Sharp, "Hymn Society of Great Britain and Ireland," CDH.

55. Eskew was editor of *The Hymn*, a publication of the Hymn Society of the United States and Canada, from 1976 to 1984.

56. Harry Eskew, "An Interview with Erik Routley," *The Hymn*, October 1981, ii–34.

57. Erik Routley, "George Wallace Briggs 1875–1959," the *Bulletin* (14/88), Summer 1960.

58. Patrick, a Scot, studied at St. Andrews. Detecting a need for a collection of songs, St Andrews gathered *The Scottish Students' Song Book* committee under the editorial convenorship of Patrick. The book launched in March 1891 and sold out in three weeks. Subsequent editions and revisions were published well into the twentieth century. These books are public domain and are available in their entirety on Haithi Trust.

59. *Bulletin*, vol. II, January 1948.

60. *Bulletin*, vol. II, April 1948.

61. Massey held the role in two separate terms, for a total of twenty-eight years. To date, there have been five editors: Patrick, Routley, Massey, Christopher Idle (b. 1938), and Andrew Pratt (b. 1948).

62. Ideally, the *Bulletin* was a quarterly publication, but this regularity varied, usually due to Routley's attention to other concerns.

63. Harry Eskew, "An Interview with John Wilson," *The Hymn* (33:4), October 1982, 215.

64. Robin A. Leaver, "John Wilson: Our Generation's Most Devoted Encourager of Fine Hymns," *The Hymn* (37:4), Autumn 2006, 20.

65. In Britain, there is no clear-cut definition of a public school. Today the term is generally used in a historical context. Traditionally, a public school was of an independent foundation and often a boarding school. These schools served as preparation for university education and were called "public" to attract a wide range of students throughout the country. In the early nineteenth century, chapel expectations were tightened in these schools and hymnals began to appear appropriate to each institution. In 1902 an anonymous committee of members of the Headmasters' Conference compiled *The Public School Hymn Book* from these singular sources. Revisions, supplements, and adaptations continued through the twentieth century. In 1937 another revision was begun but, like *Congregational Praise*, was disrupted by the war. When the work resumed and was published in 1949, an embarrassing number of errors and inconsistencies had been overlooked.

66. "Hymns for Young Methodists," the *Bulletin*, July 1950.

67. "*The Public School Hymn Book* (1949)," the *Bulletin*. (2:11:17), July 1950, 1–2.

68. Various Wilson-Routley letters between 1950 and 1958.

69. Eskew, "An Interview with Erik Routley."

70. Vernon Butcher, "The Public Schools' Contribution to Hymnody," the *Bulletin* (3:16), Autumn 1955, 254–59.

71. JWW, July 11, 1960.

72. JWW, July 17, 1960.

73. Donald Coggins, foreword, *Hymns for Church and School* (Novello: London, 1964). At the time, Coggins was the archbishop of York, following which he was named archbishop of Canterbury.

74. This may be found on the website of the HSGBI (www.hymnsocietygbi.org.uk) as an occasional paper.

75. Eskew, "An Interview with Erik Routley."

76. Eskew, "An Interview with John Wilson," 215–16.

77. Erik Routley, *A Panorama of Christian Hymnody* (GIA: Chicago) first edition 1979, second edition edited and expanded by Paul A. Richardson, 2005.

78. Ibid.

79. *Panorama*, second edition, preface.

80. Erik Routley, *The Church and Music: An Enquiry into the History, the Nature, and the Scope of Christian Judgment on Music* (J. J. Murray/Gerald Duckworth: London, 1950).

81. Appendix A.

82. Romilly Micklem, "The Church and Music," *Mansfield* magazine, July 1950, 32–33.

83. Erik Routley, *The Church and Music*.

84. Micklem, "The Church and Music."

85. Erik Routley, *I'll Praise My Maker*.

86. Clifford W. Towlson, "Review," *Bulletin* (III:2), Spring 1952, 36.

87. Rowland Edmund Prothero, 1st Baron of Ernle, agriculturalist, author, politician.

88. Phillips, Anglican priest and Hymn Society member, had written the highly regarded *Hymnody Past and Present* in 1937 and was on the editorial committee for *Hymns Ancient and Modern*, 1940.

89. Routley was frustrated that the publisher chose the title. He felt it suggested that life was somehow related to hymns.

90. Erik Routley, *Hymns and Human Life*, 2–3.

91. The title is *A Historical Study of Christian Hymnology: Its Development and Discipline* (Oxford University, 1952). This study is unpublished, but it served as the basis for several books and lectures throughout Routley's career. *The Music of Christian Hymnody* (Independent Press: London, 1957) and its revision in 1981 (GIA), *The Music of Christian Hymns*, contain much of the dissertation. The manuscript is in the Routley Collection in the Talbott Library.

92. Erik Routley, *The Story of Congregationalism*, 146.

93. K. L. Parry and Erik Routley (eds.), *Companion to Congregational Praise*.

94. TCM, September 21, 1949.

95. Erik Routley, *Hymns and the Faith*, preface.

96. Ibid.

97. George Huddleston, "*Hymns and the Faith*, Review," *Historical Magazine of the Protestant Episcopal Church* (Austin, TX), vol. 26, no. 2, June 1, 1957, 197.

98. Harry Eskew interview.

99. Ibid.

100. Seabury Press: Greenwich, CT, 1956.

101. Jane Stoddart (1863–1944), author and journalist, was de facto editor until her retirement in 1934. The *Dictionary of Nineteenth Century Journalism in Great Britain and Ireland* refers to her as "A central voice is shaping and reforming the Nonconformist conscience," 456.

102. www.churchnewspaper.com.

103. He served as editor 1956–57.

104. McMaster is a public research university in Hamilton, Ontario.

105. These lectures are in the Routley Collection as "The McMaster Lectures."

106. A college within Victoria University.

107. Alexander Dawson Matheson (1889–1962), principal of Emmanuel College, A. D. Matheson Papers, Queen's University archives.

108. A visit suggested by Daniel Jenkins, visiting professor of Ecumenical Theology. This school was absorbed into the Divinity School at the university.

109. A graduate of Amherst, Mansfield, and Union Theological Seminary, Walz served with the World Council of Churches and held pastorates at Oceanside, Second, and Fifth Avenue Presbyterian churches in New York City.

110. This field is often known as Liturgical Studies. In the early 1980s, Routley was part of a team that created the Liturgical Studies graduate program at Drew University in Madison, New Jersey.

111. A. D. Matheson Papers.

112. *Mansfield College Calendar Reports*, 1955–56, 9.

113. TCM, September 21, 1949.

114. Daniel Jenkins, 1940; William Pennar Davies (1911–1996), 1942; George Caird, Horton Davies, Erik Routley, and Peter Scott, 1943.

115. Geoffrey Beck, "Our New President," *Congregational Monthly*, June 1970, 4.

116. Beck was ordained in 1946. In 1950 he became minister at the Summertown Congregationalist Church, which became a URC church in 1972. The last service for this congregation was held in July 2022. Through the years, Micklems, Cairds, and Routleys attended. Ecumenical clergy team, Beck, David Jenkins (1925–2016), and Harry Carpenter (1901–1993), "inspired a radical experiment in joint evangelism at the Church of the Holy Family in Blackbird Leys, at the new estate established to help house the 25,000 workers at the Morris Car Factory." *Traditions and Transitions*, 21–22.

117. A middle-order batsman, Beck played for Oxford in 1943 and 1945. He was high scorer and played in other matches until 1951.

118. "Our New President."

119. Ibid.

120. The manuscript of this hymnal is in the Routley Collection.

121. In late March 1951, Routley organized a conference for Congregational organists at Mansfield College. Formed as part of the launch for *Congregational Praise*, when there appeared a need to educate church musicians in the opportunities of the new book, the guild was active until 1972, when it became the United Reformed Church's Musician Guild.

122. Genesis 32:22–32, which tells how Jacob wrestles with God through the night and ends up with a broken hip and a new name: Israel. Played in public by Routley and Mark Brumbaugh of Westminster Choir College.

123. S. D. Karunaratne, *Hymns and Verse* (Colombo Printers: Ceylon, 1949).

124. Valeri Ruddle, "Albert Bayly," CDH.

125. Anglican priest, tune writer, editor, and broadcaster. He was responsible for the BBC's war broadcast *The Daily Service* and later *Sunday Half-Hour* and *Lift Up Your Hearts*. His best known tune is "Abbot's Leigh."

126. Edward Jones, "Albert Frederick Bayly 1901–1984," *Bulletin*, September 1984, 202.

127. These were published in Bayly's first collection, *Rejoice O People: Hymns and Poetry of Albert Bayly* (Hymn Society of Great Britain and Ireland, 1949). The tunes are now copyrighted by Hope Publishing, 1990.

128. Erik Routley, "New Hymns from Two Generations," *Bulletin*, Summer 1968, 221.

129. Both Routley and Bayly grew up on the coast of East Sussex; these titles are all little villages in the area.

130. Based on Micah 6:6–8.

131. *100 Hymns for Today* (William Clowes & Sons, 1969). "What Does the Lord Require" is hymn #99.

132. Great-grandson of John Bacchus Dykes (1823–1876).

133. OLBP, xxii.

134. A mile down the road from Tye's Cross.

135. Kaye, 249.

136. Ibid.

137. "It might not have seemed promotion for this well-respected New Testament scholar, professor, and theological college principal to move to the position of Senior Tutor and Lecture at an Oxford PPH, with no prospect of University lectureship and a salary lower than he could have received elsewhere. But he and his family wanted to return to Britain, and he and his wife, Mollie, had a deep affection for Mansfield and aspirations for its future. Not a man to waste energy on bemoaning frustrations, it wasn't long before all the brightest Oxford theological students were flocking to Mansfield to hear this profound scholar who lectured so fluently and wittily using a Greek New Testament as his only aide." Kaye, 246.

138. GB to NWG, June 6, 2003.

139. Ibid.

140. The Reverend William B. J. Martin (1904–1983) had been the minister at Augustine-Bristo since 1951. In September 1958 he accepted a call to the University of Chicago as visiting professor. In the next year he became a visiting professor at Perkins School of Theology in Dallas and then minister to the First Community Church. He and Routley would cross paths several times over the next twenty years.

141. *Mansfield Calendar*, 1958–59.

142. Before the College Council at graduation, June 29, 1959.

143. Ibid.

Chapter 5

Edinburgh, 1959–1967

Augustine-Bristo Church invited Routley to preach both the morning and evening services on November 2; he was summoned to a church meeting on December 14 and issued a call on December 19.[1] Back at Mansfield, William Cadman had announced his retirement, leaving two faculty positions open,[2] so many of Routley's colleagues in Oxford and the Congregational Union of England and Wales felt abandoned by his new assignment. Scotland was not England. Though the bruises and anxiety of separation and relocation would become companions to the rest of his life, for Routley this move was an invigorating return to the work he loved. Buried in the *Bulletin*, behind memorials to Ralph Vaughn Williams (1872–1958) and Martin Shaw (1875–1958),[3] this little blurb appeared:

> And now the *Bulletin* moves back to Edinburgh, as your editor becomes, shortly after Easter, minister of Augustine-Bristo church. The prospect of being spatially separated from so many friends in the south country gives me sorrow.[4]

George IV Bridge in Edinburgh is a main thoroughfare built in the early nineteenth century intended as a link from the suburban south side of the city to the Old Town. It is an elevated street with only two visible supporting arches at the Cowgate and at Merchant Street; the rest of them provide cellars and vaults for the buildings along the top of the bridge.[5] The skyline still holds a tall spire, finished in 1861 and intended for the new home of the North College Street Congregational Church. The new church was given the name Augustine[6] by the minister, William Lindsay Alexander (1808–1884), known also for publishing a significant Congregational hymnal in 1849.[7]

AUGUSTINE-BRISTO CHURCH

In Scotland in the 1860s, it was improper for congregations to stand to sing. Chanting the Psalms was skeptically avant-garde, and forming a choir was considered a dangerous innovation. Indeed, Scottish Presbyterian congregations were usually put before ecclesiastical courts for such violations. At the North College Street church, Alexander was convinced that music was a valuable aid to worship. A choir emerged at Augustine Church when Alexander encouraged young members to stand beside the insecure precentor, and subsequently the congregation took to standing up to sing. Eventually, Augustine Church became known as "the best sung congregation" in Edinburgh.[8] It was one of the earliest churches to install an organ—a widely controversial inclusion. D. & T. Hamilton built the instrument and installed it at the rear of the church, and it was inaugurated on October 3, 1863. Sixty-four years later, an appeal was launched for a new instrument, made by A. E. Ingram; the console was moved to the front of the sanctuary.[9]

In 1941 the Augustine Church and the Bristo Congregational Church merged, becoming the Augustine-Bristo Church. The current congregation, Augustine United Church, professes the Nonconformist theology that follows a thread from the Scottish Reformation to the broad diversity within the Congregational tradition and the United Reformed Church. Their logo displays a stylized dandelion blossom, simultaneously a weed to adults and a delight to children. "It's small, determined seed symbolizes the work of the church carried in the breath of the Spirit to grow justice and joy in our lives."[10] The National Churches Trust describes the congregation as "increasingly inclusive and encourages freedom of thought and progressive Christianity."[11]

The Routleys arrived in Edinburgh in the late winter of 1959. Nicholas and Patrick were enrolled at George Heriot's School and Priscilla at Cranley School for Girls. Margaret began a studio for private string students and the children, now twelve, ten, and six, studied piano, cello, and oboe. The church manse had been newly refurbished.

> They've made the house look wonderful and done far more decorating than we asked for. Altogether, we have got off to a very happy start. We'll see what we feel like in twelve months' time, but my impression is that it'll be our fault if we feel much less happy than we do now.[12]

The everyday work of the church doesn't wait on ceremony, so Routley assumed the role as active minister almost immediately, well before his formal installation took place, Friday, April 10, 1959. The presiding minister at the service was Andrew Graham, chaplain of George Heriot's School and president of the congregation. John Marsh imposed the charge to the congregation.

> The induction was magnificent. I could have wished for nothing better, save only that the Congregation was unprepared for the question in the *Book of Public Worship*,[13] and remained dumbly solid when asked whether they'd have me as their minister! John Marsh was in his very best form, 35 minutes in a mighty exposition of Philippians 3: 7–14. Scots don't care for less than half an hour.[14]

The hymns were two of Routley's most important, "The Head that Once was Crowned with Thorns"[15] and "Come Down, O Love Divine,"[16] but they were not sung from *Congregational Praise*. When Augustine Church and Bristo Place Congregational Church merged, there were concessions and compromises from both corners, including adopting the Scottish *Church Hymnary* used by the Bristo congregation.[17] Keeping sentiment and their financial situation in mind, ABC held on to the old book.

> It hardly matters what hymn book you use, so long as you choose the right ones and sing 'em well. Some, like the AMR,[18] are deadly dull—about on level with the Presbyterian abomination I have to live with here. What I do is to shower bits of paper on the congregation with hymns on them by people like John Arlott and Mollie Caird![19]

Much to Routley's dismay, this decision held fast during most of his tenure. With pointed levity, however, Routley inserted lots of handouts of hymns from other sources for the weekly services and made the most of the metrical psalms in the *Hymnary*. A little ray of hope appeared when Routley and the secretary, Charles Somerville, were sitting by the fire one evening. Somerville raised the question of purchasing *Congregational Praise*:

> He's as Scottish as all the rest of these people, so I said, "Big snag. What do we do with the Psalms? There are not many in *Congregational Praise*." Somerville said, "My God!! We've never sung so many psalms as we have since YOU came here. We're all damn sick of them! Take them away and lose 'em!" True. I have put in one Psalm or paraphrase each service, and the result has been more hilariously successful than I could have dreamed. Thing is, we had three services in a row when our supply of Hymnaries was insufficient for the assembled saints. I hasten to assure you that my view is that somebody kindly sabotaged the books, and not that the congregation dramatically increased, so we mustn't count any chickens.[20]

The *Church Hymnary* remained in the stalls.

Ministerial Commitments

Membership at Augustine-Bristo was declining in the 1950s, and, like the situation at Mansfield, this was accompanied by worrisome fiscal constraint. One of the first major budgetary issues was replacing the boiler. In a letter to Geoffrey Beck, Routley says, "Our most considerable spiritual experience so far as a congregation was the direct consequence of the failure of our heating system."[21]

The boiler exploded the last day of September, leaving the cavernous ABC building quite chilly. Routley was caught unawares and openly irritated when it became clear that the deacons had known about this probability in April. The decision was made to switch to an electric furnace, but the required conversion would take the month of October and into November to finish. Working with their immediate need for heated worship space, the grumpy Dr. Routley and Church Council remembered that the former Bristo building, which had been sold to the local Seventh Day Adventists, was vacant on Sunday mornings. ABC had utilized this space before, so arrangements were made to move morning worship to this temporary location. Surprisingly, they all carried on quite comfortably.

> Our congregation filled the place to overflowing and nobody was, of course, able to sit in their "own" pew. It was all rather entertaining! The second Sunday someone forgot to turn on the organ switch, so "Who are these like stars appearing" was an unaccompanied solo by me because nobody knew it.[22]

Sunday evening services were held in the hall in the rough basement of the ABC building.

> I was furious at this, but in the end thought we'd better not pretend that these were services of an ordinary sort. So, we rearranged the chairs in a sort of Swanwick[23] pattern and had a service that began with the sermon and included no prayers until the end. As it happens, the people took to this and we introduced prose readings,[24] poetry, music, and drama here and there. They were quite reluctant to go back upstairs. At one blow we have managed to abolish the idea that the evening service should be the same shape as the morning one and we've even managed to get the congregation to agree to come and sit at the front while I preached from the Table![25]

In his first few months in town, Routley visited 270 of the 394 registered members, putting precisely 1,156 miles on his car. He was feeling comfortable with understanding the needs and delights of his congregation, telling Beck, "They're a wonderfully mixed-up crowd in all possible senses, but they come to church tolerably well."[26]

Christmas Day found him preaching at Greyfriars Kirk across the road. He was taken with the grace and dignity of the building, and when he looked out from the pulpit, he noticed that 75 percent of the congregation was from ABC. Later in the afternoon, a few blocks away, the manse was a busy place, with people coming and going, meals being prepared and served, and distributing benevolences. Sadly, there was a dramatic neighborhood problem demanding attention. On November 21, 1959, the dangerously decrepit but occupied five-story Penney Tenement, only a few blocks from the church, collapsed in the early morning hours.[27] There were no fatalities, but nineteen families were without housing. Fortunately, no ABC members lived in that building, but half a dozen families had homes nearby in equally dilapidated, shameful conditions.[28] The benevolences couldn't go far enough, but they set a precedent for the church's present commitment to break the cycle of homelessness.

David Willcocks

Part of everyone's Christmas Eve celebration was tuning in to the BBC broadcast of the annual Nine Lessons and Carols festival from King's College, Cambridge. For nearly thirty years, Boris Ord (1897–1961), as organist, carried the tradition forward from unpolished radio airings into the television age. Ord retired due to failing health in 1957, and former organ scholar David Willcocks (1919–2015) replaced him.[29] The new conductor and Routley were colleagues, and both were experts on the English carol. Until at least 1979, Willcocks often sent the order of service to Routley in early December. Following each service, the two men critiqued and analyzed every word and note in detailed correspondence.[30] When Willcocks became director, he wanted to retain the essence of the program[31] but questioned the repetitious nature of the carol accompaniments, particularly the seven verses of "O Come All Ye Faithful." Routley suggested composing a descant, varied accompaniment and some sort of departure from the four-part standard as solutions.[32] Willcocks gambled with the verses, resulting in the now-famous descant with verse 6 and the unconventional treatment of verse 7. Willcocks told Routley that the precentor at King's had a wobbly pitch problem; therefore, the "fff" (fortissimo) octaves and unison of verse 7 would secure the melody for the last verse. He also underlaid "Word" with the Tristan chord to draw attention to the final proclamation in the preceding John text and vary the accompaniment in a surprising way, a musical joke.[33] The setting was published in the 1961 *Carols for Choirs*, which Routley found irksome. He grumbled to John Wilson:

> I am <u>extremely</u> sorry that in *Carols for Choirs* he perpetuated the harmonic joke in the unison verse of *Adeste* which has now worn so thin. That sort of thing is fair enough once or twice but it's not funny now, and certainly not funny in print! Everybody tries to do it, and sometimes, like with the organist I heard yesterday at Greyfriars, it misses the way home.[34]

But the criticism wasn't personal. When Nicholas and Patrick went off to Cambridge, Routley appreciated Willcocks's watchful eye.

> We are very happy about Patrick's success at Caius. We hardly knew what to expect, and I appreciate your remarks about his cello playing. He certainly drinks deep of contemporary music. I am interested at the moment that he will fall into the hands of Tranchell,[35] because his Psalms are remarkable. And, Nicholas, thank you. I hope he is doing some work now and again—I think he must be because he is acquiring all sorts of knowledge which could only have been acquired at Cambridge, he could become quite a decent communicator![36]

Managing ABC in Its Urban Community

Routley enlivened each aspect of the ABC church and made things happen with his ebullient enthusiasm. He connected with youth groups, Bible studies, men's breakfasts, and community liaisons. He brought student ministers from New College into the work of ABC and dealt with denominational concerns. He spoke at civic events and university lectures and made regular trips to London for work with the BBC and RSCM. He even sang tenor in the chorus at church festivals.[37] Routley had no time to waste and demanded the same from his congregation.

> Worship conducted by him was an expression of joy and almost of exuberance, but every detail was worked out—every part of the service: hymns, prayers, readings, and sermon dovetailed together into a unity. One of the first things Erik said to my father [Charles Sommerville] was: "People think of me primarily as a musician, but my deepest interest is in interpreting the Bible.[38]

Most significantly, he helped the church to fully understand the meaning of Congregationalism and wrote the covenant that is still affirmed annually at the Augustine United Church, largely unchanged. Routley stressed that the purpose of the church meeting was not merely a time for dealing with routine business but was also part of the worship of the church, an attempt to see the implications of the faith proclaimed and to strengthen the community. Quite early in his ministry, Routley insisted that the church meeting should have punctual beginnings and endings, from 8:00 to 9:15 p.m. He prescribed that not more than twenty-five minutes be devoted to routine business and the rest spent in informal, social discussion about aspects of the church's life. The congregation gratefully approved the change.

Heriot Watt College, today a public research university, was located very close to ABC and had outgrown its facilities due to a rapid growth in enrollment. The college sat on a piece of land behind ABC, and in 1958 they approached the church with an offer to purchase the church property for fifteen thousand pounds. While this near windfall seemed like an answer to financial concerns, the Congregational Union of Scotland pronounced that a church in the center of Edinburgh was essential to the well-being of the city; ABC turned down the offer. Routley assumed leadership a year later, and Heriot Watt again made an offer for the property; again it was refused.[39] In the aftermath, Routley and the church officers quickly recognized that the church building, designed to seat one thousand, was too large for the current membership, and usage exclusive to Sundays amounted to poor stewardship. As a result, the church rented space to the college, thus opening the facility to other organizations. Over time, ABC and now its ecumenical partners, Greyfriars Kirk and St. Columba's-by-the-Castle, extended their mission to include offices for societies committed to social change, which today includes Christian Aid[40] and Jubilee Scotland,[41] as well the regular meeting place for nearly twenty other cultural and political groups that seek to elevate the physical, emotional, and social wellness of the city.[42] When Routley arrived in Edinburgh, he clearly, and naively, pronounced his idealistic goals for an urban church:

> When I came among you, I said that I believed in central city churches, and at every point, you have shown me how misconceived my own notions were. You have certainly shown me most of what I know about this ministry.[43]

It would take not only the experiences of ABC but also those at St James's in Newcastle before he understood what serving a city congregation entailed.

AUGUSTINE

Routley began his days deep in correspondence with his closest friends and family, and found time to write two sermons a week, eighteen books, and regular articles for the *Bulletin,* the *British Weekly,* and the LMS *Chronicle*; edit three hymnals; compose twelve hymn tunes; and embark on several speaking tours in the United States.

One morning, singing the George Herbert (1593–1633) text "Let all the world in every corner sing"[44] to LUCKINGTON,[45] Routley's son Patrick announced at lunch that the text was good but the music was lousy. The outcome was Routley's convincing tune AUGUSTINE, with twofold purpose.

Routley had often vocalized his objection to the conventional liberty taken by hymnal editors in setting the chorus by using only two refrains to balance the stanzas, where Herbert specifically wrote the opening sentence three times. Routley took care to set the text as Herbert intended. AUGUSTINE is used more in the United States and is still included in twenty-first-century hymnals, where attention is paid to Herbert's design.[46]

Loss

Bad news came from England in late spring of 1960. Romilly Micklem was playing a Sunday service at a church in Dorset the last Sunday of May and suffered a cerebral hemorrhage on the bench. He died on June 6. Erik was desolate.

> This is the first really personal bereavement I've ever suffered, a strange thing to wait so long for that. Romilly was next to none, my father in God, and I find the thought of losing him a hard one to reconcile. I'm sure that I am not alone. This news was immediately followed by a request that I come to the Memorial and speak.[47] If I live to be 100, I am not likely to receive any greater honor.[48]

THE DUNBLANE MUSIC CONSULTATIONS (1962–1969)

The Scottish Churches House

A decades-old concept of an ecumenical meeting place in Scotland was realized in 1948 after the World Council of Churches Assembly in Amsterdam. The Scottish delegation returned home envisioning a place for consultations, conceived in common by all the Scottish churches,[49] an essential factor of growing together and serving postwar Scotland.[50] The delegation soon renamed itself the Scottish Churches Ecumenical Council, whose members began actively seeking real estate halfway between Glasgow and Edinburgh, the largest cities in Scotland. When, in the mid-1950s, a row of derelict buildings next to the Dunblane Cathedral was up for demolition, the SCEC saw the location as ideal and submitted a proposal to the property owners. After settling a series of legal issues, the SCEC was given parts of the row; an architect was found, and the renovation began. The eventual house included dormitory quarters and meeting spaces, a kitchen, and bathrooms. During the rehabilitation, a tiny medieval chapel was uncovered behind the buildings. It, too, was cleaned up and renovated, making a useful space for prayer and meditation. This house was both the means and the symbol of a new stage in ecumenical cooperation in Scotland, a sign of hope.[51]

Ian Fraser

In 1960 the Council tapped Ian Fraser (1917–2018), ordained in the Church of Scotland and a member of the Iona Community, as the inaugural warden of the house. According to Douglas Gay, professor of theology at the University of Glasgow:

> Choosing Fraser was bold, but Fraser had been visibly active in ecumenical circles in the 1940s and 50s. As parish minister in Rosyth, he was both distinctive and effective, radical and evangelical. Accompanied by his notable intellect and political edge, the wardenship was obvious for the founding trustees.[52]

In the summer of 1961, Routley attended a ministerial meeting at the new house and met this warden, a social activist with the same independent spirit and thoughts on ecumenism, harmonizing with Routley's own. Both men favored straightforward, pragmatic problem-solving techniques.

Nearly sixty years later, Fraser distinctly remembered that first encounter with Routley:

> At a consultation on evangelism, one of the members produced a hymn which he said was in a new form and was the kind of hymn which was needed in our day. During a free period between sessions, some participants exchanged harsh comments. Their criticism was mainly that this hymn, and others, retained all the old stereotypes. For the umpteenth time, the cry went up, "Nobody's getting down to writing hymns for our time!" Then Erik Routley spoke out and said, "We need to do a proper job on this and not rely on individuals putting hymns forward!"[53]

Routley had been discontented with the stagnant state of English hymnody since his university days at Oxford, and in Scotland he found much the same conditions. Fraser listened to the disparaging complaints and said, "Let's stop moaning and get on with the job";[54] and so, with pointed determination and concerted vision, Fraser and Routley went to work.

Early Days

Fraser sent out feelers to the churches and found strong interest in a music consultation that functioned as a place for free provisional attention to texts, tunes, and liturgy and, possibly, extended to drama. He appointed Reginald Barrett-Ayres (1920–1981) from Aberdeen[55] as convenor and Routley as secretary. Fraser himself was the task master; he prepared the sessions and produced reports. In between consultations, it was Fraser who breathed down the necks of the working groups who had agreed to specific tasks, assuring that they brought their completed assignments to the next meetings. The encouragement and flow of ideas came quite notably from Routley, who eventually transformed the consultations into a British experience by inviting clergy and musicians from England as well as Scotland.

The first consultation was in early October 1962. For the opening speaker, Fraser singled out Ian Mackenzie (1931–2006), the Scottish secretary of the Student Christian Movement.[56] Mackenzie was renowned as a firebrand whose favored way of getting things done was to provoke and then sit back and wait.[57] The assembled two dozen regional ministers and organists were shaken when they were asked to suspend preconceived notions about what was right or wrong with the current hymnody and hymnals. Mackenzie asserted that the Consultation would do something very useful if, through corporate thinking and discussion, the members would use the existing liturgical framework and consider if rigid adherence to tradition both blocked and avoided the needs of the time and the duty of responding to them. The urgency from Mackenzie's position derived from the popularity of rock and roll and the developing recording industry, which seemed to support the notion that young people had become alienated from both mainstream society and religion.

> As our Lord consorted with publicans and sinners without making any demands that they should first of all change, so we should open ourselves to the young people of today and let them bring what they are and what they have, no matter if this involves guitars and different styles.[58]

Routley began the second session by introducing C. S. Lewis's criteria for literary criticism, in which Lewis argues that lowbrow-versus-highbrow discussions are not fruitful.[59] In applying this to hymnody, Routley warned against two stock phrases:

> "I don't like it" is said because the new music in question appears fascinating and dangerous, threatening one's self-preservation, and the second, "Only the best is good enough," is almost idolatrous. The necessary work of the Church is done if it whole-heartedly receives whatever means God is offering it.[60]

He also suggested that the purpose of the consultation was to "inject worship with a new kind of sincerity and gaiety, which are the constituents of the real Christian faith."[61] Though the consultation was colored by the 1960s social atmosphere, emphasis on youth was only one facet of the music of the wider church and its deficiencies.

The response to Routley's lecture was even more animated than the one following Mackenzie's, as the participants passionately debated the fundamentalism and prophecy within their current worship practices. This was a highly sensitive issue for those who favored sacred music in the popular style versus the expressions of traditional hymn themes.

Barrett-Ayres presented the final plenary, addressing the responsibility of professional musicians within the church to examine their repertoire. He argued that any viable church music had the qualities of unity, strength, and love. His examples to this were the cohesive elements of sixteenth-century polyphony, the strength of the economic and forthright music of the Lutheran tradition, and the ever-present folk element. Comments from the floor added plainsong to the list.

Strong arguments on the affinity between the hierarchy of the church, its clergy, and the creative arts continued right up to the end of the weekend Consultation. A consensus observed that hymn singing generally served as a fill-in or stimulant, so debate continued over music as a spiritual response. The concept of temporary and innovative hymnody was seen as relevant to the changing times and personal taste. Another developing facet of worship, televised broadcasts, brought evidence that the program producers chose worship music with an eye to performance. The members of the Consultation were appreciative of the need to have professional musicians as a suitable solution to the genre, but a deliberation over performance music was not part of the meeting.

Routley restated his earlier argument: There is no reason for believing that the everyday enjoyment of music is of less value than the appreciation for what had been termed "good music." Worship leaders must humbly find a common ground and a willingness to be educated when presented with *any* kind of music.

Implementation and the Second Consultation

A working party of six was asked to bring twelve new texts and thirty-six tunes to the next Consultation, in October 1963. The challenge was to investigate meter and secular poetry, the folk idiom, the *New English Bible*,[62] and the mandates put forth by Vatican II.[63] With unique and intentional synergy, the larger part of the Consultation was spent in discussions of the submitted hymns. Authors of the texts were identified, but the tune composers were kept anonymous.[64] Those who had never thought of themselves as contributors to hymnody were drawn in. Even in the presence of the creators, the voices of the group were necessary to add fresh perspective. Consultation members were sent to their rooms to see if they could come up with material to fill in the gaps within traditional denominational hymnody, and whatever was produced floated back to the full group. Candor was the core of the exercise from the start, and though there was often disagreement, no umbrage was taken. Routley pushed this scrutiny even further by pointing out that one must be aware of the adjective "Christian," as so often it meant a form of lasso to capture appealing concepts. In true Routley style, he lightened the general mood with his wry, witty observations and demonstrating that a sense of humor was the only way to acknowledge any shortcomings of the group.

Sydney Carter (1915–2004), the most striking and original of the active writers of the Christian folk song, was invited to this 1964 meeting.

> [Carter]was a distinctive, buoyant voice, a non-violent man in a violent world. He thought of life in strong metaphor who felt that folk song and faith joined hands in the service of peace and justice. Carter's rejection of structure and dogma may be contentious, but it is central to his art.[65]

Carter's songs hovered on the boundary of faith and doubt, thus providing the possibility of thought-provoking conversation. In his address, Carter compared the atmosphere of coffeehouses and pubs to the intimacy within a church service. An analysis of these settings revealed moments of unity, whether it was through singing or watching a football match. Folk songs are often profound and nearly subversive, but the genre attracts everyone from Roman Catholics to Communists, as demonstrated in the attraction to skiffle in the 1950s.[66] Echoing the criteria of the Consultations, Carter stressed that even though his songs had been printed many times, they were essentially unfinished. Each song was ready to be remade, and no printed version should be marked as authentic or final.

In their reflection following Carter's presentation, the group understood that "folk is the root from which contemporary things can grow."[67] But a few years after churches were introduced to Carter's work, John Wilson and Routley discussed the need to be careful when using Carter's songs in worship. Routley cautioned:

> The Carter-craze mustn't cause us to misuse his stuff. Just because something looks like a hymn doesn't mean it is one, and the [music] shouldn't be pushed around until begins to look like one. [For instance] "Bitter was the Night" should be sung by an invisible soloist with a guitar. The people must be brought to the song and not the other way around.[68]

A new working group was appointed at the 1964 gathering, retaining Routley and his energy essential to any forward movement of the Consultations. They were commissioned to find proper places in which a more dramatic view of liturgy could flourish.

Dissemination

In the antecedent to the 1965 meeting, Routley playfully invited members for "Forty-eight Hours of Composition and Consultation of Music and Words to Catch the Ear of our Time."[69] That year, special attention was paid to psalm settings and canticles. Routley was infectiously dynamic and constantly pointed to the group's responsibility to consider the theological mission in each hymn.[70]

By 1966, the musical output had flowed into many different channels across the English-speaking world. New people were drawn in over the years, involving nearly one hundred women and men of all ages and backgrounds.[71] Those who had never thought of themselves as hymn writers or composers were pleasantly surprised.

> I sat down at a reading desk and was given a bundle of words and told to set them to a tune. Within an hour, words and music had been called together. This was never meant to be long-lasting; built-in obsolescence was deliberate. Much of the material that was gleaned from the workshop was meant, in Erik's words, to renounce the tyranny of a four-part uniformity and to experiment with solo voices and separated singing groups; even the use of organ was non-obligatory.[72]

All Who Love and Serve Your City

These personal moments of revelation were experienced by their leader as well. Alan Luff, who was attracted to the Consultation by the emphasis on canticles, told this story many times:

> Coming into Dunblane was intimidating as you didn't think you had anything to give. Yet, you were challenged or encouraged to meet the situation. Somehow the Holy Spirit was abroad, and things happened, though the result might be quite different from that which was intended as in the case of Erik Routley. We had a session to identify gaps in the existing hymnaries and were all sent packing to see what we could come up with. The only way I could work was by creating a thread of a tune on which I could string the words. So, I hummed it repeatedly as I searched for the text. Erik and I had adjoining rooms and he was next door trying to write his own tune and gave up, due to my vocalizing, and in the end went on to write his magnificent hymn, "All Who Love and Serve Your City."[73] I was sorry for the frustration I had caused, but now I feel prouder of my humming and doodling as it expanded his own creative work.[74]

Many years later, Hinshaw Music, Inc., published *Westminster Praise*, a supplement designed for use in the chapel services at Westminster Choir College and its church music classes. In the subsequential companion, Routley adds this to the story:

My mind went in two directions, first to a beautiful tune by Peter Cutts[75] which had no text and [second] towards the special griefs of the American cities which at the time [1966] were suffering from riots. The contrast between the peacefulness of the Scottish country town and the condition of those cities preyed on me.[76]

Two publications stemmed directly from these consultations, *Dunblane Praises, Nos. 1 & 2*. They were intended as a means for field-testing the hymns, so only fourteen hundred copies were printed, although selected items were republished in 1969 in *New Songs for the Church*.[77] After the consultations had been discontinued, these little books showed that their purpose had been met. Decades later, Luff reflected that he had known no other group as creative or one that had a greater touch on the needs of those it served.[78]

Working Together

The integral part of the process was communal collaboration. A tenet of the Iona Community highlights forging accord between worship and daily life. The Consultations emulated this in the themes of hymns and in the approach to writing them. From the outset, Fraser and Routley envisioned not a college of hymn writers and composers but a laboratory in which members were accountable to one another, sharing the results of their endeavors and always seeking criticism and modification. The poetry and tunes emerged in many different styles, and no one community of worship would have use for all of them. Though very few of the hymns from these meetings appear in twenty-first-century hymnals, endurance was not the point. The process was and is a valuable model for future generations, as it effectively unchains the hymn from historic restraints.

At the Routley centenary celebrated in 2017 at Augustine United Church, Ian Fraser, at age one hundred, shared the impact of these Consultations on twenty-first-century hymnody:

> Though a lot of this is dated nowadays, the energy and enthusiasm were powerful at a time when people weren't writing hymns to any great extent. There was a great need for a new voice. Erik was the original hymnologist and commentator on contemporary, worthwhile trends in church music. We found his arguments compelling and today his contributions are a benchmark for future clergy and church musicians.[79]

Twentieth Century Church Music (Jenkins Publishing: London, 1967) was published in 1964 and written to stir up interest in the possibilities stemming from the Dunblane Consultations. In the preface Routley thanks the Dunblane experience and those "who have stimulated my otherwise sluggish perceptions of present day social needs." As Fraser says, the title limits twenty-first-century interest in the book, which is a shame, as Routley begins the preface with a timeless observation:

> In church music there has been no age so full of surprises and creative promise as our own. The age which has produced eccentricities which are so formidable and concessions to popular taste which are so disconcerting is one which has also produced an enormous amount of fine music. . . . Nothing is more important than that the conversation should not stop. Disagreement and dissent will not end [the conversation]; patronage and contempt will. It will probably remain true that those who contribute most fruitfully and successfully are those who listen openly. Creative counterpoint between different musical cultures, different social classes, and between the sacred and secular will, in the end, determine the course that church music takes. There is no reason for supposing that the course will not take us through more exciting and more vital experiences than it has passed through up to now.[80]

AMERICAN APPRENTICES

Robert H. Mitchell

Church musicians in the United States were becoming aware of Routley's examination of the interrelationship between music and theology. The concept held immediate relevance, and some didn't want to save their questions until Routley gave a lecture in their own locations, so they went to him. One such academic was the Reverend Robert H. Mitchell (1921–2002), an evangelical American Baptist church musician from California and an enthusiastic collector of hymnbooks. He taught courses in music and worship at the American Baptist Seminary in the West,[81] now part of the California Baptist Seminary.[82] Mitchell went to Edinburgh on sabbatical in 1964 "because no one else has written as competently concerning the church and its music."[83]

Shortly after Mitchell arrived, Routley gave the sermon at the traditional opening for the Edinburgh Festival held at St. Giles. Routley remembers it this way:

> We had some marvelous music there. The anthem was Fred Rimmer's "Sing We Merrily,"[84] which came off with great effect. I found the whole thing tremendously moving after resisting the experience for a while. The music and Dr. Whitley's[85] part of the service were so good as to make me feel that what I said hardly mattered.[86]

Mitchell's recollection is more colorful:

It was an elegant occasion including artists and civic leaders. The lively procession involved folks with gold capes and swords, kilts, ermine and scarlet robes, top hats and white wigs, and a variety of rich ecclesiastical garments. The great organ shook the building.[87] With exceptional competence, the crimson-robed choir sang a very dissonant 12-tone anthem; it was most appropriate for a context focused on contemporary art. It was magnificently sung. After the service, one of the civic leaders said, "That was a great service, but I didn't care much for the choir music." Routley's response: "Bless your heart! You weren't supposed to *like* that anthem."[88]

In an area of mutual interest, Routley and Mitchell dissected the current gospel trends, new territory for Routley, and a style that Mitchell could defend quite well. Through the years they kept in touch, and Routley lectured at the seminary in California and at Baptist conferences. Routley admired Mitchell's work in the United States and recommended Mitchell as a consultant for various church music situations, including a coveted role in the Westminster Abbey "Come and Sing" festivals led by John Wilson:

To be candid, I fancy you'll find a number of people wanting to jump on your bandwagon now that it's rolling so well. I should be pretty firm about accepting any of them if you don't know them personally; all the same, Bob Michell is one you'd like. He's my old friend and a winner. It isn't that all my American friends are swans, some of them are crows, but Bob is a first-rate man with a very wide-ranging mind.[89]

Even forty years after many of Routley's books had been written, Mitchell resolutely put Routley's work into his course syllabi. Mitchell contended that Routley's determination to initiate thought and conversation was still much needed, even approaching the twenty-first century.[90]

I acknowledge my enormous debt to his scholarship and his provocative thinking. No one else has so influenced my understanding, and the clarification of that understanding, in my interpretation of the Gospel and the whole of Christian living.[91]

Mary Oyer

Concurrently, another American hymnodist was in Edinburgh. Mary Oyer (b. 1923), faculty member of Goshen College,[92] had also scheduled a sabbatical in Edinburgh—and for the same reasons.

In the late 1950s Oyer attended a lecture at Goshen presented by Nathan A. Scott Jr. (1925–2006), a professor at the University of Chicago Divinity School. Scott was asked to speak about the current trends in church music. He had devised an interdisciplinary program on religion and the arts, featuring expansive and cutting-edge dialogue on the idioms within the field. Scott's perceptive observations and solutions melded with the essence of Oyer's own unconventional signature course, "Introduction to the Fine Arts."[93] At the conclusion of the lecture, Oyer approached Scott and asked where she might find more information on the matter of music and faith. Scott had heard Routley speak in Chicago in 1955 and was captivated by Routley's knowledge and riveting, easy demeanor, so he answered Oyer enthusiastically:

> Oh, I know just the man! Erik Routley, who's in Edinburgh, now; he knows everything about the subject. He's a little off-putting, though, his eyes go in different directions, and you might get distracted, but he's who you want to talk to![94]

A few years later, after she completed a doctorate in cello at the University of Michigan, which was highly unusual for a Mennonite, Oyer knew that her interest in the music of theology had not dimmed. She contacted Routley and asked if she could study with him, as she had a sabbatical coming in September 1963. Routley responded enthusiastically and proposed weekly meetings for the fee of one guinea per lesson.[95]

> I was such a Mennonite! Our tradition of hymn singing at the time was four-part and unaccompanied, which was wonderful, but I wanted to know what the organ and other instruments contributed to hymn singing. He introduced me to the wonders of the literary and poetic nature of a hymn and his sensitivity was very helpful; it was quite a revelation, really. Sometimes, he used the text of a hymn to support the entire service.[96]

Those were awkward questions back in Indiana, but Routley took her seriously. The first thing that put Oyer at ease was realizing that the Scots had once shared the same concerns about music in worship as the Mennonites; the most visible was the ban on instrumental music in church, particularly the organ.

Just before her sabbatical began, Oyer was appointed executive secretary of the committee to revise *The Mennonite Hymnary*, giving even more impetus for her trip, as she discovered "this man knew so much."[97] In an interview with Michael Hawn in 1999, Oyer explained that Routley made her aware of the value of reading an entire hymn text rather than only the abridged versions that are often published in hymnals, realizing that the whole text relays the nature of the hymn. While in Edinburgh, Oyer eagerly took advantage of the libraries and archives to examine primary sources that Routley recommended; she laughed at, but prized, Routley's recitation, from memory, of pertinent page numbers in various hymnals. One of Oyer's students in the early 1960s, Ken Nafziger observed, "They [Oyer and Routley] were two peas in a pod. Oyer carried all the notes from the 1969 Mennonite hymnal around in her head without notes or cards. Between 1963 and 1969 she lived and breathed hymnody."[98]

Routley was always keenly interested in Oyer's work with the hymn committee but found the Mennonites and their Amish cousins rather odd—philistine, even. He didn't know much about American hymnody, so Oyer gave him a shaped-note book that they used back in Goshen. He was astonished, as he had never seen one. Routley gave a lecture at Goshen in 1966, and, according to Oyer, "he loved the visit and found it quite exciting to sing in four parts—unaccompanied."[99] Routley gives Wilson an animated description:

> You'd be interested in Mennonite singing. The whole congregation has tune books and sings in 4-part harmony, just like Welshmen, with no accompaniment! A song leader gives the note and off they go! They have a quite impressive folk hymnody of their own. I'm having a cheerful time.[100]

When *The Mennonite Hymnal* was published in 1969, Routley praised its sophisticated and energetic approach to the contents, particularly the inclusion of folk hymns from a wide variety of American sources and the remarkably original work done by Oyer.[101]

Routley was simultaneously busy with the Dunblane Consultations during Oyer's stay, and he shared some of their work. She took the new music back to Indiana and the hymnal committee. "I was certain it would never be approved, but by the time the book was in print, the Mennonites were singing hearty versions of "I danced in the morning!"[102] Routley gave a lecture at Goshen in 1966. "He loved the visit and found it quite exciting to sing in four parts—unaccompanied."[103]

In an interview with Nancy Wicklund Gray in 2003, Oyer offered some strong words:

> I was so grateful to him for what happened to me, but after he came over [to the United States in 1975], I had a strange feeling. Many people I knew in the Hymn Society, even the ones who had invited him over, seemed very negative about him. He didn't attend the meetings[104] and that was an afront to some. I think it's important, at this stage, to set the record straight and show what a remarkable man he was.[105]

ROUTLEY'S LAST YEARS IN EDINBURGH

In England, discussing and revising the details of the anticipated union of the CCEW and the English Presbyterians had begun in earnest. As the progress gained momentum, the Congregational leaders badly wanted Routley and his prophetic touch back in England. The pulpit opened at Emmanuel, Cambridge, which seemed the obvious spot for a person of Routley's stature. At the church meeting following his sermon, there was dissention as to Erik's suitability. Questions arose about his heavy lecture load in the United States and that maybe he was a little too brilliant to fit the needs of a local congregation. They did not extend a call.[106]

> It was a funny business at Cambridge, but really a great relief. Moving just when Patrick was due for another year at school would have been difficult, and moreover, Nicholas is now at St John's, and he would have been furious to think his parents were following him around! It would also mean abandoning the postgraduate department in church music which New College has just set up with me in charge, so I was not too distressed. Augustine-Bristo is proving so delightful that I shall be very hard to get—supposing that anybody does want me![107]

In 1966 Routley spent a total of eighteen weeks in the United States at seminaries, universities, and conferences, either teaching courses or lecturing. Somewhat sadly, Routley appreciated that his frequent absences and travel demands limited his availability to contribute fairly to the next stage of ABC's development. The old building was suffering the eventual lot of all structures: The cost of upkeep versus return didn't seem fiscally advantageous, or even possible. The church was making overtures to the Scottish Churches Council for a grant for the purpose of reconfiguring the building to responsibly serve both the mission of the congregation and the humanitarian needs of the city. In November, Routley discussed his dilemma with his colleagues in the CUEW, and they suggested that a possible solution was the open pulpit at St James's Congregational Church in Newcastle. St James's was accustomed to good preachers, and Routley's scholarly reputation and musicianship enabled the congregation to concede to build a job description around his speaking and writing obligations. St. James's made the official call in mid-July, and the bittersweet rituals of parting began. He quickly saw one snag:

> When I remove myself, I may find it difficult to extricate myself from the Dunblane activities. I shall do so if it seems right, but I'll still be close enough to participate if required. After all, Scotland really begins on the north bank of the Tyne![108]

One example of Routley's pointed pastoral attention was seen in the frequently held Church Family Nights, a time to simply enjoy the company of one another in hospitality and laughter—often supplied by the Reverend Dr Routley. Beginning in the Oxford JCRs, he was known and sought after for hilarious ditties, which were often composed on the spot. Sometimes he was accompanied by Peter Scott, but it was usually a solo act. Routley did the same at ABC, à la the popular Flanders & Swann duo.[109] The songs were usually satirical and humorous attempts to lighten the seriousness of community or church issues. Nothing was spared. Routley sang about everything from theological stumbling blocks to the significance of the colors of the trash bins and buses throughout Edinburgh. The Presbyterians, Episcopalians, Baptists, Methodists, Congregationalists, and their churches were all objects of gentle parody.

Farewell

The final Family Night was on October 26,[110] the cusp of both the 450th Reformation Day and Routley's fiftieth birthday. Under the circumstances, it was a bit grander than normal, and Routley delivered extraordinarily. The first song was a lively discussion between Saints Columba[111] and Augustine concerning the qualities of their eponymous churches, all hashed out on a fairway. In the end, the holy men decided that their conflicting missions didn't matter, as they were both dead![112] The second was a self-deprecating look at the intellectual and refined graciousness of John Calvin and St. Augustine versus that of the long-haired, hardworking rapscallion, St. James. A few days later, the arrival of the moving van was bittersweet.[113]

The Routleys preserved strong connections with Edinburgh. Charles Somerville, church secretary, remained a friend and later visited the Routleys in the United States. The two men enjoyed each other's company immensely, from sermon critiques to church meetings and hospitality at their respective homes. Carol parties on Mayfield Terrace and at the Somerville house on Canaan Lane are still remembered.[114] Several years after Routley moved to Newcastle, he was asked to produce a book of sermons.[115] He used many from both ABC and St. James's, and in the preface he notes that the preacher, Apollos, over lunch with two followers, Aquila and Priscilla, discovered:

> He [Apollus] had not been preaching the Gospel of Jesus Christ at all. I am not a preacher of Apollonian standing, but I do believe I know how much he owed, or could have owed, to Aquila and Priscilla. My own Aquila and Priscilla are those who will thus speak with me about the faith, and every preacher has, or should pray for, a friend like that. My special ones live at 33 Canaan Lane, Edinburgh.

When the announcement of Routley's unexpected death reached the church, Charles Somerville memorialized his friend for the St. Columba–Augustine-Bristo newsletter:

Others will recall Erik's achievements in the wider world, but we remember him as a comforter of the bereaved, the sick and the troubled, a dynamo of energy, an encourager of all of us and a man who taught us in praise to make one music for the Lord of all.[116]

Soon after, Somerville's daughter, Elspeth Harley, remarked in a letter to her father:

I was wondering what Erik taught me and I could not think of anything specific, but only of him sitting in the library downstairs, talking, smoking his filthy pipe, and I realised that he had affected my attitude in almost everything.[117]

NOTES

1. GB, June 6, 1960. Though quick, the decision for his call was not unanimous.
2. George Caird filled Cadman's vacancy.
3. Vaughan Williams and Shaw both died a few months before Routley went to Edinburgh.
4. *Bulletin*, Winter 1959, 185–86.
5. https://www.scottish-places.info/features/featurefirst7774.html, accessed September 29, 2022.
6. The meeting places of Congregationalists were usually known by the streets on which they were situated. When the congregation moved into the new building on George IV Bridge, the members decided to name their church differently. St. Augustine was revered by the Reverend Alexander, who suggested the name in a proposal at the church meeting.
7. William Lindsay Alexander, *Selection of Hymns for Public Worship in Christian Churches* (Hugh Paton, Adam Square: Edinburgh, 1849).
8. Ibid.
9. Ibid.
10. https://www.augustine.org.uk/, accessed September 29, 2022.
11. National Churches Trust website, https://www.nationalchurchestrust.org/church/augustine-united-church-edinburgh, accessed October 1, 2022; https://www.augustine.org.uk/wp-content/uploads/2018/12/6.-People-and-buildings.pdf.
12. GB, April 11, 1959.
13. Huxtable, Marsh, R. Micklem, Todd, eds, *A Book of Public Worship* (London: Oxford University Press, 1956).
14. GB, April 11, 1959.
15. Thomas Kelly (1769–1856).
16. Bianca da Siena (d. 1434) and translated by Richard F. Littledale (1833–1890).
17. https://www.augustine.org.uk/wp-content/uploads/2018/12/5.-Unions-and-partnerships.pdf.
18. *Hymns Ancient & Modern, Revised* (Church of England, 1950).
19. GB, March 1, 1966.

20. GB, November 11, 1960.
21. GB, December 31, 1959.
22. Ibid.
23. Hayes Conference Center in Swanwick, Derbyshire, where yearly Congregational meetings took place. During World War II it was a camp for German and Italian prisoners of war.
24. A more probing insertion was the meditation on the first four pages of Aldous Huxley's *The Genius, and the Goddess*, which intrigued Routley immensely.
25. GB, December 31, 1959.
26. Ibid.
27. "The Penney Tenement Collapse that Changed Edinburgh Forever," https://www.edinburghnews.scotsman.com/whats-on/arts-and-entertainment/penny-tenement-collapse-changed-edinburgh-forever-601212, accessed October 4, 2022.
28. GB, December 31, 1959.
29. Willcocks attended King's College before the war, in which he participated in the Normandy invasion as part of the Cornwall Light Infantry. Following his discharge, he returned to Cambridge and finished his degree and then went on to organist positions at cathedrals in Salisbury and Worcester. In 1974 he became director of the Royal College of Music. CDH.
30. Routley Collection.
31. The prototype of this service was created in 1888 by Edward Benson (1829–1896), bishop of Truro. The King's version was adopted in 1918. CDH, https://hymnology.hymnsam.co.uk/n/nine-lessons-and-carols?q=Nine%20Lessons%20and%20Carols.
32. These solutions were also put forward in the upcoming Dunblane Music Consultations.
33. "A joke is a sort of rupture that opens up truth," attributed to Alain Badiou (Horowitz). An unexpected chord was customarily inserted at this point as early as 1887. HAM.
34. JWW, December 27, 1962.
35. Peter Tranchell (1922–1993) lectured in music at Cambridge from 1954 to 1989. His setting of Psalm 125 appears in *Ecumenical Praise* (7).
36. David Willcocks, December 25, 1966.
37. Appendix C.
38. Robert Somerville.
39. Mary C. Parnaby, "The History of Augustine Church and Augustine-Bristo Church," *Augustine United Church: The Challenge of our Heritage* (Augustine United Church: Edinburgh, 2005), 73.
40. An Edinburgh charity that campaigns for global changes to eradicate poverty, tackling its causes and effects.
41. This is a broad group of campaigners, faith groups, and civil societies working in solidarity, locally and globally, for the cancellation of an unpayable and unjust sovereign debt.
42. https://www.augustine.org.uk/about-us/partner-organisations/.
43. ER to the congregation, July 30, 1967.

44. This appears as "Antiphon I" in *The Temple*, published upon Herbert's death.
45. Composed by Basil Harwood (1859–1949), it is the most enduring tune for the Herbert text in Great Britain. CDH.
46. *Glory to God* (Louisville: Presbyterian Publishing Co., 2013), 636.
47. The memorial service was held in the chapel at Mansfield.
48. GB, June 10, 1960.
49. The group consisted of the Church of Scotland, the Scottish Episcopal Church, Congregationalists, Baptists, Methodists, United Free Church, and Roman Catholics. Participants in the various consultations were also non-Christian and atheist.
50. The correspondence from these discussions is in the Sir David Russell Papers archive at St. Andrews University.
51. Douglas Galbraith, email, April 12, 2021.
52. Douglas Gay, dissertation, 136.
53. *Duty and Delight* and conversation with Laurence Wareing in 2017.
54. Ibid.
55. Chair of the Department of Music at the University of Aberdeen, 1951–1981.
56. Read Music at Fettes and Divinity at Edinburgh, Scotland's BBC Religious Broadcasting organizer, 1973–1989.
57. Galbraith.
58. Jock Wilson the *British Weekly*, October 19, 1962.
59. C. S. Lewis, *An Experiment in Criticism* (Cambridge University Press, 1961).
60. *Duty and Delight: Routley Remembered*, Robin A. Leaver and James Litton, eds. (Hope Publishing: Carol Stream, 1985), 177.
61. George McPhee in conversation with Laurence Wareing, 2017.
62. The NEB New Testament was published in 1961, with the Old Testament following in 1970. Because of its scholarly translators, the *New English Bible* has been considered one of the more important translations of the Bible after World War II. It was assembled by British and Irish academics and theologians. Later translations broadened into the North American idiom and inclusive language.
63. The Second Ecumenical Council of the Vatican, 1962–1965. The spiritual renewal outlined by Vatican II challenged Roman Catholics to celebrate the liturgy in vernacular and localized congregational song.
64. Prior copyright was honored, but in the subsequent supplementary collections, the hymns were often just identified as "Dunblane."
65. J. R. Watson, "The life that'll never, never die," *Church Times*, March 26, 2004.
66. In the early twentieth century, skiffle, a style of folk music, arose in the United States. This was an amalgam of jazz, blues, country, and folk music. It disappeared in America in the 1940s but became very popular in Great Britain and Ireland, with probably close to fifty thousand homegrown groups playing in coffeehouses, churches, pubs, and parks. Everyone could create their own style of music without expensive instruments or musical skill. This phenomenon is often credited as an important precursor to the British folk movement of the 1960s. Groups like The Beatles (the Quarrymen), The Hollies, The Bee Gees, Pink Floyd, Procol Harum, and many solo performers arose from this development and is often labeled "The British Invasion."

67. *Duty and Delight*, 180.
68. JWW, December 23, 1967.
69. *Duty and Delight*, Fraser.
70. Wareing-Fraser conversation.
71. Just a few recognizable participants were Brian Wren, Peter Cutts, Caryl Micklem, Douglas Galbraith, John Geyer, Alan Luff, Alan Gaunt, George McPhee, David Goodall, and Stewart Todd.
72. George McPhee in conversation with Laurence Wareing, 2017.
73. Hope Publishing Co. Routley had never written a hymn text until this moment. He eventually wrote thirty-four.
74. *A Panorama of Christian Hymnody,* second edition, Paul A. Richardson, ed. (GIA: Chicago, 2005), forward.
75. "Birabus" was composed one afternoon in Newcastle when Peter was visiting the Routleys. Erik retired for a nap, challenging Peter to write a new tune in his absence. Cutts obliged.
76. Carlton R. Young (1926–2023) set this text to CHARLESTON for the *Methodist Hymnal*, 1966, and it is accepted as the conventional tune. At ABC, the tune EBENEZER was used successfully. In a letter to John Wilson in 1967, Routley moans that there is a sixth verse somewhere, but he can't lay his hands on it.
77. Reginald Barrett-Ayres and Erik Routley, eds. (Galliard Publishing and the Scottish Churches Council).
78. *Panorama*, second edition, foreword.
79. Fraser-Wareing conversation, 2017.
80. *Twentieth Century Church Music*, 212–13.
81. As of 2020, the Berkeley School of Theology.
82. The School of Christian Ministries at the California Baptist University and a member of the Graduate Theological Union consortium.
83. Robert H. Mitchell, *Ministry and Music* (Westminster Press: Philadelphia, 1968), preface.
84. Frederick Rimmer (1914–1998), Gardner Professor of Music, Glasgow University; director of Scottish Opera; founder of Scottish Music Archives.
85. The Rev. Dr. Henry C. Whitley (1906–1976), minister at St. Giles, High Kirk of Edinburgh.
86. JWW, August 21, 1964.
87. Ibid. Routley found the organ "horrible."
88. Robert. H. Mitchell, *I Don't Like that Music* (Hope Publishing Co.: Carol Stream, IL, 1993), 13–14.
89. JWW, June 25, 73.
90. Robert H. Mitchell, "Erik Routley on Church Music," *Foundations*, American Baptist Historical Society Journal, vol. 11, no. 3, 1994.
91. Robert H. Mitchell, *Ministry and Music* (Westminster Press: Philadelphia, 1978), 9.
92. Goshen College is a private Mennonite liberal arts college in Goshen, Indiana.
93. Mary Oyer. This course opened the historic and aesthetic dimensions of music and the arts for several generations of Goshen students. CDH.

94. NWG, Mary Oyer, July 7, 2003.
95. This was roughly £1.05.
96. Ibid.
97. Ibid.
98. Michael Hawn.
99. NWG, July 7, 2003.
100. JWW, April 26, 1966.
101. HSGBI *Bulletin*, Summer 1970, no. 119, 94–96.
102. "Sydney Carter's hymn was the most popular religious song for over a decade. It was broadcast on radio and TV, sung by congregations, always transformed by enthusiasm. Sometimes, like a pop song, it seemed that it would fade, but it survived." J. R. Watson, *Church Times*, March 26, 2004, 21.
103. NWG, July 7, 2003.
104. When Routley came to the United States in 1975, the Hymn Society conferences were held at the end of April, and he was heavily preoccupied with end-of-term concerns.
105. NWG, July 7, 2003.
106. *Who They Were in the Reformed Churches of England and Wales, 1901–2000* (URC), Clyde Binefield and John Taylor, eds. (Shaun Tyas: Donnington, 2007), 196–97.
107. GB, March 1, 1966, RC.
108. JWW, July 12, 1967.
109. Michael Flanders (1922–1975) and Donald Swann (1923–1994) were a British comedy team in the 1950s and 1960s known for their witty songs and monologues. They were well-known in Oxford during their student days at Christ Church, which overlapped Routley's time at Magdalen. They likely were acquainted at the time. Swann became a hymn writer, and he and Routley were close friends. Swann was also a lifelong friend and collaborator with Sydney Carter. The two met in the Friends Ambulance Service during World War II. CDH.
110. Mary C. Parnaby, *The History of Augustine Church, 1877–1941*, and *The History of Augustine-Bristo Church, 1941–1977*.
111. The organist at St. Columba-by-the-Castle was Sir Ronald Johnson (1913–1996). He and Routley were friends and collaborators (see appendix C). The Scottish Episcopal St. Columba's is part of the present ecumenical covenant with Augustine United Church and Greyfriars Church of Scotland.
112. Cassette recording of the event.
113. Erik's fiftieth birthday, October 31.
114. Somerville's son, Robert Somerville, grew up in the church, absorbing a strong and abiding faith through adulthood.
115. *Saul among the Prophets* (The Upper Room: Nashville, 1972).
116. Robert Somerville, "Erik as Pastor," centenary address, October 2017.
117. Elspeth Harley, in a letter to her father, Charles Somerville, upon Routley's sudden death in 1982.

Chapter 6

Newcastle upon Tyne, 1967–1974

Newcastle upon Tyne is a city built on layers of conflict and intercontinental claims. Early invaders included the Romans under the reign of Hadrian, who left in 410 CE, and the Anglo-Saxons, who prevailed until the arrival of the Danes in the late ninth century. Following the death of the first Norman king, William I, came violent discord among his heirs in the political struggle for territory. On the site of an old Roman bridge in Northumbria, one son, Robert Curthose,[1] built a *novum castellum*. Elizabeth I (1533–1603) granted the settlement town status in 1589, and it was legally declared a city in 1884 by Queen Victoria (1819–1901).

Like most of England, the world wars left Newcastle exhausted. The destruction of the bombings, crippling loss of life, and demands on the manufacturing areas of the England's northeast abruptly deflated the former prosperity of the late 1800s.[2] This, coupled with the lingering effects of the Great Depression, led to massive unemployment and business decline and an undermining lack of investors willing to risk changing the situation. Newcastle didn't catch a glimmer of solid recovery until the 1970s, when visionary city planners engaged in an all-encompassing regeneration scheme, eventually transforming an ailing northeast England into one of the most iconic areas in Britain, with Newcastle as the cultural and industrial center.

Whiffs of this renewal began in the 1950s and included a dramatic reconfiguration of the city center that involved demolition of many buildings, including St. James's Congregational church, a landmark since 1884. The congregation's strong opposition brought down the initiative, but the church carefully tapped into this civic energy; discussions arose to consider what kind of revitalization was required to apply the mission of the congregation to these efforts. By 1967 St. James's had an idea of what they wanted in a leader of this campaign. Attracted to his thought-provoking sermons and ecumenical experience, St. James's decided to call Routley to manage their wider plan. Routley had confided to Beck that, considering the projected responsibilities and constraints that accompanied the renovation at Augustine-Bristo, the offer from St. James's was irresistible, "though I thought nothing short of a hint from the diaconate would otherwise get us out of Edinburgh."[3]

After deep, uneasy contemplation, Routley decided to affirm the call:

> It is a tremendous and exciting prospect. The upheaval might be fairly gruesome. St. James's is the Congregational church right in the heart of the city, and they are looking for a complete re-evaluation of the life of the church to match the civic reconstructions that are going on in the immediate neighborhood. They have an adequate choir and an angelic organist who gets marvelous music out of an instrument which we must do something to improve.[4]

The manse in Newcastle was in ill repair and not really a good fit for the busy life of a modern minister. The Routley family structure had changed. Nicolas and Patrick were both at Cambridge, Priscilla was still in school, and Erik and Margaret needed room for a piano. They put down an offer on a house of their own, but St. James's agreed with their conclusions and the Church Council scurried around the area looking for proper housing. A suitable manse was soon located in a spacious detached house on Linden Road in the Gosforth section of Newcastle, only two and a half miles from the church.

Routley's first sermon at St. James's was right in the middle of Priscilla's school term,[5] so initially the plan was that Priscilla would stay at Cranley until Christmas. Surprisingly, she thrived as a boarder, and, considering this transformation, the family decided that she would remain at Cranley until her graduation. Newcastle was only 120 miles south and was connected by exceptional train service. The Routleys' many friends in Edinburgh proved more than willing to serve as emergency contact. Routley told John Wilson about the first days in town:

> Here we are, after the most infernal removal we've ever experienced!![6] Noah-like weather both on Wednesday when most of the stuff was coming in, and today, our first Sunday. Roof's leaking in the church, windows letting it in at the manse, books all over the place waiting to be sorted, and general ghastliness! However, the induction itself was a very happy occasion; we dispensed with the Charge, and our choir managed Britten's *Te Deum*. With the Stygian November damp, the hymns were quite a gesture! When we're settled, this is going to be a lot of fun and the house, though hardly navigable yet, is going to be splendid. We really are immensely fortunate.[7]

MUSIC AT ST. JAMES'S

From the early days of the congregation, St. James's emphasized hymnody in their worship services. Shortly after the church was built, a pipe organ was installed, so naturally St. James's was attracted to Routley's musical reputation as well as his preaching. In 1965, recognizing Routley's international impact on the revitalization of worship music after years of his work on committees, the Royal School of Church Music awarded Routley with their honorarium as "Fellow."[8] He was the first RSCM fellow who was not a professional church musician; more importantly, he was also the first Nonconformist to be admitted. When the RSCM was founded in 1927, only Anglicans were permitted to participate in the training, awards, and renown that membership implied. This requirement disappeared after an institutional reorganization in 1945.[9]

Music is often an amenity to change, and Routley's first route to fulfilling his call to this established but declining congregation was through the choir members, who were ready for his leadership. Like most choirs, it was a tradition-bound bunch, but with Routley's sense of humor and gift of persuasion, they were willing to try his suggestions, like introducing St James's to many of the new hymns from Dunblane and ones under consideration for *New Songs of the Church* and *Cantate Domino*. These included hymns sung in languages other than English plus canticles and psalm settings that were unfamiliar to a Congregational choir. It wasn't too long before the ensemble was also admitted into the RSCM as the first non-Anglican choir to receive this status. Routley's ardent ally in this transformation was the organist, Raymond Hall,[10] who helped them take artistic risks by learning works by Benjamin Britten (1913–1976) and Herbert Howells (1892–1983). In December 1968 two members of the choir were in London and heard *The Temptation of St. Anthony*[11] by Werner Egk (1901–1983). Back in Newcastle they asked Routley if they could program it during Lent. Routley had never heard of the piece but was willing to give it a go. And so they scheduled it for the Sunday evening service on March 9.

> It was exceedingly well done by two members of the choir and an imported pianist who had a Gerald Moore touch.[12] Fantastic stuff—quite new to me. When they asked if they could, I looked at it and said, "well, it's all in French, so if you produce a discreet English paraphrase, it'll probably get by." It got by with quite a bang![13]

The Organ

The eighty-year-old organ was no longer capable of supporting worship music in the way that Routley expected, but replacing the instrument was way beyond St. James's music budget. The controversial solution to this problem was installing an electric organ. This was a polemic subject in the pre-digital age of hybrid instruments. Colleagues in the Oxford Organists'

Association and the Congregational Organists' Guild,[14] including Carolyn Brock (1935–2017),[15] were shocked, alarmed, and offended that he would even consider this obviously practical answer at St. James's. In an article in the widely distributed *British Weekly*, Routley explained:

> I have not betrayed my allegiance to pipes. But, in these times, when so many of us wonder whether our buildings are going to last even another ten years, there are real difficulties about buying a new pipe organ or spending large sums on improving old ones. The electronic instrument has the enormous advantage that if you [a congregation] move, all you need do is move one console, the generators, and speakers. The technicians re-voice the instrument for the new church, and that's it. Better this than the sad sight of a fine old pipe-organ going for scrap value from a church which a changing society has caused to close. For our fluid and unpredictable age, a really good electronic [instrument] has what one might almost call a theological advantage.[16]

He adamantly cautions against "cheap entertainment organs not fit for a bar in Las Vegas" and that the common argument that an electric organ is not worth the church's funds is a hollow attack. Routley admonishes:

> If you need an organ, avoid all cheap imitations, study the market, and ask whether you want something permanent or something transferable. As in all other honest professions, what you pay for, you will get.[17]

Routley took his own advice and, for most of a year, scoured the churches and cathedrals with pipeless instruments and scrutinized the organ builders. Two builders stood out: Miller Organs of Norwich and Compton Organs of London, both of which produced the most realistic simulation of a pipe organ to date.[18] Routley traveled to Norwich and Exeter to hear the exemplar models of both firms. The one in Norwich was acceptable, especially for the price.[19] The Compton in Exeter was in use for the centenary celebration at St. Michael and All Angel's Church.[20] On his visit there, Routley enjoyed its full rich sound,[21] but he admitted that both companies produced instruments worthy of hymn accompaniment and recitals. In September 1969 Routley and Hall took a trip to Windermere to the home of John Robert Makin Pilling. Pilling, though a scion of an important manufacturing company in Rochdale,[22] was also a musician, organist, and choirmaster.[23]

> The owner has in his billiard room the latest £9000, 4-manual Compton electrostatic organ—the only one of its kind at present.[24] Absolutely superb—the first time I've felt like giving a pure alpha to an electronic job. Four generators, one of which is only for the reeds. I think Compton may at last have really broken through.[25]

Pilling and the farsighted Compton firm[26] were eager to see a similar instrument at St. James's, and Routley was eager to comply, but the price tag was high, and, as he reminded Wilson, "There is spectacular opposition from very defensive traditional organists."[27] Back in Newcastle, Raymond Hall spoke to the choir about the benefits of this type of instrument, and before long a church-wide appeal was launched. In the end, Routley and Hall settled on another outstanding builder, Copeman Hart, and one of their models was installed at St. James's in 1973.[28] When Geoffrey Beck was considering a new organ at his church in Brighton,[29] he asked Routley for suggestions:

> If anybody raises the question of pipeless organs, then you must consult Ernest Hart,[30] who built ours. Ours is, I say shamelessly, marvelous. It is bigger than you might want—thought it would be a pity to be meager about this. Hart would build you a good three-manual for, I suspect at present prices, some £7500. He is a real artist—streets ahead of any of the big firms. He builds them individually with his own hands, services them and voices them. When we asked what would happen if we have a fault on Saturday night as Hart was 270 miles away, he gave a tutorial to a hi-fi-expert in the congregation, which means that any running repairs we can easily do.[31]

Cantate Domino (1975; Music Edition, 1980)

The era of recovery and prosperity following World War II came with the determination to expose and tackle the social issues of racism, poverty, the environment, and civil rights. Hymnology was not the only thing that exploded in the 1960s. The United States was on fire; Europe was rife with protest, including the Prague Spring; the armed conflict in Vietnam was really a war; the international scourge of racism was both debilitating and exhausting. Ecumenical relationships seemed more important than ever. Says the Reverend Dr. David Cornick (b. 1954)[32]:

> Ecumenism was a dominate narrative in twentieth century church life. It was the hope of those generations who knew too well the legacies of religious hatred and the nationalisms that were potent factors in two world wars. Its achievements were considerable. Institutionally, ecumenism established a series of national and international meeting places between Christians across the world. All the raw pain of colonialism and living under totalitarianism found its way to the surface in the deliberations of the World Council of Churches.[33]

The World Student Christian Federation was established in the very early years of the ecumenical movement.[34] In the first three-quarters of the twentieth century, the organization published four editions of a little hymn book entitled *Cantante Domino*. The first book, in 1924, had sixty-seven hymns in English, French, and German, with the intention to make a book that was more representative of the worldwide Christian community. Each following edition—1930, 1938, and 1951—was prepared in this same spirit, but many hymns proved so unfamiliar that they were seldom sung, and the list of subjects became increasingly inadequate with each succeeding student generation. By 1968 the World Council of Churches[35] was feeling pressure to create a new edition, but they felt that the radical world outlook made the project too large for a student organization.

During the decade following the publication of *Congregational Praise*, Routley's expertise as an editor became widely respected. The Dunblane Consultations expanded his influence inside the ecumenical community, so in December 1968, when the WCC held a preliminary meeting for a new edition of the student hymnal, Routley was summoned and asked to lead the undertaking. With his usual self-effacing style, he tells Wilson:

> I'm just home from Geneva, having left home 0700 yesterday and arrived back 0800 today. Vulgar. I've at last been sucked into the orbit of ecumenism. It rather looks as if I shall be involved in editing the new *Cantate Domino*. Some poor fool's got to head it up, but it will be a considerable international project. We have to set up editorial trios in Germany, France, and Great Britain, and find research folk to explore the hymnody of, say, Tibet, or Nicaragua. Then we'll need to translate everything into French, English, and German. Well, if the WCC lay it all on me, it gives me a chance to take the wife to Geneva once or twice.[36]

In the hymnal's preface, Routley says that the purpose of the book was to serve the church at its growing points, as a meeting of cultures, races, and experiments in texts, music, and liturgy was "clearly called for."[37] In addition to the founding Europeans, the committee expanded to include affiliates from the Southern Hemisphere, Asia, and Africa, assuring that the new material represented a genuine ecumenical and international compilation. Much flexibility was required in the language display, as satisfactory translation was not always possible, so another committee was appointed to guide the larger group. Instead of every hymn being translated into French, German, and English, as in previous editions, it was decided that the hymn would appear in its original language with an English translation.[38] If clarification of the text was needed, then translations in other languages were provided.[39] Routley did a lot of the adaptations and paraphrasing, depending on the native speakers of the language in question for translations.

The book was designed to be used at international gatherings in a range of venues, from conference centers to ocean liners, or as a supplement to any denominational hymnal. The items are arranged in order of the church year and the Psalms with additional sections for the human condition, praise, experience, mission, and unity. Published in 1974 as a tunes-only version, a full-music edition appeared in 1980. Many hymns published for the first time in *Cantate Domino* now regularly appear in twenty-first-century hymnals, including Routley's well known paraphrases, "New songs of celebration render," harmonized by John Wilson, and Routley's translation and paraphrase, "There in God's garden," set to a traditional Hungarian melody.[40]

When evaluated in twenty-first-century expectations for a global ecumenical hymnal, *Cantate Domino* falls short. Revisionism deems it somewhat ungenuine and condescending in a guarded way, Eurocentric and Western, solidly dated, and inadequate in terms of performance practice. Yet, taken in context, the collection was groundbreaking in its day and fundamental in our time. C. Michael Hawn (b. 1948) notes, "Under Erik Routley's leadership, it [CD]served as an incipient model for ecumenical and international song."[41] True to his role as encourager and facilitator, Routley posed an abiding question in one of the editorial meetings: "How will Christians of the future sing—as members of the Universal Church, or not at all?"[42]

The Summit Choirbook (1983)

When Pope Pius XII (1876–1958) died in 1958, the Conclave elected Cardinal Angelo Roncalli (1881–1963), patriarch of Venice, as the new bishop of Rome. The Sacred College of Cardinals were attracted to Roncalli's conservatism and foresaw no major changes. But after only a few months in office, Pope John XXIII called a general council for revitalization of the Roman Church and to introduce a new sacred mystery: restoration of unity among all Christians. The resulting Second Vatican Council[43] met from 1962 to 1965, with a platform including dialogue with Protestant, Anglican, and Orthodox sectors of Christianity.[44] *Sacrosanctum Concilium* evolved as the decree on ecumenism and was passed nearly unanimously by the attending bishops. The English translation of the opening sentence reads: "The restoration of unity among all Christians is one of the principal concerns of the Second Vatican Council."[45] Within this decree, *Musicam Sacram* provided instructions for music in worship and an invitation to strengthen the celebration of the liturgy through congregational song and localization of language, accompanied by sensitive creativity. Individual parishes soon discovered that the actual manifestation of these modifications was an ambiguous prospect.

In northern New Jersey, the Dominican Monastery of Our Lady of the Rosary sits quietly in a residential neighborhood of Summit. Though fully American in its culture, this is a cloistered community dedicated to prayer and contemplation, guided by solid Dominican precepts and the Rule of St. Augustine. The nuns spend at least five or six hours a day in prayer through the seven offices of the Dominican liturgy and personal meditation. In the

1950s one of the community, Sr. Maria of the Cross, OP[46] (1937–2012), entered the monastery with well-developed musical skills and training as a composer.[47] Sr. Maria used her gifts as organist during the services and by composing settings for feast days.

Sr. Maria was eager to adopt *Musicam Sacram*, but she insisted upon preserving the solemnity and discipline of the Dominican tradition. Simple translations of the liturgy from Latin to English often brought more problems than solutions. With great care, Sr. Maria adapted the Gradual of the entire Dominican rite into English, as well as three volumes of Psalm chants and antiphons using her own arrangements and compositions. But the real challenge from the Vatican Council was hymnody and hymn singing, a practice that had never accompanied the Roman Catholic Mass. Most of this Summit community had never even sung one. In the larger Roman Catholic sphere, satisfying this part of the decree "caused a great explosion of new songs for the people's praise. Some are a surprise, and some are regrettable and embarrassing."[48] Though the need for a hymnal became apparent, Sr. Maria didn't know how to start, as most new hymn books are greatly influenced by their predecessors and draw on the heritage of their constituency.[49] She was starting from scratch. But this stumbling block proved musically and theologically liberating, as the customary pairings of tunes and texts expected by Protestant worshippers didn't exist.

Sr. Maria began study texts and tunes of hymns in major denominational hymnals. She found thought-provoking and theologically sound poetry in the texts of Isaac Watts and Charles Wesley. But the tunes! So many of these hymns were accompanied by tunes with lusty and majestic interpretations, which appeared contrary the dignity she was determined to maintain. In her searches, the name Erik Routley appeared regularly, and, knowing she needed help, she wrote to him for advice, sending along examples of her settings. He was immediately impressed with the "delicacy and precision of judgment, the modesty of style, the fastidious scholarship, and the remarkable depth of learning which distinguished her work."[50] Routley agreed to serve as her listening post and consultant, opening years of intimate, detailed correspondence about the future shape of the book. Most authors struggle with titles; this was no exception for the two of them. The book was intended only for Dominican use, and, as many of the songs were small anthems, rounds, antiphons, and plainsong, *The Summit Choirbook* was settled upon as an identifier of both place and use. When Routley was in Princeton for a few weeks in the summer of 1973, he made a visit to Summit—an occasion that still is remembered as a special day for the monastery. Despite the breadth of the project, there were only two people with whom Routley shared details of this work. One was Peter Scott, who, after his own Mansfield days, converted to Roman Catholicism. Routley relied on his best friend's observations of the finer details of the Mass in relation to the hymns in the book. The other was John Wilson, because there was nothing they held back in their candid critiques of hymnology.

> There's sort of an underground hymnal being produced by a learned and delightful nun in northern New Jersey for their own community. There's hope that it will be published someday. If it does, it will be a regular *Songs of Syon*,[51] which is much wanted here.[52]

The book was initially ready to print by 1975. There are over five hundred entries in two distinct parts, one for the church year and its festivals and feasts; the other is hymns for specific saint feast days, a valuable resource in a Catholic church.

> I admire with particular gratitude the sensitive way the Editor has handled the classic Protestant hymn writers, and in which she has made provision for special Holy Days, on which occasions hymnody often appears at its most sentimental and tiresome.[53]

The contributors from within the order, including the general editor, Sr. Maria, are only listed as "The Dominican Nuns of Summit NJ," and copyright is held by the cloister. This anonymity removes any focus from the artists to that of simple praise, where it belongs.

Sr. Maria and Routley considered releasing the book as a national Catholic hymnal but decided that exclusive use in Dominican monasteries better served the integrity of the book. Consequently, finding a publisher was difficult due to the intended exclusive distribution. Even Routley could not find a publisher willing to take it on, and eventually the monastery obtained private means for publication. There was only one printing of four thousand hymnals; only a few unused books remain, as the choir books are used daily in Summit and the other Dominican communities in the United States. When a monastery closes, their hymnals are returned to Our Lady of the Rosary.

The Summit Choirbook was finally published in 1983, a year after Routley died.[54] In a letter to Margaret, Sr. Maria mentioned that the monastery would send a first edition to her, catching Margaret unaware of the extent of her husband's contribution to this quiet and authoritative voice in modern hymnody. When the book arrived, Margaret admired all of it, including the way the texts and tunes were set on the page. She wistfully remarked, "I do wish Erik could have seen your book. I know what a delight it would have given him."[55]

Chapter 6

THE MINISTRY AT ST. JAMES'S

In Newcastle, Routley's working ministry went on. Serving St. James's was not very different from serving Augustine-Bristo. Routley's pastoral duties included visiting members across the city and dealing with their issues of rehousing and living expenses, but mostly he was needed to just pop in and spend some time over tea.

> To some extent one's got to accept the condition of people whose religion still means something and this just about the required size for them. I've taken the line that the minister's part is not so much to preach at them as to keep an eye on them at home. This could well mean that "good hymns" are "good Sankeys,"[56] but I do think there a little spark of genuine faith in my old dears.[57]

Routley affectionately refer to St James's as "The Cathedral of Northern Nonconformity" in his letters, which are full of newsy bits of problems and excitement—the same script from every modern congregation but with the Newcastle flair. The congregation engaged in community outreach, women's groups, men's Bible studies, services on Wednesday and Sunday, youth clubs, deacons' meetings, ailing buildings, and financial concerns. As in Edinburgh, Routley took a poorly organized concept of an inner-city ecumenical collaboration of churches and turned it into a strong, and still thriving, City Central Churches Council.

> Newcastle is a toughish nut to crack, but after five years' tentative nudging we've a Central Churches Council off the ground. The joke is that we have no [larger] Council of Churches—well, a Cathedral canon tried to get something going for years. Now the blighters have asked ME, of all people, to try to revive it. Haven't the least idea of what to do but somebody else's idea will appear in due course and give us a clue.[58]

While St. James's congregation worked outside the church on the problems of urban Newcastle, the music ministry also flourished. Under the direction of Mr. Hall, a new organ was finally commissioned, and Mr. Hart spent most of 1973 working on the specifications. The console was delivered on March 1, and Routley sent this wry comment to Wilson:

> The organ console was delivered on Thursday and got stuck in the door like the hippopotamus. So, we've sawn the door down. Reformation without tarrying for years.[59]

The initial inauguration of the instrument featured a recital by Lionel Dakers (1924–2003).[60] Routley called it a "nice, friendly program," and the church was packed. By early October the organ was 98 percent complete, and Ronald Perrin (1931–1997), organist at Ripon Cathedral, presented an introductory recital; Routley gave another for the Monday Women's Club.

> It really is a fantastic instrument; we've now got a tuba and a trumpet réal! The sound of the machine is astonishing! It should fool both the romantics and the baroquists. This afternoon, I have the astounding assignment of demonstrating it to our women's meeting (a sort of old-fashioned "mission" meeting for pensioners who live in our central city high-rises). I can fool them for a half an hour, but the builder will be there as well as Carys Hughes (1949–2003).[61]

The choir sang often for BBC programs broadcast from the Newcastle Tyne Tees television studios, though sometimes the recording venue was in the sanctuary at St. James's. The church used *Congregational Praise* as their regular hymnal, and at Daker's suggestion, in anticipation of the union with the English Presbyterians, Routley put together a supplement for the church that highlighted some new work and hymns from the Presbyterian tradition and his own challenge to "sing local." It holds texts from the new writers, like Brian Wren and Fred Pratt Green, tunes from the Scottish Psalter, and one by Erik's first music teacher at Fonthill[62]—a total of twenty-three hymns, two canticles,[63] and five Psalm settings. Even fifty years and other hymnals and supplements later, St. James's still uses the little book from time to time.

THE PURITAN PLEASURES OF THE DETECTIVE STORY (1972)

From his school days, Routley had loved detective novels, and as he matured, he found theological connections to the basic detective formula. This was well known to anyone who heard his sermons and lectures or spent any time in conversation with him by the allusions to one story or another. Routley viewed Puritanism as a lay culture that is argumentative rather than dogmatic, intelligent rather than fanatical. Encouraged by his son Patrick, Routley wrote a book on the subject. The title, *The Puritan Pleasures of the Detective Novel*, is certainly intriguing, however one defines "Puritan." In the prologue, Routley says that things are required in good detective fiction: (1) a tradition of integrity in the police force; (2) a detective who never fails; and (3) an eagerness in the reader to take pleasure in observation.[64] The book is vintage Routley in that he writes as he speaks, and there is a bit of stream of consciousness in his style. He discusses the undercurrents of primary detectives like Sherlock Holmes, Hercule Poirot, Lord Peter Wimsey, and Father Brown and authors like Conan Doyle, Agatha Christie, and Ngaio Marsh. In 1973 he was invited by Christie to address her famous Detection Club[65] and the Crime Writers' Association at the Hotel Café Royale in London. In *Talking about Detective Fiction*, P.D. James (1920–2014) wrote her own ideas of the attraction of the detective story and quotes Routley:

> My hope is that this short personal account will interest and entertain not only my readers, but the many who share our pleasure in a form of popular literature which for over fifty years has fascinated and engaged me as a writer.[66]

AGING

The years were passing, and in correspondence between Routley and his friends Geoffrey Beck and John Wilson, there appear occasional complaints of gout, high blood pressure, kidney stones, and other stress-related ailments that strike middle-aged men who work too hard. Routley and Beck were in their fifties; Wilson, ten years older. All the men had been told by their GPs to slow down and make room for some rest, usually easier said than done.

> Taking leisure time makes me feel guilty, and afraid that unless I make my own job untenable or lose it, I am positively certain that the family would be out in the street on public assistance! I am already at war with those who offer the Christian faith as a permanent "Outward Bound" course,[67] staffed by professional scolds. We must form a Drones Club[68] for the revival of relaxation.[69]

Wilson also suffered stiffness and movement issues that drove Routley to suggest a visit to his brother-in-law, Peter Scott:

> I am concerned and troubled to hear about your vexatious physical difficulties, but I believe that I can seriously put you in touch with somebody who specialized in this. He's done a very great deal of good with musicians and others who have got into occupational ruts like yours. He teaches the right use of muscles and other mechanical bits & pieces which one has to live with. I feel you might be glad to be told of this because it's entirely possible that he might deliver you from the dog-collar—oh, and he's an excellent musician, but I must declare that he is Margaret's brother![70]

BECOMING THE UNITED REFORMED CHURCH

Routley certainly didn't slow down. As with every other Congregational church at the time, the focal point for discussion and action at St. James's was the upcoming union of the Congregational and English

Presbyterian denominations. In the age of ecumenism and unity following world war, Protestants in England launched several schemes for union and reformation, most notably between the Church of England, the Methodists, the Presbyterians, and the Congregationalists. The only plan that succeeded was the agreement between the Congregational Church in England and Wales[71] and the English Presbyterian Church.

> The URC was the first denomination to be formed in England by union rather than by schism. When a church is born of a split, it begins life asserting its rightness and continues fighting its corner. The URC started life in consultation for common ground. It was born listening.[72]

This didn't happen overnight. There had been years of discussions and formal committees as the idea of union waxed and waned. Doctrinal issues of baptism and the Lord's Supper and eligible ministries had been sorted in the 1950s. Efforts originating in the assemblies of both churches produced the "Scheme of Union" in 1963. Similarities and differences were evaluated, and controversial subjects of polity were at least made bearable, if not totally accepted.[73] In fact, the two denominations were very much alike.

> That which they have developed as tradition derives from a profound respect for intellect. Preaching is central to both, and sacramentalism was secondary for a long time. A public service of worship can be complete without the Lord's Supper, but not without the Word.[74]

PRESIDENT OF THE CCEW, 1970–1971

At the May Meeting in 1969, the CCEW elected Routley as their President for the 1970–1971 term. Among congregations, hope grew that choosing Routley would put a new emphasis on the prophetic nature of the Church, rather than the "ecclesiastic jockeying"[75] that had lately accompanied much of every denominational activity.

> Neither friend or critic would be surprised to find [Routley] presiding over any society for purposes of music, hymnody, or worship. That we should have elected such a downright, no-nonsense, outspoken blow-away-the-cobwebs, Chestertonian type of man to be President of our Church does us quite as much honor and credit as it does him. . . . [We] owe more to him than we are aware, and he is one of our liveliest and most theologically trenchant preachers. His sense of humour and sweeping honesty of mind have no respect of persons, yet his pastoral care knows no limits.[76]

Routley was in the thick of it. He perceived that careful communication was the key to a reasonable transition, and there was a lot of explaining and reassuring to be done. The president's responsibility was to represent the denomination in inter-church gatherings and lead all nonbusiness meetings of the Assembly,[77] but his title did not come with membership on the Joint Negotiating Committee or any voting role. Accompanied by his foresight, drive, and persuasive leadership, he visited untold numbers of congregations offering encouragement, understanding, and explanations of the coming changes.

> There could be no more fitting person than Erik Routley to guide Congregationalism towards the transition of the next few years. With the conviction of unfragmented faith, [Routley] refuses to be bound by outworn traditions, though equally unwilling to adopt modern methods that he deems unworthy or meretricious.[78]

The Reverend Arthur Macarthur (1913–2008) held the post of general secretary of the Presbyterian Church of England and convener of the national denomination's Inter-Church Relations Committee throughout the 1960s. Concurrently, Macarthur served as minister at St. Columba's Presbyterian Church in the Tyneside town of New Shields while Routley was at St. James's. The two men frequently worked together on concerns within Greater Newcastle before they became partners in the preparation for church union. When Routley was elected president of the CCEW in 1971, Alexander was elected moderator of the General Assembly in the Presbyterian Church. The two had different roles and venues but were frequently at the same meetings and each other's sounding board, as the path to union was inevitable at this point. Final agreement was reached in 1972, and the obligatory Bill of Establishment was put before the House of Commons that June. Upon waking on the morning of October 5, Presbyterian Macarthur and Congregationalist Routley found themselves both ministers of the United Reformed Church.

WORSHIP IN THE URC

In the first united agenda, Routley was appointed chair of the Doctrine and Worship Committee. Macarthur says:

> This was a strategic appointment helping to carry us on from the worship patterns of the separate churches at a time when there was a movement of change in theological thinking brought about by the disturbing questions raised by Bishop John Robinson in his book, *Honest to God*.[79] We needed Erik's strong faith, to build bridges with the familiar.[80]

Worship was a major concern for the Joint Committee, particularly when it came to hymnody. The Congregationalists used *Congregational Praise* (1951); the Presbyterians, *The Church Hymnary* (1927). Each book represented the character of the respective denominations with some overlaps, but neither reflected the strenuous and fast-moving changes in hymnody or the celebratory atmosphere of a new church.[81] Prior to the union, a new hymnal was suggested, but there were several objections to that route. Expense was the most obvious. Hymnals take years to assemble, and one wouldn't be ready until long after the launch of the denomination. *The Presbyterian Church Hymnary, No. 3* was about to be released, and though *Congregational Praise* was widely used by Congregational churches, the decision to use it in worship had been determined by each congregation. It seemed that a supplement, not a replacement, was the solution until a compelling denominational hymnal could be envisioned. Almost every major hymnal in Great Britain and the United States had an accompanying supplement to fill in the liturgical, social, and political gaps of the hardback hymnals in the pew rack, so this idea was not confusing. In a supplement, new hymnody stands next to the traditional parent hymnals to complete the hymnal, not disregard it.

Informal discussion on a supplement occurred during the 1960s, but at the 1973 May Meeting,[82] the General Assembly officially passed a resolution to authorize the production of a hymn book supplement. This process included electing a committee that would be responsible to the Doctrine and Worship Committee, over which John Huxtable (1912–1990)[83] had been appointed at the end of Routley's term. Routley would be part of the *New Church Praise* panel,[84] and the completed supplement was released at the 1975 General Assembly. The book contains 109 hymns and service music, most written by living authors and composers, to accompany the widely welcomed *Order of Worship for the Lord's Supper*,[85] which, as Routley says in the preface, was exactly what was needed. Forty-six texts and eight tunes[86] eventually found their way into the URC *Rejoice and Sing*, and many entries appear in denominational hymns throughout the world.

ST. JAMES'S AND THE URC

The St. James's United Reformed Church was introduced to the changes in worship structure, slowly but surely, as anticipated. Churches are always reluctant to change. St. James's was a conservative place, and they were unsettled by the new definitions of former practice. Terms and responsibilities that had been worked out over the last several years in joint committees seemed like sudden changes on a local level. What is the difference between a congregation and a church? Why are elders ordained for life? Will there be a General Assembly or May Meeting?

> This Elders business is beginning to crunch us a bit. The erstwhile deacons have terrible visions of being mini-ministers sipping tea with the Gosforth matrons—we have to say that the ministers don't do this *now*, before persuading them that they needn't! With all this innovation what about a demythologization of pastoralia??[87]

The "Order of Worship" in the back of *New Church Praise* was unfamiliar and threatening in its authority. Congregational churches had traditionally been "suspicious of any attempt to codify the words and even the structure of the church's worship."[88] Historically, the Lord's Supper was not part of Congregational worship but celebrated after the service, as Communion was not part of a Congregationalist's spirituality, and members would often leave before the sacrament was offered.

Routley and the Doctrine and Worship Committee had been working on the wording and shape of this service and before it was put before the URC in 1975, but an early draft was released to congregations in February 1974 to use and examine. St. James's church meeting had proposed trying out the order on March 1, 1974. Routley was warily optimistic.

> Since my days in Brighton, I never met a more unsacramentally-minded bunch. Wednesbury, Dartford, and even Edinburgh—nobody went out before Communion. Here, a quarter of them do. (Mornings of course, evenings are for the forty righteous.) Whether it's discussions at Church Meeting, social calls, you name it, they dig in their heels. There's still a good bit of popping out before Communion, though less than formerly. I'm worried still that too many people, despite all our precautionary warnings and instructions, will hate it. I'm not having anything to do with the ICET Lord's Prayer[89]—the poor dears must have one landmark left! If it goes down here, it'll go down everywhere, if not this will probably generate a resolution to join the Congregational Federation! We must persevere.[90]

St. James's members tackled the situation with some creative solutions. A network of conversation groups was set up to consider the difficulties presented by the union. They held an all-congregation weekend conference and invited Daniel Jenkins (1914–2002) to lead the sessions.

> More than 100 people are actively participating in a pull-the-roof-down operation. They may decide to move the minister on, but never mind! It's already doing a lot for morale. I beam around and let them get on with it—being the one person who may not attend the small group meetings unless I'm invited for some information. But—I attend the leaders' committees all right! It's all

being quite good, clean fun—persuading St James's to enjoy having an entirely unpredictable future instead of the accustomed boneheaded security has been a surprisingly rewarding exercise.[91]

And suddenly, it was the clergyman himself who decided to move the minister on.[92]

NOTES

1. Robert II of Normandy (1051–2234), eldest son of William the Conqueror.
2. For most of World War II, the heavily industrial riverside areas of the Tyne, the Wears, and the Tee suffered the Newcastle Blitz and constant Luftwaffe raids. Shipyards, steelworks, collieries, and the associated residential areas of their workforce were all targets.
3. ABC received a substantial grant to alter the premises to house the offices of Christian Aid and the Scottish Churches Council and allow for a space for community meetings This involved major reworking of the interior, removing galleys, putting up partitions, adding a staircase, and moving the organ console. Routley remarked to Beck: "The new minister is magnificent—the right combination of high humour, ruthlessness, and an unsentimental concern for people, which they need. They are in capital shape." February 15, 1969.
4. JWW, August 6, 1967.
5. November 2, 1967. Routley celebrated his fiftieth birthday, October 31, with the arrival of the moving van at Mayfield Terrace in Edinburgh. JWW, October 9, 1967.
6. JWW, November 2, 1967.
7. JWW, November 5, 1967.
8. Routley cherished this honor and served on committees for several years in the UK and the United States. Lee Hastings Bristol (1923–1979) was made Fellow in 1969; he was the first American so honored. Bristol was president of Westminster Choir College from 1962 to 1969
9. In 2022 the RSCM is interdenominational, though still under the umbrella of the Church of England.
10. Biographical dates are unavailable, but Hall was concurrently director of the Durham Choral Society until his retirement in 1884.
11. *La tentation de Sainte Antoine*. Known as The Great or St. Anthony of the Desert, the monk renounced his worldly life and went into the Egyptian desert and faced supernatural temptations. Composed in 1952 and revised as a ballet in 1969.
12. Gerald Moore (1899–1987). Well-respected accompanist credited for raising the role of the accompanist to an equal artistic partner with the performer.
13. JWW, March 10, 1969.
14. Both of which he founded in 1950–1951.
15. Music director at Mansfield for thirty-five years, 1961–1996. She was the first woman to have that position in an Oxford college.
16. BW, October 10, 1968, 10.

17. Ibid.

18. They used an electrostatic method of producing sound, a version of the Van der Graaff generator, the precursor of the ubiquitous digital organs of the twenty-first century.

19. Miller installed their largest organ, the Sprouston model, as a demonstration organ in St. Peter Parmentergate. The price was £6,700. According to Routley (BW, 10-10-68) it had the true Miller authenticity of tone but lacked a certain necessary weight in the pedal, though it had some delicious sounds. There was a permanent Norman and Beard pipe organ, which was moved to Norwich School when the church closed in 1980.

20. In 2022 the Compton is on a portable platform and moved into the chapel and other areas.

21. This one bore a price of £5,575.

22. J&J Makin of outer Greater Manchester—purveyors of paper products, specializing in tinfoil papers, art paper, and coated paper.

23. Pilling attended Charterhouse School and learned to play the school's Harrison & Harrison and overlapped the music director, John Wilson, by a year. Pilling, with no heirs, founded a trust that generously supports music programs in all parts of the UK.

24. In 1965 he commissioned a four-manual electrostatic organ from Compton Organs of London. Hart voiced it to Routley's specifications.

25. JWW, September 6, 1969.

26. Pilling acquired part of Compton Organs Ltd. in 1970 and founded Makin Organs.

27. Op. cit., JWW.

28. The organ has been maintained and modified and is still in use at the now St. James's United Reformed Church.

29. The same church that Routley grew up in, but by 1974 it was URC.

30. Ernest Hart (1934–2022), founder of Copeman Hart & Company, Ltd. In 1960, Hart was managing director for fifty years.

31. GB, July 22, 1974.

32. Minister, United Reformed Church; general secretary of Churches Together in England; principal of Westminster College, Cambridge, 1996–2001.

33. Martin Camroux, *Ecumenism in Retreat* (Wife & Stock: Eugene, OR, 2016), preface by David Cornick.

34. Founded in 1885 by John R. Mott, it was an integral contributor to the creation of the World Council of Churches.

35. First organized in 1938, but opening was delayed until 1948 due to the war. From their website: "The World Council of Churches is a worldwide fellowship of churches in search of Christian unity, common witness, and service to all people, as a global expression of the modern ecumenical movement." Headquarters are in Geneva.

36. JWW, December 18, 1968.

37. The methods and materials initiated at Dunblane were adapted in this process to gather new and vital hymns.

38. Many of the text translations were done by Fred Kaan, particularly those in Swedish.

39. The index lists twenty-six languages.

40. Today this is commonly paired with "Shades Mountain" by K. Lee. Scott (b. 1950). Other hymn writers who gained recognition are Fred Pratt Green (1901–2000), Fred Kaan (1929–2009), I-to Loh (b. 1936), Pablo Sosa (1933–2020), João Faustini (1931–2023), and Brian Wren (b. 1936).

41. C. Michael Hawn, "*Cantate Domino*: Erik Routley and Global Song," *The Hymn*, October 2004, 13.

42. *Cantate Domino: Music Edition*, preface, ix.

43. There have been many Roman Catholic church councils, but this was only the second one to be held in the Vatican. They met for four weeks a year from 1962 to 1965. John XXIII died in 1963, and his successor, Paul VI, closed the Council and took responsibility for implementing the reforms.

44. George Caird represented the Congregational Union of England and Wales.

45. https://www.vatican.va/archive/hist_councils/ii_vatican_council/documents/vat-ii_decree_19641121_unitatis-redintegratio_en.html.

46. Order of Preachers, a mendicant pontifical order founded in 1215 by the Dominicans.

47. Born Marianne Gennaro, Sr. Maria grew up in Brooklyn and attended Manhattanville College, then known as the College of the Sacred Heart. She became a nun in the Order of Preachers in 1961.

48. Erik Routley, preface, *The Summit Choir Book*.

49. Bernard Massey, "*The Summit Choirbook*," the HSGBI *Bulletin*, vol. 11, no. 1, January 1985, 6.

50. Erik Routley, preface, *The Summit Choir Book*.

51. Edited by George Woodard, the texts were published by the Plainsong and Medieval Music Society and printed at the Convent at Wantage, near Oxford, 1904. CDH.

52. JWW, November 1975.

53. Ibid.

54. Revisions were made to the 1975 manuscript, but the content is largely unchanged.

55. MR, Sr. Maria, October 3, 1984. Both Erik Routley and Peter Scott are held in perpetual prayer at the monastery.

56. Ira D. Sankey (1840–1908). Raised in New Castle, Pennsylvania, Sankey is widely known for his tunes to evangelical gospel hymns, characterized by a strong, rhythmic beat and an easily learned melody.

57. JWW, December 14, 1967.

58. GB, February 12, 1974.

59. JWW, March 3, 1973.

60. This concert is available on YouTube. https://www.youtube.com/@URCStJamessNewcastlehymns.

61. Carys Hughes was a well-known organist and recording artist throughout Great Britain. St James's had commissioned three organ programs to display the new instrument. Hughes performed one of these.

62. Margaret McWilliams (1891–1972), set to text by John Webster Grant (1919–2006), "The flaming banners of our King," and another by Donald Hughes (1911–1967), "Creator of the earth and skies."

63. Luff joined the Dunblane Consultations in 1964 when there was an emphasis on canticles. He and Routley collaborated on several.

64. Not surprisingly, Routley turns to C. S. Lewis, in this case *The Pilgrim's Regress*, and Lewis's analysis of the requirements of romantic literature for his criteria.

65. The Oath: "Do you promise that your detectives shall well and truly detect the crimes presented to them using those wits which it may please you to bestow upon them and not placing reliance on nor making use of Divine Revelation, Feminine Intuition, Mumbo Jumbo, Jiggery-Pokery, Coincidence, or Act of God?"

66. P. D. James, viii.

67. An organization founded in the UK in 1941 to foster personal growth and social skills through outdoor expeditions and public service.

68. A fictional location generally for stereotypical rich, idle gentlemen in the stories of P. G. Wodehouse (1881–1975).

69. GB, February 3, 1969.

70. JWW, June 23, 1969. Scott was a well-known practitioner and teacher of the Alexander Technique.

71. "Union" was changed to "Church" in 1966.

72. Stephen Tomkin, *That They All May Be One* (URC: London, 2022), 15.

73. Two major hurdles were that the governing elders in the Presbyterian church were ordained for life, and the comparable Congregational deacons were elected for a specific period of time. The URC was to have only one label for the members of the governing body of the congregation: "elder."

74. Routley, "The United Reformed Church," sermon, 1972, private collection.

75. *Monthly Messenger*, May 1970 (Congregational Church of Mount Road, Tettenhall Wood, Wales).

76. Geoffrey Beck, "Our New President," *Congregational Monthly*, June 1970.

77. NWG, Gwen Hall (b. 1926), April 2007. Gwen held the post of president of the CCEW from 1969 to 1972. She chaired all business meetings. After union, she became chair of the Church Life department.

78. *The Congregational Yearbook*, 1970–1971, 28.

79. Upon publication, *Honest to God* touched off an intense polemic debate about Christian belief amid the tumult of civil unrest in the world. In 1964 Routley contributed to the controversy in "A Man for Others," a long essay vindicating and reinterpreting the ideas put forth by Bishop Robinson.

80. Arthur Macarthur letter to Nancy Wicklund Gray, March 24, 2003, private collection.

81. Ibid.

82. *United Reformed Church Reports of Committee*, May 5–9, 1973.

83. Co-general secretary of the United Reformed Church along with Arthur Macarthur.

84. Other members were Carolyn Brock, Percy Bush, J. K. Gregory, Donald Hilton, R. Jacquet, Donald McIlhagga, Caryl Micklem, C. E. Strange, A. D. Thomas, Brian Wren, and John Wilson as musical advisor. Several of these members were on the editorial committee appointed in 1985 for the purpose of creating the URC hymnal, *Rejoice and Sing*.

85. Preface, *Rejoice and Sing*.

86. David Goodall, "United Reformed Church Hymnody," CDH.

87. GW, November 22, 1973.

88. Goodall, CDH.

89. The International Consultation on English Texts was established in 1969 as an independent ecumenical organization commissioned to produce common liturgical texts in English (Tra/Trad), 224.

90. GB, January 26, 1974. The Congregation Federation was formed in 1972 by the congregations that did not choose to join the Union.

91. GB, February 24, 1974.

92. Appendix E.

Chapter 7

Princeton, 1975–1982

EARLY LECTURE TOURS

Austin P. Lovelace (1919–2010) was an instructor at the Garrett Theological Seminary in Evanston[1] and fresh from the School of Sacred Music at Union Theological Seminary in New York City. Lovelace read everything written by Routley that he could lay his hands on, ordering many books directly from England.[2] In the summer of 1959, Austin and his family embarked on a two-month tour of Europe and Great Britain and in July visited the Routleys in Edinburgh. Routley and Lovelace found much to talk about in a nonstop exchange of their common experiences, accompanied by their ribald and witty parley.[3] Routley told Lovelace that he would be giving a lecture in Chicago in a couple of years, and they agreed to get together again.

While Routley was still in Oxford, the Reverend Dr. Robert Harley Fischer (1918–2004) came to Mansfield as the first participant of the Lutheran Tutorship, sponsored by the Lutheran World Federation.[4] Fischer, a professor at what is now the Lutheran School of Theology in Chicago, got to know Routley and arranged for Routley to go to Chicago to teach a two-week course on hymns in the summer of 1962. This included an opportunity to preach at the University of Chicago's Rockefeller Chapel. Hearing this plan, Lovelace invited Routley to Garrett to be part of an editorial meeting for the *Methodist Hymnal* (1966) as an authoritative voice concerning some of the new work coming out of the UK.[5] At this same meeting, Routley first connected with Carlton R. Young (1926–2023).[6] Recognizing their collaborative possibilities, Routley, Lovelace, and Young became colleagues almost immediately, working closely on all manner of hymnological projects for the next twenty years.[7]

Following the Chicago engagement, Routley was scheduled to speak at Union Theological Seminary at the invitation of Robert S. Baker (1917–2005), renowned organist and director of the School of Sacred Music. The Rev.

Dr. James I. McCord (1920–1970), president of the Princeton Theological Seminary, attended the lecture and, impressed with Routley's knowledge and preaching skills, secured Routley for the April 1966 Stone Lectures[8] at PTS.[9] McCord mentioned this to Lee Hastings Bristol (1923–1979),[10] president of Westminster Choir College, also in Princeton, and Bristol arranged for Routley to speak at WCC that same week. Wanting to make the most of his travel visa, Routley also responded to his friends Bob Mitchell and Mary Oyer, agreeing to present the Drexel Lectures at the Baptist Theological Seminary in California and speak at the Mennonite Seminary in Goshen and Elkhart.

CONCERNS IN NEWCASTLE

He was out of the country for five weeks when health issues struck. When a flood of invitations from universities, seminaries, and denominational offices in the United States and Canada followed these first invitations to the States,[11] Erik realized that he had to respond seriously to the symptoms of overwork and pay close attention to his diet.[12] He was very relieved to return to Edinburgh and a familiar routine.

> I'm mighty glad to be back home; it was a strenuous tour, but exceedingly interesting. The innards bothered me almost all the time I was away but are now behaving better. Nothing serious, I think only some loose chips from the original rock. I am looking in with the surgeon next week and am trusting that it will be a friendly occasion.[13]

Despite the allure of the lecture circuit, Erik's primary consideration was his family and ministerial obligations. The congregations in Edinburgh and Newcastle usually allowed only summer travel during the long holidays. He tried to keep to this schedule while serving both churches, though there was the occasional exception. During 1970–71,[14] as president of the CCEW, Routley had only one short visit to Fort Worth, and that had been arranged in 1968. The years surrounding the formation of the United Reformed Church were rough on St. James's, a typical condition in most Congregational churches. Though Routley was quite focused on this process, he was finding that he wasn't as physically tuned to the demands of an active ministry as he had been. Even though he felt ministry was his calling, Routley sensed a pull to give attention to his books, compositions, editorships, etc., which were in practice only very important and influential avocations.

Clergy salaries in Great Britain were decidedly low,[15] and Routley's slow-arriving royalties and stipends were often the much needed supplements to the demands of a family of five. A university position, free from the persistent dailiness of a city congregation, was appealing. But that was the issue. In Great Britain there were professorships in church history and theology, but he had discovered that there were also academic posts in church music in America. St. James's sensed his dilemma, and with casual chats and informal meetings, both the congregation and Routley began to look to the future.

> I have begun to wonder what would happen when I've outrun my useful life here,[16] which I estimate will become apparent, or perhaps grossly, inescapably apparent, by about next March. It's time for somebody of 37 with independent means and three young children to come and do their stuff. The troops are marvelous, and if I stay in church ministry, I wouldn't want to move to another because they are so splendid here, even if the management is perhaps a shade aloof.[17]

BIRTH OF *ECUMENICAL PRAISE* (1977)

In the summer of 1972, Austin Lovelace suggested to Sam Young that there was a real need for an American multidenominational supplement to offset the rejection of the new, alternative hymns by the editors of recent hymnals.[18] Young took the suggestion to George Shorney (1931–2012) at Hope Publishing Company, who became convinced that this would not only be a useful supplement but also saw that it would bring a new group of hymn writers into the HPC fold. By 1974 Routley was already heavily involved, and living in Princeton would make travel to Chicago and New York much easier.

In choosing an editorial board, Lovelace and Young strongly recommended Routley as their number-one choice of partner. Shorney only knew Routley by reputation and his work with *Cantate Domino*, but, as he trusted Lovelace and Young, Shorney agreed. Filling out the committee was Alec Wyton (1921–2007), the organist and choir master at St. John the Divine, widely celebrated for his knowledge of three sacred music repertoires: British, American, and that which was emerging outside the church.[19] The committee met twice a year for four years, often around Routley's schedule and arrival at O'Hare. At one meeting, at the University Club in Chicago, the subject was the title. The group wrangled over it an entire afternoon because Routley pressed that "ecumenical," "inclusive," and "experimental" were not synonyms. Finally, it was Routley who stopped and said, "We've kicked this around long enough; I suggest we go with *Ecumenical Praise* and get on with it!"[20] The supplement was published in 1977, and though never a bestseller, the contents were influential and significant. Some of the writers and composers were barely known in North America, and today many of their hymns are standard fare for new hymnals.[21]

Concurrently, Routley was having conversations with the elders and deacons at St. James's about his retirement, and from experience Routley knew that a very important concern of a new minister would be housing. When Erik and Margaret moved into the manse on Linden Road in 1967, they were thrilled with the size and promise of the place. As their family changed and the inevitable problems with the house appeared, St. James's anticipated that when Routley moved on, a suitable home for the next minister had to be first on the agenda to ensure a comfortable start for a new minister. With that in mind, the search for another place began in the autumn of 1973, but there was full understanding with the Routleys that if they stayed in Newcastle, the congregation would be very happy. Of course timing is never perfect, and when a new manse was purchased on The Riding and the one on Linden Road sold, Routley had no plans to move on. Erik and Margaret had to relocate to The Riding 21, for what turned out to be less than a year.

THE INVITATION TO PRINCETON

Routley's summer tour in 1973 was jammed with engagements and even more exhausting than usual. He was in North America for forty-three days, and only two of them found him neither traveling nor speaking, and "in one or two cases accommodation was rather boy-scout."[22] The backbone of the trip was three weeklong conferences at Montreat and Mo Ranch and one in Denver. He was asked to talk on hymnody and introduce the new Presbyterian hymnal, *The Worshipbook*, plus a "Come and Sing" at each. Then there was a Psalm class at Perkins and a session with the Missouri Synod, followed by another week in Princeton.

> The weekends were occupied usually in preaching and talking on the previous Saturday nights at various churches: 2 Methodists, 1 Baptist and one Disciples of Christ. You don't choose your hymns if you are a visitor over there, and I constantly seemed to get "Joyful, joyful, we adore Thee" to Beethoven. I suppose they thought I should like it because I'm musical, but I find it detestable.[23]

While in Princeton, Jim McCord broached the subject of a visiting professorship at the seminary, perhaps for the 1974–75 year. The original music director at PTS, David Hugh Jones (1900–1983)[24] had retired in 1970, and PTS had been searching for someone of suitable experience and accomplishment to fill his role. It appeared likely that there would not be a candidate available permanently until the fall of 1975,[25] though there were people in the area who could fulfill the chapel and music responsibilities temporarily.[26]

In February of 1974 Routley told McCord that he was interested. Simultaneously, Routley was contacted by Ray Robinson, Bristol's successor as president of Westminster Choir College. He wondered whether Routley was available for a two-semester position beginning in 1975. But actual manifestation of these possibilities moved slowly. It was the end of June before PTS had a full idea of what they wanted or needed from Routley. They proposed a yearlong position that included the summer months. He would be organist and lecturer, working alongside Arlo Duba (1929–2023), director of chapel and professor of liturgy.[27] The offer was to begin in September through the next August. Routley was disgruntled, as there was no way he could get to Princeton that fast. His responsibilities to St James's and the URC had to be considered, as well as organizing his personal departure. *New Church Praise* and *Cantate Domino*, important projects, were not yet released. McCord then suggested that Routley's position could begin in January 1975 and last eight months. This was still quick for Erik and Margaret, but workable. WCC proposed a visiting lectureship for the 1975–76 academic year, with the possibility of renewal. Routley told both PTS and WCC that he would accept. In a letter to Wilson, he frets:

> I've suddenly become very nostalgic about Newcastle. But it may be, as it were, the last bus home, and maybe I should catch it.[28]

Getting Routley to Princeton had strings attached to every involved party. There were endless questions regarding immigration procedure, course load, salary, housing, travel expenses, and family priorities. Conferences are planned years in advance, and in the early 1970s Routley had already committed to several that would occur in 1974 and 1975. Just as important were the ties to sever in England, feathers to be unruffled, and promises made to keep in touch.

Leaving the HSGBI

One of the more pressing detachments was ending his long editorship of the *Bulletin*. From his first issue in 1948 through 1974, Routley's articles are a history of the changes in hymns, personalities, and all the controversy and confusion of the postwar recovery period. In American terms, he covers church music of "the greatest generation," the baby boomers, Generation X, and even, prophetically, squeaks into the millennials. With his usual straightforward and humorous self-deprecation, softened by genuine warmth, he broke some hearts in his final editorial:

> The time has come to say goodbye—high time too. I am telling everybody that there is no job that I have managed to hold down for as much as 27 years but this. Heavens, but how patient you have all been! I think it is 91 issues, about fourteen hundred pages, and an astronomical number of misprints (until the good John Wilson came to my rescue as proof-reader) that you have endured from my various addresses. And, personally, I find that I have been editing this Bulletin for nearly half my lifetime. More credit to your patience than to my assiduity; twice I tried to resign but you wouldn't let me. Now I must because I am going to America.[29]

Routley's announcement brought sharp reactions within the Hymn Society. Seeing only what appeared to be an abrupt departure, many members felt abandoned; others felt resentment at the thought of losing their brilliant, infuriating, unique, candid Erik Routley and his biting, suffers-no-fools sense of humour. Members like Caryl Micklem, David Goodall, and Peter Cutts[30] who had been encouraged and supported by Routley despaired his loss. In what appeared to be "a plot hatched by Erik Routley and John Wilson,"[31] Bernard S. Massey (1927–2011) became the editor and outlasted Routley's tenure by a year.[32]

> Desperate situations call for desperate measures. The finger of fate pointed at one with no relevant qualifications beyond the ability to spell. This luckless character was given just a week or two to think of a convincing excuse for not taking over the vacant chair with no brief but, "We want a *Bulletin*; you produce it."[33]

Travel Preparation

Between July and September, Routley and McCord debated their method of travel—plane or ship. At first Erik and Margaret decided to fly for what seemed like a practicality. Margaret had neither been to the United States nor on a plane, and mingled with the pangs of separation was a real excitement for what lay ahead. McCord assured them that their apartment would be furnished, and he promised to have a piano in place when they arrived. So most of their furniture and household belongings remained in England at their cottage in Northumbria; their piano was loaned to Newcastle University until they returned. As the length of their stay in the United States was unclear, they didn't want to get rid of everything if they were going to be back in England within a year. Of primary concern were Erik's library and Margaret's violin. Margaret did not want the instrument out of her sight—or hands. Though Routley wanted to take all his books to Princeton, the freight charge by air was enormous.[34] Traveling by ship was more expensive per person, but storage on the boat was negligible; and on board, Margaret would have her violin where she could see it. So, ship it was, and at Southampton they ascended the ramp of the MV *Kungsholm*, part of the Swedish American Line, on the day they had hoped for, December 23, 1974.[35]

> The Atlantic crossing was spectacular—force 10 or 11 winds from Christmas Eve to New Year's Day. We didn't stop in Bermuda [as planned] as we were so far behind, but we didn't miss any meals, and had a wonderful time eating, sleeping, drinking Bloody Marys, and doing precious little else! We came into New York on a calm, crisp and cloudless morning [January 2, 1975] to see the Manhattan skyline and the Statue of Liberty.[36]

But a flawless move is never the case.

PRINCETON THEOLOGICAL SEMINARY

When the Routleys disembarked, there was no one there to meet them and no one to take their cargo off the ship. After a few uncertain and inquiring phone calls, an endless wait, and patchy solutions, Erik and Margaret got to Princeton via a pickup truck driven by the PTS property manager. The campus was on holiday and nearly vacant when Erik and Margaret arrived. After searching for the location of their housing and its corresponding keys, the driver/property manager took them to their apartment. They were underwhelmed: no piano and very sparse furnishings. Erik and Margaret were pretty much on their own until PTS reopened on January 14. All in all, though, they explored Princeton, enjoying each other and the anonymity. Located in central New Jersey, Princeton's beginnings date to the early eighteenth century. For identification, "Princeton" signifies the university, "Princeton Theological Seminary" is the "Seminary," and Westminster Choir College is either "Westminster" or "the Choir College." All three academic institutions were founded by Presbyterians and are located in what was once "The Borough."[37] The university, with architecture strongly reminiscent of Cambridge colleges, occupies the middle of the town; the Seminary borders the university's southwest side; and Westminster is one and a half miles to the northeast. Nassau Street holds all three together. When Erik and Margaret moved to town, Nassau Street was lined with shops like Landau, Hulit's, and Woolworth's. These were interspersed with a mom-and-pop hardware store, The Annex, PJs Pancakes, a movie theater, a grocery, a pharmacy, and, way down by Westminster, Hoagie Haven. The residents were, both then and now, quintessentially town and gown—which the Routleys understood.

> Princeton is a lovely little town of about 25,000, and we live 100 yards from a bus service and 200 yards from the railway station, so we aren't crippled by the absence of a car. I'm at present on a campus which has much piety and NO musical sense and shall soon move to one that has lots of music and no theology. I already note that people hope I may be able to form some sort of interpretative link between these two places, which at present, have nothing at all to say to each other. We'll see![38]

Erik stewed around, worrying about teaching space and where his books would go, but Margaret was thrilled to have time to practice, wander the streets, and discover potential students. In their first few days in town, Erik was out walking and met a familiar figure:

> Yesterday, I was walking along Nassau Street and ran into Lee Bristol, who accosted me in his genial way and handed me a copy of music in your familiar handwriting which turned out to be a nice coda for "What Wondrous Love." This was a delightful reminder of the other half of our life![39]

With the blessing of the Seminary, Howard G. Hageman (1922–1992), president of the New Brunswick Theological Seminary,[40] had secured Routley for a weeklong seminar beginning January 5, as the semester classes at PTS didn't start until January 30. Routley was picked up by a driver each morning, transported to New Brunswick, and brought back later in the afternoon. Ray Robinson also got McCord's permission to use Routley at an annual conference in Fort Lauderdale sponsored by the Choir College. Routley's first actual PTS assignment was opening chapel on Wednesday, January 16, which was a memorial service for Martin Luther King Jr. (1929–1968).

Getting Down to Work

The PTS chapel services were scheduled daily from Monday to Friday, as most of the seminarians had weekend responsibilities in local churches. The services lasted twenty minutes and were student led and student organized. An informal but competent seminary choir sang an anthem on Thursdays, and on the other days a group was formed on the spot with whoever attended. Prior to Routley's arrival these "choirs" were held together by James Litton;[41] "it was a fun, jovial group, not very well rehearsed but comfortable."[42] When Routley arrived, Arlo Duba oversaw the program and approved the selection of student preacher of the day and the music choices, but he generally gave Routley full reign of the organ.

> It was a great privilege to be so closely related to him and his wife Margaret during this time. It was here that he [Routley] worked out his transition from Britain

to the United States. His musical knowledge and his humor were infectious. I often said that for me, it amounted to a graduate course in church music![43]

An older graduate student, Jim Shannon (b. 1934), was president of the Student Chapel Committee; Duba put him in charge of Erik and Margaret's arrival to assure it was as smooth as possible. Though there wasn't much to unpack, Shannon organized a crew to sort Routley's books and music—most of which didn't actually start arriving until term began.[44] The students showed up anyway and assembled some bookcases one afternoon—by all accounts, an experience filled with hearty laughter as all of them, including Erik and Margaret, made sardonic remarks about the ineptitude of academics to handle DIY projects by simply following the enclosed instructions! The bookcases got assembled and placed against the walls, which brought more caustic chuckles as the students admired the expanse of empty shelves. But in a college town, pizza and beer breaks the ice and fixes just about everything, and it did.

McCord had asked Routley to teach a course on hymnology, something new to the Seminary. Shannon enrolled in the course, and as he was an older student and had experience editing hymns and hymnals, he was expecting a superficial syllabus aimed toward eager freshmen seminarians. A few days after the class started, he realized that he was going to have to struggle to stay afloat.

> He was an encyclopedia and had memorized *The Worshipbook*! He had anecdotes for every author and composer and critiques each one in a way that had us in stitches. All of a sudden, in the midst of a very austere and almost pompous lecture, he would stop, and laugh at his own foibles![45]

Preregistration for the course was nineteen students, but when word of Routley's magnetism got around the Seminary, thirteen more registered and squeezed into every space in the room. Soon the course was oversubscribed and had to be capped. Routley set the campus on fire in a new way, and those that had to be refused were quite disappointed, especially since they realized this would be a one-time offering.[46]

Shannon, a US Navy chaplain, signed up for a weekly tutorial with Routley. Shannon had served on the editorial committee for the *Armed Forces Hymnal* and had edited *The Book of Worship for the United States Military*. He was working on a companion to the hymnal[47] and intended to use this work for the project that Routley required. Routley strongly critiqued each entry, demanding frequent rewrites, and citations were particularly scrutinized. But Shannon loved the challenges and responded appropriately with no complaint.

Holy Week 1974

Arlo Duba's liturgical training and experience was extensive. He studied liturgy with Roman Catholics and Orthodox Christians at institutes in France and Asia and was a founding member of the North American Academy of Liturgy.[48] He had been moved by the beauty of the Paschal Vigil and had conducted this ritual at PTS for the triduum of 1973 and 1974. Easter was early in 1975, March 30. Duba approached Routley about being involved that year; he expected an indifferent response, but Routley was honored to be part of the feast. Routley had participated in a joint Easter Vigil in Edinburgh, but he had never experienced or planned a full Tenebrae.[49]

> Tenebrae is magnificent, isn't it? Our liturgical professor here recently studied liturgics in Paris and is very keen on the sort of thing that the Orthodox church does. You'll know about the tradition in both eastern and western churches of lighting the Paschal Candle and blessing the water of Baptism on Easter Eve. Well, here it began Thursday night from 8 pm until 11:30 and took up again at 3 pm on Good Friday. We called it the "Watch of Mourning and Hope" which meant that the chapel was inhabited by somebody, or sometimes a congregation, all the way until 7:30 Saturday night, with Scripture readings every quarter hour. Many of us had Easter duties elsewhere so the choir was depleted, but we coped with the 3 hour service on Good Friday across the street at the Episcopal Church; three hymns and five Gelineau psalms and 5 hymns and 2 metrical psalms from *The Worshipbook* during the middle hours and then on Saturday, the choir finished the "watch" with *Les Reproaches* and four plainsong psalms. Then we began the Easter Vigil, Part I being Genesis and Exodus and unaccompanied singing. The Chapel was full to bursting. At the end [of this part] we sang the *Exultet* plainsong, CWM RHONDDA, and Psalm 114 to *Tonus Peregrinus*, with a cymbal crashing into the middle of every verse. Part II didn't concern me. "Prophecy and the Incarnation" were dealt with by a gifted but raucous pop group in a building on the other side of campus, to which everybody went in procession with lighted candles. Back in the Chapel for Part III, we renewed our Baptism vows and had Eucharist. So, we got in ST PATRICK'S BREASTPLATE for the baptism bit, AVE VIRGO, and then the EASTER HYMN, of course, with a brass band! It was immensely dramatic and somewhat indigestible—a pertinent metaphor because some of the participants and choristers had been fasting since Thursday night. At midnight we all sat down to a gargantuan breakfast![50]

Margaret and The Borough

Margaret, despite all the chaos and clutter, was enjoying Princeton. Hazel McCord had become a friend and introduced Margaret to members of a good orchestra, set up chamber music opportunities, and took Margaret to the Princeton Music Club. Relieved, Erik told John Wilson:

> She turns me out of the flat two hours a day so that she can practice—except that she's still waiting for her music, too, except the Bach unaccompanied sonatas. We have found Americans immensely easier to live with on their own soil. She's off to see friends in Virginia and North Carolina. I tell her that she needn't take a job unless it pays more than I'm paid! I'm terribly pleased that it is, so far, working out so well.[51]

The Routleys began attending the Episcopalian Trinity Church, where the atmosphere reminded them of home.

After Easter, the semester quickly came to an end with all the fuss that entails, and classes ended May 8. Routley spent most weekends either out of town or preaching in local churches. His spring travel included Birmingham, Alabama; Boston; Charlotte, North Carolina; Minneapolis; Baton Rouge, Louisiana; and New Haven, Connecticut.

TRANSITION TO THE CHOIR COLLEGE

For most of the term, Routley had preparatory conversations with Charles Schisler (1932–2011)[52] and John Kemp (1916–1997)[53] concerning his participation in the Summer Sessions, an annual mini-Westminster experience that Schisler began when he arrived in 1969. Kemp was chair of the Church Music department and eager to have Routley on campus. McCord told both men that Routley could probably straddle the summer program at PTS, and he hoped Routley would be available at the Seminary on a part-time basis when he moved campuses.[54] The acting WCC dean, Peter Wright,[55] and Kemp were also trying to assemble a workload that complemented Routley's travel and writing.

It was decided that Routley would teach three courses each term and one course at the Seminary. The chapel situation was casual, as there had been no chaplain for years,[56] but a student committee had worked very hard to conduct respectable services in the interim.[57] Though they were impressed with Routley's presence, the students were concerned that the chapel would be run differently and that they would have no voice in the preparation for services. Routley met with the chairman of the student committee in June, assuring him that his own intention was keeping the status quo. Schisler and Kemp agreed that any official chapel responsibilities for Routley should be on hold until the second semester, but they did ask if Routley would take four services that fall.

One thing that has proved unexpectedly rewarding is that they unwisely asked my advice about what to do with chapel—10am on Tuesdays. I asked, "What do you usually do?" I was told, "Oh, we have a concert of sacred music now and again." So, I asked them, "What about having a worship service?" They asked me to go on and I further said, "Make it 30 minutes instead of 50 and see what happens." The result? 200–300 people in a voluntary chapel every Tuesday singing with a congregation that is a trained choir, which is out of this world![58]

New Housing

The month of May at the Seminary was full of alumni and graduation events, which involved Routley playing the organ in the Miller Chapel. Simultaneously, with the help of Hazel McCord and other new acquaintances, Margaret and Erik searched for housing, needed when the contract with the Seminary expired in August. They decided to rent for a year to better understand their circumstances with Westminster.[59]

> Our life here is developing interestingly. We now have a car, which we haven't yet crashed and a house for next year—a little honey of a place that we are renting from July 1 and shall hope to be in by July 10. [The house] is in Kingston, just over the border to the north from Princeton, separated from it by a nice narrow lake, wooded and quiet, and the house has three bedrooms, a living room, a kitchen, a lovely basement for my books—the best study I've ever had, 35' x 15' of beautiful space. Three days before we moved the books in, we had 18" of rain in seven days, which meant 3" of water in the basement. Needless to say, my books are all two feet off the floor. But there's lots of garden in the American style which need only to be run over now and then with a motor mower. We decided to rent for a year to see whether Westminster's contract is renewed. I'm agnostic about that at present; some things about the place suggest that I might not be eager for it to be renewed. But I think I can stand a year of it. The Seminary has been very kind to us.[60]

Priscilla spent the month of July with her parents, just in time to help with the move and rescue the books. The first week of August, Erik had a lecture engagement at Massanetta Springs, and Margaret went along. This was followed with a little holiday exploration of the middle Appalachians and the Smoky Mountains before beginning yet another new chapter.

> For the first time in 32 years of married life, I took off without a forwarding address, and I must say it was a blissful time in magnificent scenery, all along the East Tennessee valleys where these lovely American folk hymns come from! Not that I heard any; I was on vacation![61]

WESTMINSTER CHOIR COLLEGE

The semester at Westminster began easily: two classes on Monday and Wednesday, "Hymns and Church History" and "Liturgy and Worship," plus one at PTS on hymnody, chapel Tuesdays, and a graduate and first-year student practicum.

> The great thing about American classes is how slowly they move and therefore how thin you can beat stuff out. When you can't think of anything to say you have what they call a "bull session" where they ask questions. I aim to survive.[62]

Hoping that the student committee would soften to his presence, Routley's choice to be only peripherally involved with the chapel services surprised some people in England. He tried to explain it to Fred Pratt Green:

> Westminster has allowed its weekly Tuesday chapel services to fall into some disarray, through not having any competent chaplain to direct them. I'm not chaplain, at the moment, but I have been allowed to get something going there, which is usually a 30 minute service with brisk behaviour and, of course superb hymn singing.[63]

WESTMINSTER PRAISE

In one of their first on-campus meetings, Ray Robinson, with promises of funding from Lee Bristol, asked Routley if he would consider making a supplement hymnal especially for the Choir College. Westminster used *The Pilgrim Hymnal*,[64] which Routley told Wilson was quite acceptable and intelligent; but sensing potential, Routley quickly set about turning the concept of *Westminster Praise* into a reality.

> It's great fun, though a responsibility for me as no one here knows ANYTHING AT ALL about hymns, and so they are just leaving me to it. How I wish you were here to hold my hand! Still, on production methods there are people who know the ropes. We're likely to be producing an 80 page, stapled booklet. To get it all in the space, I may have to bow to the habit of interlining words, it certainly does save paper. Good American material is really in short supply, but still, it's out there, and it's coming up on 1976, so I'm getting pressure not to make it too ENGLISH.[65]

An editorial board was set up with Routley, John Kemp, and Greg Funfgeld (b. 1953).[66] The *Preface* states that, rather than produce one more contemporary supplement, the editors chose a balance of the best of eminent composers that did not appear in *The Pilgrim's Hymnal*, some international representation from *Cantante Domino*, and commendable pieces from "our own generation."

> Our supplement will be designed to include things that musicians can enjoy and respect. There a tolerable amount of John Wilson and disciplined modern US stuff as I have been able to assemble. My instincts would have been to include pretty well the whole corpus of FPG, but that was perhaps too extravagant![67]

Aside from Routley, contributions came from three other faculty members: Theodore R. Lorah Jr. (1948–2009), David S. York (ret. 1985), and Alice Parker (b. 1924).[68] Not surprisingly, Margaret McWilliams, Erik's teacher at Fonthill, and Alexander Brent Smith, John Wilson, Brian Wren, Fred Pratt Green, and Peter Cutts are also represented. It fit the perimeters of the Westminster services in that some hymns were more suitable for choral anthems and were antiphonal with choir and congregation, and as the community consisted of trained singers, the tunes were often pitched higher than one intended for wider use. The booklet, what Wilson called "a hymnodist's idea of bliss,"[69] was published by Hinshaw and released in the spring of 1976.[70]

ADAPTING TO A NEW CULTURE

To the delight of both Erik and Margaret, reports of the famous fall colors were not exaggerated, and they were both relieved that their current lifestyle allowed them time to walk through it all without the guilt that they should be doing something else. Several friends from Great Britain visited Academy Road that season, and though both Erik and Margaret complained that there were no moors in the United States, they were comfortable with their choice to relocate.

By Thanksgiving, however, Routley was ready for a break. He found the American design of daily lectures to be quite tiring, yet all in all he enjoyed it and was looking forward to the spring semester when his courses would change to include music-based classes rather than just history. John Kemp wanted Routley to have a study on campus so he would be more visible to the college community. Routley balked at this because he usually wrote until midnight, and he didn't want to leave Margaret at home by herself for that long every night. After some pointed dickering, Routley agreed to holding regular office hours in the little room at the landing of the staircase leading to Bristol Chapel, where there was just enough space for a desk and phone.

Erik and Margaret sent out their first Christmas letter in December, and all in all it was a thoughtful and appreciative look on their last year:

Despite what you may be told, we find the American people hospitable, accepting, and it's not too much to say, relaxed. Part of this must be due to the bigness of the place, even in New Jersey, the most densely populated state in the country, the more ferocious effects of crowdedness aren't all-pervasive. If you ask, "What's it <u>like</u> living over there?"—it depends on, I suppose, who you are and what you want to do. It's a bit like Kent—one end is monstrously metropolitan and contains what must be the ugliest twenty-mile tract in all America. The other end is rustic, agricultural, and undulating. Princeton is just about on the line between the two, being itself wooded, quiet, and academic, but only a few miles from the New York sprawl.

In September, I began to teach at Westminster Choir College, which has turned out to be an impressive institution. I am teaching (or more exact, occupying a classroom in which students are also present) and have a chance to conduct weekly chapel now and again. The most exciting thing for me has been the sound of the singing of 200–400 students in chapel. The whole congregation being a trained choir. Just think of that! No complaints about unknown tunes—they can read them—or about tunes being too high—they can all climb up anywhere. There is something about American singers that lifts the heart when they take hold of something. Their lack of shyness—which in older days was sometimes an embarrassment—comes out when they sing and when they say responses in church in a most heartwarming way. We don't have a chaplain, but I seem to have added a ministry of this sort to my official teaching duties and I'm glad to do it.[71]

Not surprisingly, Routley wrote relatively little for journals that year. Getting to his lectures around the country was a bit easier because he wasn't flying from England. He usually found himself in New York once a week for RSCM meetings, consultations with publishers, and preaching. The churches in and around Princeton and Philadelphia saw a lot of him too. Two books, written previously, were published,[72] and he continued to work on *Ecumenical Praise*, traveling regularly to Chicago.

TRILOGY OF TEXTBOOKS

At both PTS and WCC, Routley taught a class entitled "Hymns and Theology." In hopes of saving American church music from itself, he proposed to "make students aware of the inner meaning of hymn texts, tolerant of language and critical of misleading theology."[73] It was no secret that Routley thought the whole problem with hymnody in the United States stemmed from the editorial decision to interlay the text and tune. British hymnals print the tune and text separately. He noticed that in the United States hymns were judged "good" or "bad" by how well one did or didn't know the tune, paying no attention to the poetry. One of his students in 1981, Mark Trautman (b. 1960) remembers Routley entertaining the class with this little parody attributed to Nathaniel Micklem:

> *Lord, keep us safe this night, beneath the stars and moon;*
> *Pay though no heed to the words we sing, we only like the tune!*[74]

But then Routley had an inspiration. Hymnals were his class textbooks, but a more comprehensive resource would work better.

> I have an idea in my mind to rescue hymnody in the USA by getting together a book simply containing an anthology of texts without tunes—not for use in church, but for devotion and study. I am so tired of trying to get people to see hymns as literature, and appreciate their theological and scriptural overtones, with the texts all scrambles the way they always are in American hymnals. (I'm beginning to get near a date when this happened. I'm putting it about 1920–25, thanks to the influence of Sankey and his followers.) I knew, and you must have known, people who read their hymn books along with their Bibles. Not here, not anymore. So, it becomes so flat and brutal when they come to singing them. I dunno. Nobody may take it, but I'm thinking that since I need a textbook, I might as well make one.[75]

The result was *A Panorama of Christian Hymnody*,[76] a classic study of twentieth-century hymn texts. He starts with Luther and plunges right into metrical psalms, going straight from Isaac Watts, "the liberator of English hymnody,"[77] into the output of the 1970s. However, through the years, Routley's persuasive argument that hymns must always be honestly appraised in the context of theology and pastoral ministry[78] has hit a wall of trepidation. In the twenty-first century, those who study theological concepts are often bound by the societal literalism that has gradually crept into the classroom. Never having heard Routley's biting epigrams and strongly stated opinions in person, readers are often affronted by his style and perceive his ideas as authoritatively undebatable. In fact, as told by all who knew him:

> Routley's style is meant to stimulate thought and discussion, a step that contemporary students are often afraid to take, not trusting in the validity of their own ideas. It's safer to believe that all that one reads in a classroom is irrefutable.[79]

An academic trilogy was produced with two other books: *An English Speaking Hymnal Guide*, a companion to the hymnals that Routley used, and *The Music of Christian Hymns*, an updated, second reworking of his doctoral thesis. This was published by GIA in 1981, which took over the rights to *Panorama* and the *Hymnal Guide* in 1984. In the 1990s GIA saw that demand for this trio had not diminished, but taking in the future drawbacks to understanding Routley's original works, GIA approached Peter Cutts, Paul A. Richardson, and Paul Westermeyer with the possibility of writing revisions using contemporary vocabulary and updating the musical references still further. The HSUSC and GIA negotiated their ideas with Margaret Routley, and Cutts, Richardson, and Westermeyer began their work. Westermeyer quickly assessed that there could be no revision of *The Music of Christian Hymns* that maintained the scholarly integrity of Routley's text, so GIA and Westermeyer decided to let Routley's work stand; Westermeyer would write a new book, but one utilizing his own experience and interpretation of the subject. What followed was *Let the People Sing: Hymn Tunes in Perspective* (GIA, 2005). These upgrades were a huge undertaking by all three men and GIA, but by 2005 the revised volumes were published.[80]

SPRING SEMESTER 1976

January 1976 brought proliferous preparation for the coming US Bicentennial celebration, and in administrative meetings, Routley often had to wryly remind the group that the event was viewed a little differently in England. There was a spurt of patriotic interest in Southern folk hymnody and music presentations of every kind carried representative examples. Routley's thoughts on folk music and hymnody are well known: "Hymns are the folk-song of the church militant. They are, essentially, the people's music."[81] Thus, for the most part, this national anniversary was an enjoyable learning experience for Routley, as ever since Mary Oyer introduced him to the variety of unstructured music of America, he had eagerly tried each new one he came across. Wanting to add his blessing to the Bicentennial, he bragged to Wilson that he had inserted "Land of Rest," "Consolation," and "Wondrous Love" into chapel services! Lee Bristol was on the bandwagon. He was scheduled to lead an "Act of Praise" sing at Westminster Abbey in May and had programmed an all-America event.[82] John and Erik poked fun at Bristol's endless self-centered gossiping, but he (LHB) was using Richard Dirksen's (1921–2003) "Vineyard Haven" for the opening hymn:

> I suspect that LHB's humdinger is indeed VINEYARD HAVEN. The original setting was made for an enthronement in Washington [DC] Cathedral, where Dirksen is on the music staff. Doreen Potter told me it was also a great success at the WCC.[83]

But, despite the sarcasm, Routley admired Bristol's choice. He had the tune on his most-important-of-the-twentieth-century list,[84] and had himself put it into *Westminster Praise*.

The designation, Spring Semester, always seems an anomaly in the winter weather of January. The race to graduation begins slowly. In January there was a repeat of the Westminster conference in Fort Lauderdale with the Kemps and Joseph Flummerfelt (1937–2019). The Routleys chose to drive down early via the Everglades. At the end of the week, Margaret drove back to Princeton and Erik flew to Oklahoma City. Margaret's mother was having some health problems, and she was on her way to London to help with her care.

> We're now preparing here for a visit by Margaret to England; news about her 87-yr-old mother is not too good, and it was suggested that she might pay a visit. So, she will be boarding a plane for the first time in her life, and since you get the fare half price if you stay more than three weeks, she'll be there for about a month from March 9th. She is quite excited at the prospect of renewing contacts in Britain. She will certainly go to Newcastle and to Glasgow where Priscilla is now teaching and singing in Paisley Abbey choir—one of our greatest choirs, one of our finest organs—Cavaille Coll—and one of our best organists.[85] She's so lucky![86]

Delay of *Ecumenical Praise*

Westminster Praise was scheduled to be in Routley's hands by May 1, finished in a record seven months, but publication of *Ecumenical Praise* had been pushed back to the fall of 1976.

> They [Hope] keep sending bundles of proofs round our 4-strong committee and then getting snarled up. You know what's in it anyway, but still, there's some pretty surprising pages. The four of us, Lovelace, Wyton, Sam Young, and me, have so little in common (though we have a great time in each other's company) that any critic will be able to see exactly what suggestions were made by whom.[87]

An outside contributor to *Ecumenical Praise* was Calvin Hampton (1938–1984). Two of Hampton's tunes, "De Tar"[88] and "Pike," appeared in *Ecumenical Praise* and *Westminster Praise*, respectively. Routley had met with Hampton a few times in New York City and heard about Hampton's organ recitals on Friday nights at midnight. When Margaret was in England, Routley went up to Manhattan one Friday night. "Remarkable," he told Wilson.[89] Though he was impressed with Hampton's rhythmic repetitions and plainsong tunes, Routley wasn't entirely convinced of Hampton's validity as a tune writer:

> It's a bit affected, and I can't quite admit yet to be in the charmed circle of hymn composer fellows who write tunes without words in mind. Also, I wish he wouldn't compose AMENS into his tunes![90]

Gibbons

Margaret came back to Princeton the first week of April with a surprise:

> Margaret returns from England on Monday and bringing our dog! That will ensure our staying here a while, because when we return, the dog will have to go in quarantine for a while—at hideous expense—and I must save up. But the creature was one of the things she most hated leaving behind, so there it is.[91]

In reality, Gibbons, a Norwich terrier, was beloved by both of them; "she brings much good humour to our lives and now barks with a New Jersey accent!"[92]

Accreditation Strain

Educational institutions in the United States are accredited by rigorous peer review every five to ten years, and the results are held in a database with the United States Department of Education. The criteria examined are determined by the mission of the rated institution. Accreditation is not mandatory, but the results determine the amount of public funding granted to the school and students, and the legitimacy of the credits earned toward the appropriate degree sought. At Westminster Choir College there was a level of professional excellence that demanded accreditation for the outside evaluation of their graduates. Westminster's reaccreditation visit was due in April, and, as is always the case, this audit had loomed over the campus all year. Tensions are high when the visit approaches.

> We have all been warned since September that this week we should be visited by a bunch of inspectors who could decide whether we were fit to continue our accreditation (and get needful bucks from central sources) so everybody has been thinking of this as the day of judgement for months. The fellows come and sit in on classes and peek about everything, but they have turned out to be a very nice group indeed. However, we were supposed to be musically on show in chapel, so we go our best student organist,[93] and he IS good. He set up the EASTER HYMN with a descant which he wrote, and the chapel was full to bursting.[94]

Westminster passed and got their accreditation for another ten years. Commencement was a glorious affair held in the cathedral-like Princeton University chapel, which in 1976 was the second-largest university chapel in the world, behind King's College Cambridge. An important tradition allows the graduating class to choose the commencement speaker, and that year they chose Bob Hope, much to the embarrassment of Dean Schisler. Nonetheless, Leslie Townes Hope (1903–2003) was made a Fellow. Routley observed that Hope was not comfortable speaking to musicians from a pulpit, but "he was a good deal less tedious than most." Hope ended his address with his own wit: "Well, you're graduating with Hope, and I have to leave the Faith and Charity to you."[95]

JULY THROUGH AUGUST 1976

Just after graduation both Margaret and Erik flew to Colorado for a long weekend at Central Presbyterian Church in downtown Denver.

> We have just returned from five days in Colorado, which were memorable. The Presbyterian church in the city centre invited me to preach and give 3 lectures. For this they paid a fee plus expenses and hotel for self and the wife. Denver is Colorado's biggest city, a mile above the sea, and the Rockies go up about 20 miles to the west. We borrowed a car and took an extra day and drove 200 miles into the mountains spending a lot of our time above 10,000′, and what with the fauna and flora and views, we had a superb day. It's 1600 miles away from here [Princeton] so it was a chance not to be missed. Happily, the church has a first-rate organ and organist—an alumnus of WCC.[96]

Back home in Princeton, Routley worked on *Panorama* and began a companion to *Westminster Praise*. The hymnbook had been very well received, despite embarrassing printing errors. The editorial board decided to publish with Donald Hinshaw (1934–1996), as he had just started his publishing business and they wanted to support him. He didn't quite have the swing of it.

> Hinshaw hasn't published a book before, and he doesn't know much about doing it yet; he certainly doesn't have a reader, though few do these days. But there it is, and I must live with it until the thing is redone.[97]

San Anselmo and the West Coast

Westminster Praise would be featured at all his summer workshops across the country, and he hoped a new, corrected printing would take place in September. San Anselmo, and the San Francisco Theological Seminary, was the next conference after Denver, and Margaret was invited there as well. But despite the trip home in the spring, flying was not her preferred method of transportation. "Why fly when you can drive? I came to see the place, not fly about!" she justified to Erik.[98] She creatively answered an advertisement from somebody who wanted a co-driver to California.

> She teamed up with a delightful lady and her two teenage children and a Volkswagen. She survived triumphantly and they drove across the country, seeing the New Mexico mountains, the Arizona desert, stopping at the Grand Canyon, and, as she told her husband, "Even the most garrulous American just stares in silence." And for good measure, they took in Los Angeles.[99]

Margaret met up with Erik at the seminary, located north of San Francisco, across the Golden Gate Bridge, in Marin County. "California is lovely. This part, just north of San Francisco, is more like England than anything we have seen—like Exmoor."[100] At the end of the week they rented a car and enjoyed a two-week holiday, beginning by driving through the Sierras and spending a night at Yosemite. They continued up into Oregon, and Margaret swam in the Pacific Ocean. "It was beautiful, beyond description."[101]

Move to Skillman

Westminster offered Routley another yearlong contract, and as he signed it, he and Margaret realized that they had to decide what to do about their housing. The lease on Academy Road was up in August, and the discussion was whether to renew or look for a place to buy. They decided on the latter, thinking that despite a mortgage, there would be a little resale nest egg when Erik retired and they returned to England. Before setting out on the back-to-back summer lectures, they found a place that would do.

> Our immediate thrill, by the way, is that conceivably, we are going to buy a house! It's too expensive and we shouldn't, but it is nice and if we get it, we won't even need a change of address because it's only about a mile from this one. The owner ought to get more than we offered, so at this moment, we are cliffhanging.[102]

And, as everything often happens at once, the first house didn't come through but a second one did.

End of Summer

In a whirlwind of legal documents, Erik was off to Texas, Denver again, North Carolina, and Virginia. Margaret drove to Denver and spent a few days with friends in the mountains while Erik was working. They drove to Montreat, followed by another week at Massanetta Springs. The semester started August 21, and they moved house on the 30th amid torrid New Jersey heat and humidity. Margaret went back to London two days later.

> Margaret went off to London to take over her mother while her brother and sister-in-law take a holiday and she'll be there another ten days. So—at our ripe years we have entered on our first mortgage, and I have to try to live another 20 years! But the house is delightful, and we are glad to have it.[103]

AUTUMN 1976

Once more, the launching of *Ecumenical Praise* was deferred, but unlike Hinshaw, Hope Publishing was well-run, and Routley felt that the printing and promotion were likely to be done right. Sam Young was a little annoyed with Routley by the release *Westminster Praise*, but he petulantly, and correctly, accepted that Routley had been pushed by his superior, Ray Robinson, to finish it. In October, Young invited Routley to Nashville[104] to introduce the new supplement with a hymn festival at Christ Church, an Episcopal congregation.[105] HPC had furnished a sampler, and Routley's word for the event was "splendid." Young adds a little more detail:

> Erik was the genial host, moving up and down the center aisle leading, gesturing, ad libbing [*sic*] who would sing what in the next stanza, lecturing all the time. This was a revelation for me since I'd always seen him behind a podium and then moving to a piano. It was an overwhelming success.[106]

Work at WCC

Fall semester 1976 was full of college activities and whizzing about the country for weekend seminars and preaching at least one sermon every weekend. In November there was a welcome break in the daily schedule when the Westminster Symphonic Choir went to New York. The Routleys were able to get to Lincoln Center and hear the choir and the New York Philharmonic perform *Gloria* (1959) by Francis Poulenc (1899–1963) and Franz Josef Haydn's (1732–1809) the *Nelson Mass* (Hob. XXII/11), with Leonard Bernstein (1918–1990) conducting. Again, Routley's one-word description was "splendid."[107] The Student Chapel Committee organized WCCs first Advent Lessons and Carols service, and as it was well received, they vowed to make it an annual tradition. Then Routley enjoyed three travel-free weeks and attended Trinity Church just to worship, not preach.

End of an Era

Over the years, Nathaniel Micklem and Routley kept up their own correspondence. In November, Routley sensed a frailness in Micklem and confided in Wilson that he thought he could go anytime. Micklem died on December 26, but Routley didn't hear of it until Horton Davies (1916–2005)[108] sent over the obituary from *The Times*. In correspondence with John Huxtable and Caryl Micklem (Nathaniel's nephew), all three men remarked that it was an end of an important era. His thoughts to Wilson ended up in the dedication of *A Panorama of Christian Hymnody*:

> I was sad to hear that Nathaniel Micklem died the day after Christmas. He was my mentor in every way, teacher, preacher, and scholar, and he guided my feet on this path of hymnody.[109]

MOVING FORWARD

The year 1977 began with more than a full load of teaching, and all Routley's classes were totally subscribed with a waiting list. January through May was crammed with engagements in the United States and Canada, *Panorama* was accepted by Liturgical Press, *English-Speaking Hymnody* was complete, and Routley began work on his revision of the *Music of Christian Hymnody*. A particularly satisfying opportunity was unfolding in central New Jersey between the seminaries. For several years there was talk of a Liturgical Studies Institute being formed somewhere that offered degrees at all levels. Horton Davies (1917–2005), professor of religion at Princeton,[110] and Howard G. Hageman, president of New Brunswick Theological Seminary, were looking for a way to organize the courses taught by visiting professors into an accredited program. The requirements were hashed out, permissions granted, and logistics considered; in the late winter of 1977, brochures were distributed detailing the new Liturgical Studies Institute at Drew University.[111] Routley, who had taught visiting courses at PTS during his semesters at WCC, was one of the distinguished faculty selected to facilitate the course.[112]

Graduation

The repertoire for the annual commencement ceremony usually required the entire semester to prepare. The student graduation committee asked Routley's old friend, the composer Donald Swann (1923–1994), to give the address and approached Routley for an original hymn for the ceremony.[113]

I was staggered to be asked, and I went away to give my ego the needed reducing treatment. Wondering what to set, I remembered that Commencement would fall on Ascension Day, though nobody present would notice that. I turned to a dramatic and magnificent Latin text by an ancient Christian, the Venerable Bede, who lived his whole life in the part of England I have just left, Tyneside, in the far north where all the sea chanties come from.[114]

For many years the music in these ceremonies at the Princeton University chapel was conducted by Joe Flummerfelt with Joan H. Lippincott (b. 1935)[115] at the organ, working together to fill the space with a disciplined, yet spiritually powerful sound. Routley had to run down to Baltimore after the ceremony, but he sent this to Joe from there:

> As always, the Commencement was musically memorable, and everything was handled with your characteristic warmth and distinction. Thank you very much for making my trivial offering sound convincingly like music. I was much moved by the trouble you took with it; the tempo was just right and so was the general spirit of the thing. I shall continue to take some considerable pride in the recollection of it having actually been conducted by Joe Flummerfelt and sung by the Westminster Choir.[116]

"Sound like music" is a beloved and often quoted line around the Choir College. The source stems from a student in the organ studio of L. Eugene Roan (1931–2006), and it was frequently retold in many a lesson and classroom.[117] Alums can repeat it by heart, but this version is in Larry G. Biser's *Joan Lippincott: The Gift of Music*:[118]

> When teaching baroque articulation, a student was playing her Bach piece in a slow legato. Roan, knowing she played the violin, asked her to pretend that she was playing the violin and sing along with the line. What immerged was a beautiful melodic line using her imagined bowings. Roan said, "That's it! Play it exactly like that!" The student looked at her teacher and replied, "Oh . . . like music, not like organ."[119]

Routley, particularly delighted with the story, adopted his own version, "Oh! Like music, not like hymn playing." He worked closely with the organ department for the weekly chapel services and special occasions. Aside from seeking advice from them for his hymn anthologies, he helped develop hymn-playing studies and the departmental jury requirements. He dedicated his *25 Festive Hymns* to Lippincott.[120]

The Green Cards

Just before graduation, Erik and Margaret received a surprising and much welcomed letter from the US Department of Immigration containing their "green cards." Their initial visas had been obtained by PTS in November 1974, accompanied by the caveat that the documents must be renewed when Routley began working at Westminster. Erik and Margaret did just that and applied for a permanent resident green card, which was swiftly denied—for some reason, Westminster had forgotten their part in the process. The Routleys were informed that with expired visas, they were in the United States illegally. Immigration was a hot topic in Congress, and though Routley fit the criterion for residency,[121] both he and Margaret would be considered illegals for at least another eight weeks. Furious correspondence on behalf of the Routleys by attorneys and sponsors went on for more than two years. Routley had asked several colleagues in the United States to write letters, and one person who, from the initial applications, never stopped writing was Routley's friend from the 1960s, Lloyd Pfautsch.

> I hasten to tell you that yesterday, 10 May 1977, my wife and I received our final clearances and were issued with those green cards containing hideous passport pictures which permit us to come and go as we will. After 33 and a half months of hanging about this is a great relief, and we remember that you helped to achieve it.[122]

RETURN VISIT TO ENGLAND AND RELEASE OF *ECUMENICAL PRAISE*

Late May brought Routley's first visit back to England. The occasion was the fiftieth anniversary of the RSCM, but he and Margaret spent a lot of the month of May and into June visiting family and friends from London to Glasgow. Routley struggled to keep his calendar filled with things he wanted to do rather than things he had to do. Routley attended a Hymn Society meeting, an overnight and hymn sing with John Wilson at the Abbey, a visit to Lancing for their graduation, and a call on Timothy Dudley-Smith (b. 1926) in Norwich. After the engagement at Lancing, he called on Geoffrey Beck, who was now, ironically, minister to the congregation of the URC church in which Routley grew up as a Congregationalist.

At last, *Ecumenical Praise* was released in the spring, and when the fall semester began, the first big event was a three-day workshop at Westminster. John Kemp coordinated the conference involving all four editors, George Shorney, and several of the composers, including Heinz Werner Zimmermann

(1930–2022) and William Albright (1944–1998). The Choir College provided a student accompanist, and Routley told Wilson that the student did a reasonable job, as they had to sight-read everything. Some composers wouldn't conduct their own works, however, as they felt the playing was inadequate. Zimmermann handed his packet to Young and said, "Here, you take over." Routley was also rather testy and walked out of a brainstorming session on the direction of modern hymnody, claiming the group was unqualified to deal with the subject.[123] But a very complimentary Routley described the book to Pfautsch:

> I suppose you have seen *Ecumenical Praise*? It has at last been published and very well, I think. It's a wonderful mixture of mad and delightful things. Certainly, when you turn the pages, you haven't the least idea what crazy thing you will on next—which is a hymn book I find very satisfying.[124]

MELLOWING

In October, Erik turned sixty and mused to both John Wilson and Geoffrey Beck about what that entailed and revealed some retirement plans:

> I have just begun my seventh decade, and I suppose we are becoming old gentlemen. If I look into the matter, I'd say that I feel all right, though heaven knows I am getting slower, and there's a depressing tendence to have to look up a number in the telephone book![125]

As Erik looked at the ages of his colleagues in England, he felt a bit younger. Wilson was nearly seventy-three, and Fred Pratt Green was a year older than Wilson.

> And I can reply to you both that the good example set by my so-creative seniors is enough to make the seventh decade look not too formidable. I think I am probably doing too much, and not doing a lot of well, but I should hate not to have enough to do. I kid myself that if I retired tomorrow, I should still be busy, but there's much to be said for having a timetable. I must say that it's something of a relief to be able to say when your official day's work is done—which in my other line of business one could not. It's been altogether better than I deserve these last three years.[126]

The Thanksgiving holiday brought the beginning of a quiet respite. The students held their second Advent service with a new level of mutual trust and appreciation in their vision for chapel. Christmas was quiet, and the New Year came in with a mammoth snowstorm—17 inches in Princeton and up to

14 feet across the country. Schools were closed and the Routleys couldn't get their driveway cleared fast enough for Erik to make it to Trinity to preach. Someone came with a plow to finish what they had started, and he made it, but spoke to a very diminished congregation.

John Wilson and *Sixteen Hymns of Today*

While still in Newcastle, Routley and John Wilson co-edited a little supplement for the RSCM *Hymns for Celebration* featuring new and old songs from across Great Britain for use in the Eucharist. When Wilson's wife, Mary, died in August 1974, the regularity of Erik's letters were a great comfort and a distraction. Wilson filled his hours with hymnological pursuits and a new interest, the barrel organ.[127] For the better part of a year he roamed sites and documented organs around England. Erik was quite anxious about John's isolation, and he came up with a scheme to keep John busy—compile his own hymnal.

> I occasionally have an empty house for five or six weeks when Margaret must go to England, and I know a wee bit of what an empty home is like and how strangely difficult it is to get down to things. I can only imagine how it is for you. What I really want to say, wondering whether this was the time to say it, is there any chance at all of a full John Wilson hymnbook finding its way to birth? Maybe not; however, should the gate suddenly swing open, I do hope you'll canter through it. I must think whom I should ask to do the unlocking. I am not suggesting a transatlantic collaboration, but if you are thinking of a new project—and you should—nobody could do it better. Please let this simmer.[128]

A short while later, the RSCM and Fred Pratt Green opened the gate; the result was *Sixteen Hymns of Today*,[129] which was published in June 1978.

> WOW!! Sixteen Hymns has come! It is magnificent—as I knew it would be. The whole thing is chaste, modest, and distinguished. Not a trace of turgid academicism nor of contemporary irresponsibility. Isn't that your own handwriting on the cover? How praiseworthy to have reproducible handwriting![130]

Life in Skillman

The Routley property in Skillman covered about half an acre, and half of that was wooded. In the summer of 1977, Margaret, with a bit of help from her husband, reclaimed some of it for a rather substantial vegetable garden. Soon the plot was good and ready for what turned out to be a bumper crop[131] of beans, tomatoes, peas, peppers, potatoes, and greens, which gave them independence from frequent trips to the grocer.

Growing your own stuff is very fashionable in these parts, quite a new idea. Not quite as religious, though, as jogging. Jogging is getting yourself up in a track suit and running with great dignity along Route 518, filling your lungs with the choicest petrol fumes and then setting up a movement to prove that this has all sorts of transcendental effects.[132]

Erik and Margaret did not jog. Margaret "threatened to buy a bicycle, which would mean subscribing to yet another "GREAT MOVEMENT of the late seventies!"[133] So they walked Gibbons regularly and ignored trendsetting.

DIRECTOR OF CHAPEL

That spring, Routley reworked his contract with Schisler and Kemp, including a new title: Director of Chapel. The student committee had become comfortable with Routley and leaned on him more and more for direction, no longer worried that their thoughts wouldn't be heard. Routley was hoping to have chapel celebrated as an official part of the college by guiding it into his job description. There was some faculty disgruntlement with Routley, however. On the surface it appeared to some that Routley was never there, though of the fifty-two trips that took Routley around the United States and Canada in 1977–78, he was only absent from class four times. Many of the workshops were arranged by Robinson, who felt that Routley was the perfect ambassador for Westminster Choir College. Other faculty members often joined him at various weekend locations—Joe Flummerfelt, John Kemp, Helen Kemp, Joan Lippincott, and Gerard Farrell, to name only a few. After much negotiation, both in person and through letter, it was agreed that Routley would be named Director of Chapel, with responsibilities for all that chapel entailed—from speakers to bulletins, and choosing liturgy, hymns, and scripture. Routley again agreed that he would hold regular office hours in that little cubby up the stairs by the inside door to Bristol Chapel.

> I was installed as Director of Chapel this morning at an amusing service, the last of the academic year and set up by the Seniors. The end of their time at the Choir College is a tremendous tear-jerker—they make a huge thing of flying away from the nest. It's always a huge success. Now all that's left is the Commencement that happens next week at the Princeton University Chapel that, once again, jerks tears.[134]

Pi Kappa Lambda is a national prestigious, invitation-only music honor society that awards membership yearly to student and faculty who have demonstrated superior musical and academic achievement. Part of the commencement service that year established a chapter at the Choir College.

Routley approved of the chapter, but these types of organizations were puzzling and humorous.

> These fraternities which sport Greek letters are a great feature of the United States and most of them are just secret societies, but this one is the only one for musicians. I gather that the College is honored by this, though it's a foreign language to me. We sang both FPG's music hymns, which came in mighty useful.[135]

SUMMER SESSIONS AND HOLIDAYS

The summer of 1978 had Routley back on the road, but unlike 1977, in between travel to Seattle, Wisconsin, Texas, and Montreat, written into the new contract was the expectation that he would offer seminars in the summer sessions. A new, and very popular, addition to the program included weekly hymn sings, which soon became a traditional part of summers at the Princeton campus on Walnut Street. The first one was held in June and, according to Routley and the *Town Topics*,[136] it was wonderful.

> There's something about American singers that lifts the heart when they take hold of something. Their lack of shyness—which in older days was sometimes an embarrassment—comes out when they sing, and say responses in church, in a most heartwarming way.[137]

Between graduation and the start of the summer program, Erik and Margaret managed to slip away to Vermont for ten days, "wooded and beautiful when you can see it, so much like the Lake District in that way."[138] After visits from Patrick and Priscilla, Margaret was off to England to spend time with her mother. For Routley, the new fall semester passed in a flurry of conferences in places like Toronto and Boulder. The weekly sermons, the revision of *Church Music and Theology* as *Church Music and the Christian Faith*, teaching, input into the new Lutheran hymnal, and several articles finally paused with the blessed relief of Thanksgiving and Christmas breaks.

LOSING PETER SCOTT

News from home during the autumn was that Peter Scott had been ill, but Erik and Margaret got word of just how serious on December 28. He died on December 30, and Margaret left for England immediately. Several months later Erik, confided to Sr. Maria in Summit:

My wife's brother Peter, and my best friend, died at 60 (ten months my junior). He meant so much to us that we just looked at each other and said, "The only person I could have borne less to lose would have been you." Among other things, I might add, he was the best musician I think I have ever known. There are two people I have relied upon for musical education and refreshment, and Peter Scott was one.[139]

1979–80 Academic Year

Routley traveled more than forty thousand miles in 1979, much of it in the summer months, which this year also included preparation for John Kemp's sabbatical.

> I have a hideous prospect ahead. My revered department head, John Kemp, and his wife, Helen, are taking a sabbatical from January to May, and guess whom that leaves to be acting head of department? Since this will be as honorary as directing Chapel, and not near as much fun, I propose to organize the whole administration in the direction of my own personal convenience. The assignment only lasts until June, so perhaps even my surpassing ingenuity won't be able to ruin the Church Music Department.[140]

Family and Friends

In Skillman, Margaret had organized quartets that met regularly at the house along with her other students. The garden fell prey to a hurricane that blew down a huge willow tree and suffered some neglect during July, when both Margaret and Erik were out of town, though in different directions. Margaret went to England. Erik took off to all his many conferences. Yet it was the summer of visitors. George McPhee and Charles Somerville and other folk from Edinburgh came in August. All the children made it to the United States that summer, and each was doing well in their respective situations. Patrick, who had left editing for law school, was called to the bar in July, and Margaret was able to be there and witness it in person. Priscilla wrote every week, without fail, and was happily busy with her students. Nicholas spent most the month of October with his parents.

> He has a sabbatical from Sydney, partly for pleasure and partly for research. He is giving some concerts and accompanies, for which he is becoming very distinguished. He is now well-established in New South Wales as a teacher and choral director. His specialty is Josquin des Prez, and he's giving some lectures on our campus. His first one made quite an impression. This is the longest time he has spent in our company since he went to Cambridge 14 years ago! We had

a freak snowstorm but stayed cheerful throughout. I achieved my ambition to say upon answering the phone, "Which Dr. Routley do you wish?"[141]

Routley and Wilson spent much of the autumn months organizing a jam-packed visit to the RSCM for twenty-six Westminster students in January 1980. Helen and John Kemp and Ray Robinson were going as well, marking a huge turnaround for both men, who were suspicious of the RSCM. Lionel Dakers[142] had come for a summer session and convinced them that the RSCM was more than English cathedrals and Anglicanism, which brought both Kemp and Robinson on board.

Establishing Chapel

Routley had seen an entire cohort graduate by May 1979, so the Student Chapel Committee in September now consisted of students that didn't see Routley as a stranger.

> Routley transformed the undistinguished weekly event into a model of well-crafted liturgy. Erik's unerring memory for the hymnic repertoire, his pastoral and liturgical skills, and his enthusiasm to get on with it, provided the leadership that met the needs of the increasingly diverse Westminster community.[143]

At the beginning of the school year, the Chapel Committee approached Routley about the possibility of presenting Lloyd Pfautsch's *A Day for Dancing*, a thirty-minute piece that included song, dance, and theater.[144] Routley, who had heard the work in Dallas, contacted Pfautsch, inquiring about the possibility of Pfautsch attending the performance. Pfautsch agreed; Routley was thrilled; the students were ecstatic. The evening in April was attended by members of the Princeton community as well as WCC folk. The chapel was packed, and the performance was a remarkable success.

First Glimpse of Retirement

In May 1980, Routley again went to London both for RSCM business and to conduct two of Wilson's "Come and Sing" programs in Westminster Abbey. When Routley returned from England, Schisler notified him that he had been granted tenure—barely. Nonetheless, this meant that in 1982, Routley would be eligible for a sabbatical.

> That's the sort of thing that means a great deal to anybody half my age. To me it comes through as a Nice Thought. An incurious member of the Board of Trustees, perhaps in his cups, told me that the voting was 4–3, so I suppose it could have been nearly a Nasty Thought. It means that I must do something

158   *Chapter 7*

deliciously and notably immoral before they can fire me. I am due for a bit of sabbatical in the first half of 1983, and our regulations say you must teach for at least a year after or hand back your pay. So, you see where that gets us.[145]

The summer of 1980 ran its predictable, but usually erratic, course through workshops, weekend preaching, visits from family and friends, holiday travel, and the ever-surprising garden. The beans flourished, and artichokes, spinach, and collards rounded out the usual abundant return of tomatoes. Margaret went to England to help her mother and Anne Scott move to Oxford from Ealing for easier daily living and the academic stimulation. September put Routley back in his chapel and lecturing slot at Westminster, as the Kemps had returned from their sabbatical.

REJOICE IN THE LORD

New Brunswick Theological Seminary was the theological center of the Reformed Church in America, and for many years Routley had been associated with NBTS through collaborations with Howard Hageman, PTS, and the liturgical studies program at Drew. During the late 1970s, the RCA was seriously contemplating replacing both their denominational hymnal, which was seventy years old, and the one they borrowed from the Presbyterians in 1955. They wanted a book with a theologically solid representation of Christianity in the contents, hymns with singable tunes, and familiar texts. A committee was appointed to explore the matter, and in 1979 they reported to the General Synod their assessment that a new hymnal was necessary. A committee of seven was assembled, with Howard Hageman as chair. One of their first tasks was securing an editor, and Routley, though not the only consideration, was their first choice; but they were not confident that he would have the time to devote to this project, sure to last few years. Hageman presented the entire proposition to Routley, who immediately accepted; Routley told Wilson about it straightaway:

> They're a small company, not much bigger than the URC, and rather intelligent. They haven't had their own book for quite a time and have shared T*he Presbyterian Hymnbook* of 1955. They have become restless about this and want no part of the *Worshipbook.* Unofficially, somebody asked me what I thought, and I said that if they produced a book which every campus must buy, they'd immediately sell twice as many copies, and they might catch some of the Presbyterian market. They took the idea to their synod and the thing was authorized without a dissenting vote. I'm to be like an architect advising people to put up an aquarium. I am rather chuffed,[146] because this is a bus I thought I had missed.[147]

The meetings were usually held three or four times a year at the seminary in Princeton and lasted two or three days. Routley was to appear before the committee on the second day of the first meeting, and he was anxiously agonizing about his ability to produce something he had assumed he wouldn't be able to do. Likewise, the committee was intimidated by a man they knew only by name and reputation. A member of the committee, Norman Kansfield (b. 1940) recalls:

> When I saw him in the flesh, he was nothing that I had presumed—a rather tall, slender, marginally reserved British person. There suddenly was Erik! This absolute imp came in, all action, smoking his pipe and smoke whirling around everywhere. I loved him immediately.[148]

Rather like his approach to *Congregational Praise*, Routley gave the committee his detailed and authoritative steps of a disciplined procedure and his own expectations for respectful remuneration. After his presentation, Routley was asked to leave the room. The committee debated for about thirty minutes and, aware of how much Routley would add to the project, brought him back and told Routley that he was their choice for editor. Without hesitation, Routley welcomed their bid, and they all got to work that very afternoon.

It was not all smooth sailing, and a few months later Routley left the group, with their blessing. Fortunately, after brushing aside some abrasive interaction and friction, work on the hymnal—with Routley—continued, and the scratchy start faded away.

> All is well now, and our committee of seven has been working very happily. We are up to something quite new, at any rate in the USA—a lyric companion to the Bible. Watch this space about November 1984! The Reformed Church was really begun by the Dutch people on the *Mayflower*, and it's kept its theological head remarkably well during the age of lunacies.[149]

From the time he formulated his thoughts on the relationship between theology and music in the 1950s, Routley envisioned a hymnal formatted in scriptural order, a companion to the Bible, as he saw this as the only way to unite the minister and church musician, symbiotic artists in the conversational drama of worship. One of Routley's more insistent editorial suggestions was that the hymnal should be constructed according to the arrangement of the books of the Bible:

> Just as the Bible is a book of books, which can be read either as a precious collection of sacred oracles or as a continuous record of God's dealings with humanity, so a hymnal which really expresses the church's faith ought to be

usable either as a collection of sacred lyrics or as a book which can be read as a kind of commentary on the story the Bible tells.[150]

According to the final preface, "the book follows the canonical order of the Bible as the outline for the selection of hymns. It begins with God's act of creation and concludes with the great vision of God's eternal city.[151]

Discussion of the compelling problem of sexist and gender-specific vocabulary of older hymnody was always on the agenda of the RIL committee meetings. Routley firmly believed that theologically, literary integrity and inclusive language carried equal weight in determining the contents of a hymnal. The decision was reached to make changes in the pronouns and female/male representations only if the poetry was not damaged in the process. Examining and adjusting the texts was an exhausting, emotional task. The selection of hymns was generally approved if the modifications fit both the meter and intent of the original. If a hymn didn't fit, it was excluded. The committee grasped the complexity of the predicament, but the larger, cultural problem could not be resolved in their time frame. In the end, the group decided there were only four hymns that had to be included that did not respond well to alterations. Routley wit prevailed. These hymns have a little printed dagger, (†), after the title.[152]

The title took a while to reach consensus. Routley suggested the phrase "Rejoice in the Lord" because it appears in both the Old and New Testaments. It became the working title and then stuck, adding: *A Hymn Companion to the Scriptures*. A brilliant but easily missed musical subtlety that Routley insisted upon that is easily missed, is that the book begins and ends with the words of Isaac Watts, respectively: "O God, our help in ages past" and "We give immortal praise." But it's their tunes, "St. Anne" and "Croft's 136" that complete Routley's vision:

> The hymns of creation begin in the perfect concord of C major, in the first chord of ST ANNE, and that the hymns of the new creation conclude with the perfect, untroubled, but emphatic final chord of CROFT'S 136th.[153]

CROSSING THE UNITED STATES AND CANADA

In 1981 Margaret and Erik finally took a proper holiday between graduation and the start of the summer sessions involving more lectures at SFTS, Montreat, and Massanetta. Some friends in New Jersey were moving to Oregon. This couple had three little children and two cars. They had prepared themselves for an arduous journey until the Routleys, remembering the success of Margaret's previous drive across the country, suggested that they drive one car, giving each car two drivers. The seven of them, two in a Rabbit and five in a station wagon, hopped across the country from one Motel 6 to the next. They made stops at Yellowstone and Grand Teton National Parks. The family went on to their new home in Portland, and Erik and Margaret went up to Olympia and Mount Rainier. They took the Rabbit back to Portland and then boarded a bus to Vancouver, following the coastline of the Pacific Northwest. In Vancouver they got the cross-Canada train to Montreal. As they appreciated all the stunning scenery, they began to work out their plans for Erik's sabbatical. One thing on the list was discovering more about Europe. Margaret had only been to the Netherlands and Luxembourg, and Erik had only a couple of student trips and his visits to Geneva to his credit. One of Peter and Anne's children lived in Rome, which seemed like a perfect place to start. When they got back to Skillman, Margaret caught up with her students and Erik returned to his correspondence, describing the whole experience with his favorite one word sentence: "Splendid!!"

ANTICIPATING THE SABBATICAL

By the summer of 1982, specifics for Erik's upcoming sabbatical were being finalized. Erik and Margaret would spend the month of January 1983 in England. Routley had committed to preach in Paisley and Edinburgh toward the end of the month, and there were a few meetings he had to see to in London—and there would likely be a family wedding to attend. Their length of stay would be determined by their pocketbooks and returning to Margaret's full load of students back in Princeton.

At the Choir College, Routley began to get everything in order for his absence in the spring. He and John Kemp were finding capable persons to teach the scheduled hymnology and liturgy classes. Routley and the Chapel Committee set the upcoming spring weekly schedule, and speakers for the services were lined up until graduation in May.

Tribute to Helen Kemp

Helen Kemp (1918–2015), internationally known for her work with children's choirs, was planning on retiring in May 1983. She was beloved by her students and esteemed by the faculty, and Schisler was hoping that Sue Ellen Page (1949–2016) would be available to slip in to teach Helen's class load. Westminster was organizing a "Festival of Singing Children" during the spring alumni and graduation festivities. John Rutter (b. 1945), Hal Hopson (b. 1933), Natalie Sleeth (1930–1992), Page, and Routley had been commissioned to compose hymns and anthems. Nearly fifty children's choirs in the Princeton area, including eastern Pennsylvania, were invited to mark the occasion.

> I have the daunting assignment of devising something for a huge festival with children's choir of 600, due next May, celebrating the retirement of my boss's wife, who is a coast-to-coast authority (and deservedly) on children's music in church. I don't know how to do it.[154]

But he figured it out, organizing the liturgy and writing an orchestral setting of his newly composed tune, "Orchard Road." Knowing he would be on sabbatical during the spring semester, and somewhat unsure of his schedule, Routley gave it all to John Kemp in mid-September.[155]

Tribute to Warren Martin

Another big occasion had Routley's attention. Warren Martin (1916–1982), a member of the Westminster faculty for more than thirty years, had died in April. His presence was much missed on campus, so a memorial had been arranged for him during the fall semester, when faculty and students would all be back in session. As the Kemp celebration was being planned, Charles Schisler, Routley, and others were also designing Martin's service and chose November 14 in Bristol Chapel. Though the occasion was more of a concert than worship service, Routley found the appropriate arrangements of the hymns and agreed to write the prayers. Again, recognizing the pressure of his schedule, Routley gave his pieces to Schisler when the term began.

SEPTEMBER 1982

The first week of September, Routley took the *RIL* manuscript to New York City to be printed, and he presented the photocopies to the committee's final meeting at the end of the month. A satisfied Routley quickly wrote to John Wilson:

> There's one piece of good hymnic news. We have just finished our last meeting, though there are lots of nuts and bolts for me to tighten up. I suppose the very last decision we made was to restore "Rock of Ages"!! They didn't want it, any of them, but thought they'd better. Not to the American tune—that would have been too much! And I managed to surprise them by writing a text for the tune of "How Great thou art." We were a bit stumped by that because it's monstrously popular in the rather cumbersome well-known version, and it's also very expensive to buy! I reharmonized it and hope we're not vandalized.[156]

In two letters and a postcard to Kansfield, Routley voiced detailed concerns about the presentation of two hymns in the book.[157] The *RIL* committee scheduled an introductory presentation of the hymnal for Thursday, October 7, at the Second Reformed Church of New Brunswick[158] across College Avenue from NBTS and a more formal presentation at the Seminary on Saturday, the 9th. Routley would lead both sessions, and though Routley had to get to a conference in Tennessee immediately following the debut Thursday, he intended to fly back Friday night.

Preparing for the atmosphere in England, Routley wrote a despairing letter to Caryl Micklem about the goings on in the URC and the demise of Mansfield College. The decision to become a PPC in 1954 didn't produce the expected revenue, and an appreciation for an academic setting for good ministers and thoughtful theologians was disappearing. They agreed to discuss the subject in January.[159]

NASHVILLE

The week of October 3 was, as usual, a busy one. At chapel on Tuesday, the theme was "Youth." Routley brought chuckles when he said in his sermon that when he began his ministry in 1943, it never occurred to him that the last days of his ministry would be given to persons young enough to be his grandchildren; but he added that never did he think this ministry to the young would have enriched him so much. In three weeks hence, junior classman James Brumm, a Routley student from the beginning of his freshman year at Westminster, was scheduled as the weekly chapel coordinator.[160] Brumm had heard Routley's new tune LITTON when it premiered in the summer[161] and wanted to include it in the liturgy; in a conversation with Dr. Routley, Brumm asked if he could have a copy of the tune. On Thursday morning, October 7, as Routley was leaving the campus for the program in New Brunswick, he and Brumm crossed paths on the quad outside the chapel. Routley pulled out an envelope containing a copy of LITTON and handed it to Brumm, insisting that if he (Routley) didn't give it to Brumm that day, he was sure he'd never get around to it.[162]

Following the talk at the church, Routley got a flight from Newark to Nashville to present three lectures at Scarritt College, a Methodist center for church musicians. He was scheduled to speak in the late afternoon and then have dinner with Hal Hopson (b. 1933) and his wife, Martha. After a long, collegial evening, Routley wished them a good night and said he would see them in the morning.

On Friday morning, October 8, Routley was uncharacteristically late for his second lecture. Darryl Ray Miller (b. 1949) was the administrative assistant at Scarritt and responsible for the practical side of the workshop, which was headlined by Routley. Miller had sent a graduate student, Clark Morrell (b. 1958), to bring Routley to the site. When Routley was not waiting for him and there was no answer in his room, Morrell called Miller. Miller suggested that Morrell retrace his route and see if, by chance, Routley had decided to walk to Scarritt. James I. Warren (b. 1934),[163] speaker for the next session, was in the room for the Routley lecture, and when Routley was late, Warren volunteered to give his own presentation first. Morrell returned to Scarritt, telling Miller that Routley was nowhere to be found. The two men returned to the hotel and convinced Reception to take them to Routley's room. Upon opening the door, they found Dr. Routley in bed, having died in his sleep. The bedside table held a bookmarked detective novel.[164]

NOTES

1. Now known as Garrett-Evangelical Theological Seminary on the campus of Northwestern University in Evanston and affiliated with the United Methodist Church. The two institutions associate closely but are independent of each other. Northwestern was founded by Methodist Episcopal clergy but is now nonsectarian.

2. Letter from Loveless to NWG, June 2, 2003.

3. Ibid.

4. Nathaniel Micklem, *National Socialism and the Roman Catholic Church*, 243. Rhodes scholar Adam von Trott (1909–1944) studied at Mansfield in 1929 and was one of the leaders of the plot to assassinate Hitler; he was arrested and hanged for treason in 1944. In the 1980s, Elaine Kaye and Geoffrey Beck organized the Adam von Trott Memorial Appeal in his memory. There is a plaque at Mansfield, a memorial lecture series, and the Living Memorial Scholarship, which allows a German student to come to Mansfield College every two years to study for a master's degree in politics. This appeal absorbed the Lutheran Tutorship. In 2014 the German government awarded Kaye and Beck the Cross of the Order of Merit of the Federal Republic of Germany.

5. Particularly that of Peter Cutts, whose tune "Wylde Green" was included in the hymnal. Many years later, Lovelace visited St. James's one Sunday and Peter Cutts was the organist. Routley inserted John Monsell's (1811–1875) "God Is Love, by Him Upholden," set to "Wylde Green." Quite a treat for Lovelace. Lovelace letter to NWG.

6. Routley wrote a review of this hymnal for the *Bulletin*, vol. 6, no. 108, 106–111.

7. At the time, Young was music editor of Abingdon Press, and he immediately contracted Routley for *Hymns Today and Tomorrow* (1964), followed by *Music Leadership in the Church* (1967) and *Words, Music, and the Church* (1968).

8. Endowed by Levi P. Stone (1802–1884) in 1871; lectures are given biannually.

9. *Words, Music, and the Church* is based on the contents of these lectures. On the strength of his reception, Routley was invited to address several summer sessions at

PTS in the years before his faculty position at the Seminary began in 1975. For the next twenty years, Routley was a recurring speaker at many other Presbyterian locations, Montreat Conference Center in North Carolina, Mo Ranch northwest of San Antonio, and Massanetta Springs Conference Center near Harrisonburg, Virginia, and at Presbyterian colleges and churches across the country.

10. Bristol was a hymnologist, hymnal editor, and composer. His well-known tune "Dickinson College" is often linked with Fred Pratt Green's text, "The church of Christ in every age." At Routley's suggestion, this pairing was included in *The Hymnal 1982* (Church Hymnal Corporation, 1985); it is currently in many major denominational hymnals in the United States and Canada. In 1969, at Routley's recommendation, Bristol was the first American to be admitted to the RSCM. Every May beginning in the 1960s, John Wilson organized weekly "Come and Sing" events at Westminster Abbey. Bristol eagerly led at least four of these sessions through the years.

11. Attempts to list all of these over the years are always incomplete.

12. Kidney stones and stress-related maladies necessitated a ten-week health leave from the pulpit in Edinburgh.

13. JWW, May 25, 1966.

14. The term was from May 1970 to May 1971.

15. Numbers are approximate, but in 1970 the range in pounds was £2,000–£4,000/year. Routley's salary was about £2,500. In dollars, that was about $5,000/year.

16. This year (1974) would mark thirty-one years of Congregational ministry for Routley, and he was eligible to retire.

17. Letter to Beck, July 20, 1974. "Management" refers to Routley.

18. Carlton Young, *I'll Sing On*, 127.

19. Ibid.

20. *The Hymn*, vol. 53, no. 4, October 2002, 17.

21. Ibid. Names like Brian Wren, Fred Pratt Green, Tom Colvin, Fred Kaan, and many others.

22. JWW, August 8, 1973.

23. Ibid.

24. And active member of the HSUSC, Jones was a founding faculty member of Westminster Choir College. In 1939 Jones became the first music faculty member at the Seminary directing the well-known choir, chapel, and teaching organ and hymnology. CDH.

25. Permanent positions were complicated to arrange due to immigration requirements.

26. One of these persons was James Litton (1934–2022), music director at Trinity Church, Princeton.

27. Duba had been chaplain at Westminster Choir College from 1960 to 1968.

28. JWW, June 7, 1974.

29. For the full article see, *Bulletin*, VIII, no. 131, Winter 1974, 1–3.

30. Ironically, Cutts moved to the United States in 1989 to become director of music at Andover-Newton School of Theology.

31. Massey, *Bulletin*, vol. 16, no. 8, October 2001, 229.

32. Massey served twice, 1975–2001 and 2003–2004.32.
33. Massey, *Bulletin*, vol. 16, no. 229, October 2001.
34. At the time of his death, there were more than two thousand books and hymnals in his library, and most of them were in regular use.
35. For more information on her curious history, see https://en.wikipedia.org/wiki/MV_Kungsholm_(1965)#Peace_Boat.
36. JWW, January 11, 1975.
37. Princeton Borough bordered on Princeton Township. Each had separate governments until 2013, when the two municipalities merged.
38. JWW, January 11, 1975.
39. Ibid.
40. Sixteen miles northeast of Princeton.
41. Director of music at the nearby Trinity Episcopal Church.
42. NWG, Litton, August 7, 2003.
43. Arlo Duba, *Presbyterian Worship in the Twentieth Century*, chapter 5.
44. NWG, Shannon, August 2003.
45. Ibid.
46. Ibid. Though, later in the summer, PTS and WCC worked out an arrangement allowing Routley to teach a course at the seminary.
47. *Book of Worship for the United States Armed Forces* (US Government Printing Office, 1974).
48. This is an ecumenical and interreligious association of liturgical scholars who collaborate in research concerning public worship. www.naal-liturgy.org.
49. The Paschal Triduum is a period of three days that begins with the liturgy on Holy (Maundy) Thursday, reaches its high point at the Easter Vigil, and closes with evening prayer on Easter Sunday.
50. JWW, April 3, 1975.
51. JWW, February 28, 1975.
52. Appointed dean in 1975.
53. Chair of the Church Music Department.
54. ER letters to John Kemp to James McCord, April 1975.
55. Wright was interim Dean 1971–1975; Schisler was made dean in 1975 and served in that position until 1988.
56. Arlo Duba was the chaplain until 1968.
57. There was one member of each class and a president on the committee. Services were planned to accommodate experimental worship in many denominational styles.
58. Lloyd Pfautsch (1921–2003), November 20, 1975.
59. JWW, May 30, 1975, and August 5, 1975.
60. ER/MR Christmas letter, 1976.
61. JWW, August 25, 1975.
62. JWW, September 8, 1975.
63. FPG, November 25, 1975.
64. *The Pilgrim Hymnal* (Pilgrim Press: Boston, 1958), United Church of Christ.
65. JWW, October 18, 1975.

66. Funfgeld directed the Bach Choir of Bethlehem, Pennsylvania, from 1983 to 2022. WCC, 1976.
67. FPG, November 9, 1975.
68. This was first published in *The Mennonite Hymnal*, 1966.
69. JWW to ER, December 15, 1975.
70. Routley introduced *Westminster Praise* at the traditional anthem reading session during Alumni Week.
71. Christmas letter, 1975.
72. *Exploring the Psalms* and *Martin Shaw: A Centenary Appreciation* (E. M. Campbell: London, 1975).
73. Class syllabus, 1976.
74. The original words are a vesper hymn, "Lord keep us safe this night," thought to be written by John Leland (1754–1841).
75. JWW, November 22, 2976.
76. *A Panorama of Christian Hymnody* (GIA Publications: Chicago, 1979).
77. Ibid., 16.
78. Paul A. Richardson, "The Influence of Routley's Writings in the Classroom Today," *The Hymn* (the Hymn Society of the United States and Canada), vol. 53, no. 4, October 2002, 15–16.
79. Paul Richardson, introduction.
80. Erik Routley, *An English Speaking Hymnal Guide*, edited and expanded by Peter Cutts (GIA: Chicago, 2005, 1979); Routley, *A Panorama of Christian Hymnody*, edited and expanded by Paul A. Richardson (GIA: Chicago, 2005, 1979); Paul Westermeyer, *Let the People Sing: Hymn Tunes in Perspective* (GIA: Chicago, 2005).
81. *Hymns and Human Life* (J. J. Murray Press: London, 1953), preface.
82. These sings had been John Wilson's responsibility every May since the late 1960s, and Bristol was always ready to conduct.
83. World Council of Churches in this case. JWW, February 19, 1976.
84. Essay in the Routley Collection.
85. George McPhee.
86. JWW, February 19, 1976. Wilson
87. JWW, May 2, 1976.
88. Set to the fifteenth-century text "O Love, How Deep, How Broad."
89. JWW, May 4, 1976.
90. JWW, May 17, 1976.
91. JWW, April 4, 1976.
92. Christmas letter, 1976.
93. Greg Funfgeld.
94. JWW, April 26, 1976.
95. Christmas letter, 1976.
96. JWW, June 8, 1976.
97. JWW, February 14, 1977.
98. Christmas letter, 1976.
99. Christmas letter, 1976
100. June 29, 1976.

101. Christmas letter, 1976.
102. Ibid.
103. September 20, 1976.
104. Young had left Perkins and taken up the directorship of the master's program at Scarritt College.
105. The music directors were Lois Fyfe (1927–2014) and Peter Fyfe. Lois founded Lois Fyfe Music in Nashville, a company specializing in sacred music distribution and advice. The couple and Routley became friends. He recommended them to Trinity Church in Princeton when Jim Litton left for St. Bartholomew in New York. The church hired John Bertalot (b. 1931).
106. Carlton R. Young, *I'll Sing On* (GIA: Chicago, 2022), 152.
107. The Routleys had received the tickets for this event as a gift. He was astonished that they were eleven dollars each, and there was no way they could have afforded the evening otherwise.
108. Davies, a renowned theologian, was a member of the JCR at Mansfield with Routley. He was a professor at Princeton University for nearly fifty years and had access to *The Times*.
109. JWW, January 28,1977.
110. In the Mansfield JCR with Routley.
111. Drew Theological Seminary is a seminary of the United Methodist Church in Madison, New Jersey.
112. Founding faculty also included James H. Pain (1930–2022), Drew; Gabriel M Corless, OSB (b. 1929), Drew; Bard Thompson (1925–1987), Drew; and Frank Estocin (1939–2010), president, Saint Sophia Orthodox Seminary. The program has been absorbed into other courses at Drew.
113. The result was an SATB, brass-organ setting of a text from the Venerable Bede (673–735) and published by Hinshaw.
114. RSCM newsletter, vol. 13, no. 3, Summer 1979.
115. Lippincott was appointed department chair in 1967 and served until her retirement in 2000. A virtuosic organist, she performed widely in the United States, Canada, and Europe and is known for her presentation of pieces by J. S. Bach and her teachings on rhythm, touch, and baroque articulation.
116. To Flummerfelt, May 21, 1977.
117. During Routley's tenure, the Westminster organ department was Joan Lippincott, head; Mary Krimmel, Virginia Cheeseman, George Markey, Donald McDonald, Eugene Roan, Robert Carwithen, William Hays, Robert Schuneman, Harald Vogel, and Mark Brombaugh.
118. Larry G. Biser, ed. *Joan Lippincott: The Gift of Music*, 32.
119. Biser, 32.
120. *25 Festive Hymns for Organ and Choir* (Augsburg: Minneapolis, 1982).
121. The 1975 Immigration and Nationality Act Amendment.
122. Pfautsch letter, May 11, 1977.
123. *I'll Sing On*, 127.
124. Pfautsch letter, May 11,1977.
125. GB, November 7, 1977.

126. JWW, November 1, 1977.

127. In 1970 John and Mary were in Woodrising, Norfolk, and encoded some music for the instrument. When he returned in 1975, he was startled, saddened, then comforted by the sound of her voice on a recording.

128. JWW, August 23, 1973.

129. John Wilson, ed., *Sixteen Hymns of Today for Use as Simple Anthems*, the Royal School of Church Music (Halstan & Co: Amersham, England, 1978).

130. JWW, June 14, 1978.

131. The state's nickname is the Garden State; it's well earned.

132. Christmas letter, 1978.

133. Christmas letter, 1978.

134. JWW, April 26, 1978.

135. JWW, May 9, 1978.

136. This is a weekly Princeton community newspaper. June 27, 1978.

137. JWW, June 30, 1978.

138. JWW, June 4, 1978.

139. Letter to Sr. Maria of the Cross, July 20, 1979. The other person was John W. Wilson.

140. Christmas letter, 1979.

141. Alice Fanstone (from Brighton), October 10, 1979.

142. Dakers was director of the RSCM.

143. Carlton Young, "The Memorial Service," *The Hymn*, January 1983, 20.

144. Lawson-Gould Music Publishers, 1969. From Michael Hawn: *A Day for Dancing* (1969) was written for the University Chorale at SMU. Because Meadows School of the Arts includes programs in all the arts, Pfautsch also included the dance (choreography) and theater departments (lighting and narration). The idea for *Day for Dancing* came from Britten's *Ceremony of Carols*. Most of the carol texts came from the *Oxford Book of Carols* (1928). It was Pfautsch's most performed work, taken around the world.

145. Christmas letter, 1980.

146. Informally, "very pleased" in Great Britain; not generally used in the United States.

147. JWW, July 8, 1980.

148. NWG, Kansfield, July 30, 2003.

149. Christmas letter, 1981.

150. *Hymns Today and Tomorrow*, 145.

151. *Rejoice in the Lord*, preface.

152. #159, "Sometimes a light surprises"; #209, "God rest you merry gentlemen"; #252, "At even, when the sun was set"; and #522, "Our Father, by whose name."

153. Robin Leaver, "Review: *Rejoice in the Lord*," *News of Hymnody Quarterly* (Grove books Ltd. and SPCK: London), no. 15, July 1985.

154. JWW, August 1982.

155. "Good News for All: A Choral Hymn," Op. 36 (Orchard Road), words by Edward J. Burns (b. 1938) (Hinshaw, 1983).

156. JWW, September 27, 1982.

157. Routley Collection.
158. In 2022 the name of the church is Community Church of New Brunswick.
159. TCM, October 1, 1982.
160. In August, students in their junior and senior years were assigned to organize the Tuesday chapel services for the semester.
161. Routley wrote this for his friend and colleague, as Litton was leaving Trinity Church in Princeton for a position at the historic St. Bartholomew's Church in Manhattan.
162. Email, November 2022.
163. Taught hymnology at Scarritt.
164. Recollections and emails from Morrell, October and November 2022, private collection.

Epilogue

Charles Schisler received the call from Nashville around 10:00 a.m. on that Friday. He called John Kemp, Howard Hageman, and then went to find Ray Robinson, who was attending a meeting. The Westminster Symphonic Choir[1] rehearsed in the Playhouse every day at 11:00 under the direction of Joe Flummerfelt. Charles went to the Playhouse and asked Joe to step outside. Having been told about Routley, Dr. Flummerfelt went back to his podium and said, "I am sorry to have to tell you that Dr. Routley died this morning in Nashville." In the shocked silence, and amid his own disbelief, Flummerfelt said, "We cannot rehearse today." Further away, Norman Kansfield was in his office in New Brunswick answering the questions in Routley's letters. As he was writing, the phone rang. It was his friend Howard with the inconceivable news.

After John Kemp ended the call with Schisler, he turned to Helen and said, "I have to tell Margaret. I can't go by myself."[2] They worked out their words as they made their way to Skillman. Neither Helen nor John really knew Margaret very well, and they realized that showing up unexpected and uninvited would tell Margaret immediately that something was wrong. Margaret opened the door and John simply said, "We've got to talk to you." Margaret stiffened and let them in the house. As word spread, many more people arrived, including Ray and Ruth Robinson. Phone calls were made to Australia, Glasgow, Oxford, and London, and all three adult children got to Princeton by Monday the 11th. That same day, faculty, friends, and students gathered in the chapel at noon for a short silent five minutes, and then Dr. Flummerfelt led the group in the Choir College's signature blessing, Peter Lutkin's "Benediction."[3] The next plans included an evening vigil with the casket at Trinity Church so the mourning community could stop in for reflection from 6:00 p.m. until midnight, broken by a small prayer service at 8:00. On Tuesday morning, October 12, the casket was taken across town to Bristol Chapel.

Epilogue

BRISTOL CHAPEL, OCTOBER 12, 1982

It was the appropriate place to bring all of Erik Routley—the place where the faithful minister and teacher had so significantly and joyfully led the college's worshipping community.[4] The funeral began at 10:00 a.m., the usual day and hour for chapel, and Bristol was filled beyond capacity, with no livestream to handle the overflow. The casket was placed in front of the chancel area by the faculty and student pallbearers.[5] Several witnesses noted that the floral blanket on top of the casket was the only color amid the somber brown-and-white decor.[6] "The low ceiling and stunning congregational singing, "returned us for a moment to the sounds of a Reformed chapel, bringing us close to Routley's roots."[7]

Margaret carefully framed the liturgy to sidestep overstatement and triumphism, which her husband would have avoided, letting the music tell his story; the opening and closing Bach chorales, *Allein Gott in der Höh' sei Ehr* and *Nun danket alle Gott*, would have been enough.[8] The hymns were two that spoke most importantly to Routley, "I'll praise my Maker while I've breath" and "The head which once was crowned with thorns." "The Call," composed by his old Lancing housemaster and organ teacher, Alexander Brent Smith, and Routley's anthem "Praise" were sung by all the people, in true Congregationalist style. *A Prayer Canticle* by Routley and Alan Luff emphasized the enormous contribution to hymnody made by the Dunblane Consultations. Erik's old classmate Daniel Jenkins, a visiting professor at PTS that year, had immediately agreed to give the address.[9] As a personal link to Mansfield College, he reminded those present of Erik's integrity, generosity, independent spirit, and pastoral dedication. Jenkins underscored his friend Erik's synthesis with his ministry as the guiding light of his whole life.[10] Sam Young described it simply:

> Beyond the remembrance and the remembering of Erik's genius and his life and work, we were also assured in scripture prayer, and in Professor Jenkins' words, Erik Routley, that superb singer of the Gospel of Jesus Christ, had already taken his place with "David who stands with harp in hands."[11]

For Margaret and the family, the days that followed were a blur of condolences, visitors, food, and sadness. The messages from their dear friends in England and Scotland did not arrive until a few days after the service.[12] Bereft, John Wilson assured the Routleys that Erik had just raised the standard of the heavenly choir.[13] Jenkins and Caryl Micklem arranged for an obituary to appear in the *London Times*.

WESTMINSTER ABBEY, FEBRUARY 8, 1983

When Patrick returned to London at the end of October, he began to plan for a public memorial in England. After contacting Alan Luff, then minor canon and precentor at Westminster Abbey, Patrick got in touch with Caryl Micklem to see that the appropriate participants were gathered to plan the event. There was some discussion of location: Mansfield Chapel or Westminster Abbey. The Abbey seemed to be better suited in both location and the envisioned type of service and the anticipated large number of guests and participants. As Secretary of the HSGBI, Luff used his role at the Abbey to coordinate the arrangements between the United Kingdom and the United States.

The service complemented the one in Princeton, adopting some of the same the elements of Routley's professional and public contributions and adding others. There was purposefully no choir,[14] forcing the congregational singing to dominate the service, though John Wilson arranged for the choir from Charterhouse to lead the hymns.[15] The opening of the memorial contained two different Routley works, "Let all the world in every corner sing," set to AUGUSTINE, and Routley's paraphrase of Psalm 98, "New songs of celebration render," set to the Genevan tune RENDEZ A DIEU. *A Prayer Canticle* was repeated, except this time, Luff himself was the cantor, providing an intimate touch to the antiphon. George Caird gave the sermon, sprinkled with anecdotes from Mansfield days, examples of Routley's influence on the music of the Church, and ending with the measure of Routley's life:

The great glory of God and the contemporary circumstances of man need to collide in modern verse. This seems to me to be the hymnologist's version of the Great Commandment. Anyone who is preoccupied with the great glory of God and the need of man is not likely to have much time left over for self-concern.[16]

Between October and February, there were many suggestions for some sort of permanent memorial. Robin Leaver contacted HPC and proposed some type of Festschrift as a "new collection of essays which would not only provide for some focus on the life of Erik Routley but would also commission fresh contributions to the bibliography of church music and hymnody."[17] Luff invited some of those attending the memorial to dinner in his rooms after the memorial to devise and outline the book.[18] In *Panorama*, Routley remarks that the epigrammatic style is always the mark of a good hymn writer: "The memorable phrase, packing immense amounts into a few simple works is what makes a hymn live."[19] Those gathered knew from experience that Routley communicated with epigrams to bring the glory of God to the people. Leaver recognized this epigrammatic power in the opening line, "In praise of God meet duty and delight,"[20] and there was no need to look any further for a title. When these ideas were presented to Margaret, she was encouraging; but in a letter to George Shorney, she had a major request:

His long service in the ministry should not be overlooked. If a biographical article is included then it should be written by someone who knew Erik for longer than the years he spent in the US. Caryl Micklem's name springs to mind as the perfect choice, a man who has been very close to Erik's mind for forty years, as a friend, churchman, and church musician, and who could write with real understanding.[21]

Caryl gave the editors[22] exactly what Margaret hoped for:

Erik was Erik. You could not slow him down. And though all who loved him feel irreparable loss, he gives us a new notion of everlasting rest. Erik could convey the mystery and wonder of the Glory of God as well as he could relay the compelling "down-to-earthness" of the Bible. This thrusting, self-assertive, know-it-all man was perpetually awestruck. He spoke of what he knew, devoting all of himself to getting out of the way, to let us see what he had seen.[23]

NOTES

1. The Westminster Symphonic Choir is made of all sophomore, junior, and senior students and most graduate students as well. This choir performs with the New York Philharmonic, the Philadelphia Orchestra, and other major orchestras. In 1982 they rehearsed every day.

2. NWG, Helen Kemp, August 5, 2001.

3. Written in 1900, CPDL.

4. Carlton Young, "The Memorial Service," *The Hymn*, January 1983, 22.

5. Joseph Flummerfelt, conductor; Dean Charles Schisler; voice faculty, Daniel Pratt (b. 1938); church music faculty, Gerard Farrell, OSB (1919–2000); John Kemp; Brian-Paul Thomas (1960–2021), president of the Student Chapel Committee. Honorary: theory faculty, Harriet Chase (b. 1931); organ faculty, Joan Lippincott; Helen Kemp; Sue-Ellen Page.

6. Margaret and a friend made this arrangement.

7. Carlton Young, "The Memorial Service," *The Hymn*, January 1983, 22.

8. "All glory be to God on high" (BWV 662) and "Now thank we all our God" (BWV 657).

9. Except for Margaret, Jenkins had known Routley longer than anyone else in the room.

10. There was one eerie moment. Erik's office was at the top of the stairs just outside the doors to the chapel. Stephen Schall (b. 1962), a student at the college, remembers that in the middle of the service, the phone rang insistently, and went unanswered.

11. Op. cit., Carlton Young. The line is from the hymn "Jerusalem, my happy home," which Jenkins quoted in his address.

12. Caryl and Ruth Micklem wrote immediately, and their words to Margaret tell of the first few days after hearing the news about their beloved friend, Erik; this letter remains in a private collection. The tributes that Ruth and Caryl added in *Duty and Delight* carry all the love and faithful promises of their initial grief and their gratitude for Erik.

13. Letter to Margaret, October 11, 1982.

14. Ordinarily the custom in an English service at the Abbey.

15. Wilson was the music director at Charterhouse from 1932 to 1965.

16. In January 1982 Brian Wren wrote to Caird and shared Routley's words from the famous letter Routley wrote responding to Wren's early attempt at hymn writing. At the Abbey, Caird paraphrased Routley's advice.

17. *Duty and Delight: Routley Remembered*, Robin A. Leaver and James Litton, eds. (Hope Publishing: Carol Stream, 1985), preface.

18. This included Robin Leaver, Carlton Young, George Shorney, and Ray Robinson.

19. *Panorama*, introduction.

20. This hymn, "For Musicians," is the basis for the anthem "Praise," sung at the funeral in Princeton. It was commissioned by the Westminster Presbyterian Church of Lincoln, Nebraska, in 1976.

21. Letter to George Shorney, March 10, 1983.

22. Leaver and James Litton; Carton R Young, executive editor.

23. DD, 11–14.

Acknowledgments

In mid-March 2020, when the world shut down, I was in conversations with Raymond Gray and Nicholas Routley concerning writing this biography. For thirty years, Ray's late wife, Nancy Wicklund Gray, had collected material toward recounting the life of Dr. Routley, and though no book materialized, both Ray and Nicholas wanted to move forward with the project. Based on my friendship with Nancy and my CV, the two felt I was the perfect candidate to get Routley's story to the public. I had lived in Mobile for four months and found myself with excess time on my hands, so I reluctantly and tentatively agreed to take it on, though I had no idea of how to begin, or even why to begin.

In isolation, I traveled to Doylestown, Pennsylvania, and spent five days in Nancy's study, sorting and re-sorting her piles of photocopies and her invaluable interviews with Routley's colleagues. Ray shipped eleven boxes to my front door in Mobile and my dining room, only recently cleared of moving rubble, became the Routley biography center. Ray remarried, and as he and his wife, Susan Scott, settled into their new lives, she uncovered more material and graciously sent it all to me. As I set to work, I constantly wondered if this was a worthwhile project. By October 2020 I knew I had been handed both a lifeline through the pandemic and an exceptional and essential opportunity to record and present the life of an extraordinary human being. The subsequent, continuous string of blessings and lucky breaks kept me convinced that a book was important. Though I was confined to my house, I wasn't working alone.

The Routleys—Nicholas, Patrick, Angela, and especially Priscilla—warmly welcomed me into their world with uncensored glimpses of their father through their recollections and family documents. In 2022, I spent several days in Paisley with Priscilla, combing through drawers of memorabilia, supported by her gracious hospitality. Patrick and Angela Routley dug out boxes of tapes and papers, which we sorted on the dining table in their

London flat. Nicholas Routley, who, alas, lives in Australia, kept my facts straight and my spirits lifted.

Robin Leaver, with his unique understanding of English and American church music of the twentieth century, provided three years of uninterrupted encouragement, information, and corrections while he humorously rode out my incessant badgering and rambling emails. Getting to know Carlton "Sam" Young was a delightful serendipity. Sam and Erik worked together on critical hymnals and supplements produced in the 1960s and 1970s, and his experiences were important at every stage of the book. Paul Richardson, a fellow fact detective, endured my endless pestering and quickly furnished witty, yet accurate, answers to every question. Douglas Galbraith, a participant at Dunblane, supplied most of the details from those visionary, groundbreaking consultations. Dick Watson helped me navigate the components of twentieth-century English church music but also, more importantly, guided me through Durham and the Palace Green Library. Michael Hopkins, secretary of the United Reformed Church History Society, quickly furnished and amended detail after detail of the Congregational Church and the URC. James Caird, Robert Canham, David Cornick, Michael Hawn, Simon Jenkins, Michael McMahon, Romilly Micklem, Clark Morrell, Andrew Pratt, Andrew Scott, and Adam Tice always responded promptly and enthusiastically to my unending appeals for information.

A major obstacle for my research lay with the pandemic restrictions on travel. Archives were inaccessible for two years, but the librarians from Oxford, Durham, and Princeton created ways to access resources using Zoom, Facetime, and email. Stephanie Sussmeier, former archivist of Special Collections at the Talbott Music Library of Rider University, is a star who never refused a request and always delivered more than I asked for as we immersed ourselves in the comprehensive Routley Collection. The curators at the Palace Green Library scanned and sent nearly four hundred letters to John Wilson and conducted individual research sessions on Zoom. Librarians at Mansfield found letters, minutes, and articles relating to Routley's student and professional days. The Reformed Church Center at the New Brunswick Theological Seminary in New Jersey awarded me the Poppen-Young Fellowship in 2022. Matt Gasero, former archivist for the Reformed Church in America, found an abundance of documentation relating to *Rejoice in the Lord*. I met with two of the hymnal committee members, Norman Kansfield and Gloria Norton. I am in humble debt to Sr. Mary Martin Jacobs, OP, at the Monastery of Our Lady of the Rosary in Summit, New Jersey, for her time and telling of the making of *The Summit Choirbook*. She patiently corrected my mistakes and answered so many naïve questions.

Todd T. Romoff engraved and digitized the manuscripts of many of Routley's compositions held in the Routley Collection, particularly *Hunsdon*

House, allowing easy access to performers and researchers. He also digitized cassettes of Routley's lectures and the funeral and memorial services.

In Edinburgh, Johnny Bell, Fiona Bennett, Laurence Wareing, Robert Somerville, and Mary Parnaby provided lively anecdotes from the Routley days, as did Ann Jackson, Jo and John Lumsden, Mary Dowse, Ryan Sirmons, Jackie Aitken, and Robin Beaumont in Newcastle. Hugh Banton, electronic organ expert, supplied many of the details concerning the building and installation of St. James's Copeman Hart instrument.

The Hymn Society of the United States and Canada and the United Reformed Church History Society generously supplied much-needed travel grants. Considerable support was also received from James Brumm, Kiyomi Camp, Megan Canfield, and Burgin Mathews.

My Westminster Choir College family came through as always. James Brumm and Mark Trautman, both Routley students, were part of a panel presentation on Routley's hymn writing for the 2021 Christian Congregational Music conference. Their steady support was always reassuring. Joan Lippincott invited me to her home for an interview about her recollections of working with Routley. James Busby, Altanese Cato, Deborah Holden-Holloway, Donald Nally, Phil Rowland, Stephen Schall, Ann Sears, and Thomas Simpson shared hours of candid observations and reflections.

Dear friends opened their doors as I traveled throughout the United States and the UK for eighteen months. I am especially grateful to Bridget Mason in Edinburgh and Ann Ryan and Stu Dember in Princeton. The generosity of Bob and Sofran McBride, Kiyomi Camp and Brad White, Joan and Ken Clark, and Cathey Cawthorne and Teresa Tessner must also be mentioned. Closer to home, Rebekah Abel Lamar, Randy Sheets, Monika Renee Cosson, Carol Lasater, and Whitney Wills guided me through the dark valleys, while West Nottingham Stitch-and-Chat brought new friends, and Mary Joe Crosby reminded me where I came from. Then there's my family. Brothers Mark, Kirk, Nelson, and Douglas are no doubt especially glad this work is completed, though they gave their full supportive attention when I demanded it! Scott and Sara, Whitney and Ava, you are my backbone.

Appendix A

Book Dedications

Erik Routley wrote nearly fifty books; not all of them contained a dedication, but those that did are significant.

The Church and Music

Vitae Christianae artis musicae praeceptoribus, primus optimus deilectissimis (To my first, best and beloved teachers of Christian life and the art of music), John and Eleanor Routley

I'll Praise My Maker

ERM, PWM, TCM, HSM [E. Romilly Micklem, Phyllis Winifred Micklem, Thomas Caryl Micklem, Henry Spedding Micklem], who by forbearance, friendship, hospitality, and Wisdom have interpreted to me the mystery of grace, this book is affectionately dedicated.

Hymns and Human Life

To Margaret, my wife

The Gift of Conversion

I venture to mark a conjunction of events historic and transitory by offering these pages as a token of gratitude and affection to my colleagues of the Senior Common Room: John Marsh, William Cadman, Horton Marlais Davies, and Frances Roger Tomes

The Music of Christian Hymnody

To Kenneth Lloyd Parry

Wisdom of the Fathers

To the Fellowship of Young Congregationalists of Northumbria and Durham. And to Ralph Bell [1912–1987] of Otterburn Hall, I gratefully dedicate these pages, because Ralph is the most improbably theologian I know, and one of the most effective, and because the Fellowship is the best audience I have ever encountered in discussion of the best subjects.

The English Carol

Cyrillo Vincentio Taylor. Ecclesiae Anglicanae Sacerdoti, scholae Regiae Sanctae Musicea olim Custodi, Amico adjutori praeceptori dedicatum (Cyril Vincent Taylor, Priest in the Church of England, Chaplain of the RSCM, Colleague, Teacher, Friend)

Church Music and Theology; Church Music and the Christian Faith

Ian Mackenzie, with respect

Into a Far Country

In Piam Memoriam, Edward Romilly Micklem, Viri iusti, docti, sanct Necon amatoribus iam in saeculo militantibus valde desiderati et in gratias parum persolvandas filio filiaeque Thomas Caryl and Margaret Ruth, amicis dilectissimish, hospitibus, dulcissimus in quorum fidem congaudens hunc labellum dedicate auctor (In reverent memory: Edward Romilly Micklem, and to his son and daughter-in-law, Thomas Caryl and Margaret Ruth, my dearest friends)

Music Leadership in the Church

Bob Mitchell

Twentieth Century Church Music

The Reverend Ronald Johnson, C.B., organist of St. Columba's Episcopal Church, Edinburgh, who knows, loves, and interprets in the local congregation Church Music of all ages

The Puritan Pleasures of the Detective Novel

Patrick, who said, "Why don't you send it to Gollancz?"

Words, Music, and the Church

Dedicated with respect and gratitude to Lloyd A. Pfautsch

A Panorama of Christian Hymnody

To Nathaniel Micklem, D.D., preacher, teacher, scholar, wit, who guided my feet into this path

The Music of Christian Hymns

Dedicated, with affection, to my friend and mentor, John Wilson, our generation's most devoted encourager of fine hymnody.

Appendix B

"The Books That Shaped My Life"

by Erik Routley

The Christian Century, November 2, 1977
(used by permission)
All are available in various reprints.

The Pilgrim's Regress, C. S. Lewis
(J. M. Dent and Sons, 1931)

He Came Down, Charles Williams
(Heinemann Press: London, 1938)

De Incarnatione of St. Athanasius, fourth century

What Is the Faith? Nathaniel Micklem
(Hodder & Stoughton: London, 1936)

Our Approach to God, E. R. Micklem
(Hodder & Stoughton: London, 1934)

The Hymns of Wesley and Watts, Bernard L. Manning
(Epworth Press: London, 1942)

The Courage to Be, Paul Tillich
(Collins Press: London, 1952)

The novels of C. P. Snow

Appendix B

Whyte's Bible Characters, Alexander Whyte
(Oliphant Anderson and Ferrier: Edinburgh, 1896)

Christian Maturity and the Theology of Success, Daniel Jenkins
(SCM Press: London, 1976)

Appendix C

Statement from Sir Ronald Johnson

Sir Ronald Johnson, CB, was secretary of the Scottish Home and Health Department and organist/choirmaster at St. Columba's-by-the-Castle Episcopal Church (ecumenically partnered with Greyfriars Kirk and Augustine United Church). Routley dedicated Twentieth Century Church Music *to Sir Ronald. This tribute is in the private papers of Caryl Micklem.*

Erik Routley as a Singer

Thousands of people have heard Erik Routley's musical tenor voice as he used it to illustrate a point at a choir practice or a teach-in. But comparatively few ever heard him as a soloist or as the leading tenor of a small group. He did not consider it part of his calling—the more's the pity—to arrange musical events in which he himself starred as a singer. But for a few years while he was in Edinburgh, he participated in programmes arranged by an informal group based in a neighbouring church to his own. So, it came about that, at the time when his book *The Musical Wesleys* was no doubt forming in his mind, his high, clear, and sensitive voice was heard in St. Giles' Cathedral in two motets and a solo song by Samuel Wesley. He initially exercised some influence on the group's choice of music. For instance, he encouraged them to venture on Herbert Howells's evening canticles in B minor and proved the proverbial (and much needed) tower of strength when they were performed in St. Mary's Cathedral. Erik also threw himself, with enthusiasm, into such new ideas as the group pet forward. He not only sang in the first performance of David Johnson's setting of Mary McDonald's "Jerusalem, glad I stand in your gates," he got it published by Galliard in *New Songs for the Church*.

Those who were privileged to share these events with Erik will never forget the pleasure of singing alongside a voice which was so musical and so true.

R. E. J.
25 February 1983

Appendix D

Letter to Friends

Letter to friends before leaving Newcastle for the United States, October 31, 1974

From Erik and Margaret to all our friends

We think it has probably got about by now that we are going to America for a while. This is by way of being a temporary farewell, and to let you know what our address will be.

From January 2 until the end of August we can be found at Princeton Theological Seminary, Princeton, NJ, USA, 08540. After that at Westminster Choir College, Princeton (as before). In both cases ER is to be a member of the faculty—one supposes a kind of professor—pursuing the subject of Church Music. We don't actually know at this stage how permanent the second appointment is to be, but the indications are that it will run a few years. The first one, which is temporary, involves an occasional lecture and playing the chapel organ and running the student choir; the second requires some teaching and permits some writing and travelling.

One thing we must advise you all is that you had better not try to send us Christmas cards this year. The removal is a protracted affair. We shall have had to leave our Newcastle home very soon after the first of December and for a while we shall live at our cottage in Northumberland (22 Pennine Road, Halton Lea Gate, Carlisle, CA6 7LB); about the 16th of December we shall go to London (25 Corfton Road, W 5), and on the 23rd we board the ship. Yes, no aeroplane this time, but a ship which unbelievably is running at the time we want. The MS KUNGSHOLM, Swedish-American Line, leaves Southampton that day, calls for one whole day at Bermuda (!) and lands us in New York on 2 January. We are looking forward to the enforced break that this will provide between jobs, and we rely on you all to sing daily "For those in peril on the sea."

Naturally, we shall want to keep in touch with you all, and eventually we intend to come back to England. Some of you may want to know that Margaret's mother, Dorothy Scott, will be living from 18 November with her son Peter Scott, at 25 Corfton Road, W5.

We leave our family scattered about the world. Nicholas is on his way to Australia to join the faculty of music at Sydney University; Patrick will be our senior representative in England. He is now an editor at Stainer & Bell, the music publisher. Priscilla continues for at least one more year at Glasgow [University], and plans a little further musical study after that, but at this moment we are not quite sure what.

We send you all our love,
E. R.
M. R.
Newcastle, November 1974

Appendix E

Letter to John Wilson about *Ecumenical Praise*

Letter to John Wilson in September 1973 relating the creation of Ecumenical Praise

September 7, 1973

My dear John,
This *Ecumenical Praise* hymnbook is, of course, an American idea. While I was over there, I met the other four characters [on the committee] whose names will be familiar to you. Sam Young (as we all know him) is a gifted fellow who, in his youth, was a jazz musician—who played himself twice across the Atlantic. And who I think never had a straight music degree until they made him a Professor and a MusD at Dallas—a great choral conductor, and once a considerable promoter of honkytonk church music which he says he's now had quite enough of. Austin Lovelace is the USA's answer to Eric Thiman—a facile and poised composer who turns out hymn-anthems like shelling peas. He's now organist of a big Methodist church in Dallas. Alec Wyton is a fantastic fellow who knows every musician in the US by his Christian name, who had a lot to do with the HAIR Mass at St. John the Divine, New York, where he is organist. He performs the works of every far-out electronic atonal musician who cares to write for the church. And George Shorney is the principal of Hope Publishing Company, who want to put out an ecumenical supplement for the US of good contemporary mainstream material. Hope Pub. Co. started out in the 1890s as a publisher of Gospel songs. It's sown its wild oats and now looks for something really good. My own job is to dig out likely stuff from Europe. *Cantate Domino* provides a useful quarry, of course, but naturally, I have to consult the sage of Guildford—which, when I come down, I will do. I may wickedly send off some stuff that hasn't passed the Censor, like SHILLINGFORD. So, maybe

you'd look out for a few things which you would like to see exported. We, the editors, are a curiously ill-sorted crew, as you can see, but something interesting might well come of all this. Some of our best Westminster Abbey things ought to be sent in.

Till Friday, and as ever,

Note: "*The sage of Guildford*" *is Routlese for John Wilson, who lived in Guildford.*

Appendix F

Prophetic Article from the *Church Times*

"Hymns for All Seasons"
by Erik Routley
The *Church Times*, August 1981
(used by permission)

"A new shared hymnbook for which every major Church in Britain would abandon its own hymnary has always been difficult to conceive and in the present situation seems a flight of pure fantasy, But . . . " (Reform, January 1981, p. 2).

So, it has come: the one authorized hymnal for the whole of England! As its preface says, "Here you've got the coolest hymnbook ever put out; it's the neatest, the inclusivest, the most sociodemographicalistically oriented bunch of praises we could hammer up."

The book is designed to serve the two major denominations in England—the Church of the Holy Spirit in England and the English Church of the Holy Spirit—which comprise between them ninety-seven percent of the Christian population of the country (and 1.388 percent of the population of the country).

THIRTEEN YEARS' TOIL

The committee which prepared the book originally consisted of one hundred and three members; their work has taken thirteen years, and ninety-eight of them have lived to see its fruit. Perhaps it is an indication of the vitality of Christian debate, and at the same time of the openness of the contemporary Christian mind that the number of hymns this committee agreed to include in the book is as high as 133. To these, I shall come in a moment, but it must be made clear that this is not merely a hymnal. People who have no use for hymns whatever will especially welcome it.

I am not, of course, competent to review the 282 pages of material for liturgical dance, but I think most people will agree that the photographs with which these are illustrated are artistic and mature—qualities we are always glad to find in a hymn book.

Then there is a psalter with a selection of psalms. Two psalms are presented in multiple translations so that they can be sung in the dialects of (to name a few) Oswestry, Hexham, Heckmondwike, Truro, Preston, North End, Preston Southend, Wallsend, and Brixton. Counting a number of variations on what we used to think of as Middle Eastern languages, we have seventy-three versions of each psalm—and here we must pay tribute to the editors for resisting the temptation to make this seventy-five and thus to present a 150-psalm psalter. These editors are men and women of principle, not of fancy.

There is also—for this is a sumptuous book (Why not? After 24 August 2012, it will be illegal to use any other hymnbook, and after that date any church using it will be liable to a fine of 13.8619 percent of its central assessment for every Sunday of such use, and a further 8.772 percent should it ever be used on a Tuesday.)—a collection of anthems.

A hundred years ago those who used to be called Nonconformists included anthems in their hymnals being notorious for their zeal for congregational involvement. But now what the new editors provide are lively songs about the things that mean most to modern Christians—work, eating, making love, and the godly censure of the indolent.

The tunes are simple (few use more than 4 notes), all the songs have choruses, and the pieces are adorned with useful directions for singing and for miming and illustrating the subjects sung about. There are fifty-three of these, one for each Sunday of the year and one for the extra one which comes every few years. Since this extra Sunday gives such pleasure to church finance officers, this one is on the subject of stewardship, and it opens with the haunting lines:

> *Twenty-five pounds*
> *Twenty-five pounds,*
> *Twenty-five hundred miserable*
> *pennies.*

This is a moving ballad about a young woman who, having contributed that paltry sum to a Sunday's collection, was overcome by remorse and became an announcer on Ouse Television. But observe the footnote: "If you want to substitute another adjective for the one in Italics, stick in whatever you like." Spontaneity! Edifying, biting, subtle stuff, plus spontaneity!

Now to the hymns. I need remind nobody of the recent decision of the Hierarchy of Eleven—who, by controlling all details of local church life, have caused to welcome a reduction in ecclesiastical bureaucracy and expense—that by 24 August 2012, church organs must be sold.

The Hierarchy's Guidelines for the Ordering of Spontaneous Worship (edition 2007, page 613, column 2) direct that the only instrument allowed in public worship is the bambo. Our overseas readers may need to be told that this is a stringed instrument played by a hand-held computer which will play only in the keys of B major and F minor. All hymns are set in one of these keys—none, so far as I can see, in both; they are scored with simple computer symbols, and of course, we now need no key signatures.

All we need are two symbols, both in the shape of a key—a large one indicating F minor and a small one indicating B major. One welcomes this touch of creative imagination, one might say of radical and eminently practicable dissent from convention, of built-in paradox, on the editors' part—a gesture as typographically elegant as it is mentally stimulating.

But users of the hymnal need not fear that all is unfamiliar. A quick eye will readily detect several of the great melodies of the past—at No. 66, for example, a pentatonic version of "Pop Goes the Weasel," and at No. 66, under the name SPHERA, the athletic and fascinating "One Fishball," a splendid and long-awaited alternative tune for "All people that on earth do dwell."

Occasionally an ascription goes astray. The tune of No. 97 is attributed to the musical editor, Lucien Fitzgibbon Spiegelscheibewerker, whose name appears 217 times in the book; he is no doubt the arranger, but people of my age recognize it at once as based on a theme in Telemann's 466th Concerto.

It will be noticed that the hymn tunes are in some cases more complex than the music of the psalter or the service settings and certainly than that of the anthems. Indeed, no fewer than forty-seven of the 202 tunes in the book use six or more notes of the scale, and in the Christmas section, the tunes approach a floridity that some will regard as hazardous. This is because the memories of the aged retain many of these quaint tunes; probably they will die with us, and obviously, it was wise to make the new material as easy as possible.

It will come as no surprise that nearly all the texts of the hymns are translations. The taste of the editors in selecting the texts is certainly wide-ranging; a curmudgeonly critic might call it unpredictable. But I think the only hymns that stand in their original texts are the American hymn, "Little drops of water," and that fine old English hymn, "Within the churchyard side by side." Another recondite tune from past history, set to a modern text at No. 77, is "Abide with me." Despite its difficulties, congregations will mostly manage it.

But what one most admires is the way in which texts have been translated into sturdy modern language. I offer three examples: (a) No. 9, "Hear the pleasant voices sing." Seniors will recognize it as a revision of an old hymn, "Hark the herald angels sing"; but who can fail to applaud the theological honesty of editors who fearlessly respond to the known fact that nobody believes in angels, and their linguistic precision in admitting that nobody wants to hark to anything?

In the second stanza, observe with what shrewdness they have excised the vile sexist language of past ages. They have noticed, with true professional alertness, that in America, the phrase "you guys" is acceptable when addressed to mixed company and has been for twenty-five years; so they have boldly substituted "guy" for "man" wherever "man" was used to mean "humanity." Elsewhere they make use of the valuable new pronoun "bish" (with its cognates "bash" and "bosh") to replace "his" where "his" means "his or her."

When looking a hymn up in the index, you must not be surprised when an opening line has been altered. The editors, however, assist us by printing the familiar opening in Gothic type and upside down next to the altered line. Could we ask for anything more helpful"?

(b) No. 33, an old hymn of Isaac Watts, still engages the affections of the elderly, but most people agree that it is much improved by being reduced to two stanzas, the first and last of the original. In what is now the second stanza, the editors, realizing that we do not live in an age of universal joy, very properly delete the reference to "troubles" so that the last two lines now run:

> *You'll keep your blessings*
> *Tumbling fast*
> *Until we all come home.*

In this they faithfully reflect the spirit of the age into which we have been so blissfully ushered.

(c) No. 66. Here is the editorial sensitiveness at its best. You may remember how stanza 3 used to go:

> *O enter then his gates with praise; Approach with joy his*
> *courts unto.*

Modern social conscience cannot obviously, tolerate that. "Gates" suggests that obsession for privacy, which was so typical of the old upper classes, and "courts" the stately homes which once disfigured out countryside. So, the image is altered to something more in keeping with modern social thinking:

*We'll climb the stairs with
Joyful praise;
Approach with joy his rooms unto.*

It is quaint, of course! A charming mixture of ancient and modern. But that's not all. A footnote says that you can sing this if you like: "We'll ride the lifts with joyful praise."

Can social and intellectual flexibility go further?

BLACK BORDER

Well, you must judge for yourselves. After 24 August 2012, this will be our one hymnal. It is published on a page twenty-eight inches by eleven, which is ideal for reading endways on an ironing board. The text type is 48-point. The syllables of all words are separated by hyphens to make for easier reading of polysyllables. The cover is tasteful, there is a piercing relevance about the black border surrounding a panel in puce with a picture of (a member of the committee tells me) a Phoenix descending.

The editorial committee have brought forth now the most significant production in hymnology since Sternhold's Psalms. For this it is worth renouncing all our other hymnals. Nothing is now left but to disband the Executive, bury the Editor, and embalm the Vice-Presidents of the Hymn Society in a final act of salutation and homage to the one eternal and immortal *English Hymnal*.

Erik Routley
Isle of Dogs
30 February 2010 [date intentional]

Bibliography

BOOKS BY ERIK ROUTLEY

A Panorama of Christian Hymnody. The Liturgical Press: Collegeville, MN, 1979. Second Edition, Paul A. Richardson, ed. GIA: Chicago, 2005.
An English-Speaking Hymnal Guide. The Liturgical Press: Collegeville, MN, 1979. Second Edition, Peter Cutts. GIA: Chicago, 2005.
A Historical Study of Christian Hymnody. Oxford University Press: Oxford, 1950.
An Organist's Companion to the Worshipbook. Reformed Liturgy and Music, vol. 9, no. 2. Spring 1975.
Church Music and Theology. Student Christian Movement: London, 1959.
Companion to Congregational Praise. With K. L. Parry. Independent Press: London, 1953.
Companion to Westminster Praise. Hinshaw: Chapel Hill, 1977.
Church Music and the Christian Faith. Agape: Carol Stream, IL, 1978.
Ecumenical Hymnody. Independent Press: London, 1959.
Exploring the Psalms. Westminster Press: Philadelphia, 1975.
I'll Praise My Maker. Independent Press: London, 1951.
Hymns and Human Life. J. J. Murray Press: London, 1953.
Hymns and the Faith. J. J. Murray Press: London, 1955; Seabury Press: Greenwich, CT, 1956.
Hymns Today and Tomorrow. Abingdon Press: New York, 1964.
Into a Broad Land. CCEW: London, 1970.
Into a Far Country. Independent Press: London, 1962.
Is Jazz Music Christian? Epworth Press: London, 1964.
Martin Shaw: A Centenary Appreciation. E. M. Campbell: London, 1975.
Music Leadership in the Church. Abingdon Press: Carol Stream, IL, 1967.
Music, Sacred and Profane. Independent Press: London, 1960.
Saul Among the Prophets. The Upper Room, Abingdon Press: Nashville, 1972.
The Church and Music. Duckworth: London, 1950.
The Divine Formula. Prestige Press: Princeton, NJ, 1985.
The English Carol. Jenkins Press: London, 1958; Oxford University Press: New York, 1959.

The Gift of Conversion. Butterworth Press: London, 1957; Muhlenberg Press: Philadelphia, 1958.
The History of Congregationalism. Independent Press: London, 1961.
The Man for Others. Peter Smith: Derby, 1964; Oxford University Press: New York, 1964.
The Music of Christian Hymnody. Independent Press: London, 1957.
The Music of Christian Hymns. GIA: Chicago, 1981.
The Organist's Guide to Congregational Praise. Independent Press: London, 1957.
The Puritan Pleasures of the Detective Story. Gollancz: London, 1972.
The Story of Congregationalism. Independent Press: London, 1962.
The University Carol Book. H. Freeman: London, 1961.
Twentieth Century Church Music. Jenkins Publishing: London, 1967.
Words, Music and the Church. Abingdon Press: Nashville, 1969.

GENERAL BIBLIOGRAPHY

Adey, Lionel. *Class & Idol and the English Hymn*. University of British Columbia: Vancouver, 1988.
Ahlstrom, S. E. *A Religious History of the American People*. Yale Press: New Haven, 1972.
Argent, Alan. *Elsie Chamberlain: The Independent Life of a Woman Minister*. Equinox Publishing: Sheffield, 2013.
Bayly, Albert. *Rejoice O People: Hymns and Poetry of Albert Bayly*. HSGBI, 1949.
Biser, Larry G., ed. *Joan Lippincott: The Gift of Music*. Organ Historical Society: Richmond, VA, 2013.
Bush, Geoffrey. *An Unsentimental Education*. Thames Publishing: London, 1990.
Brabazon, James. *Dorothy L. Sayers*. Charles Scribner: New York, 1981.
Bradley, Ian. *Believing in Britain: The Spiritual Identity of Britishness*. Lion Hudson: Oxford, 2007.
———. *Marching to the Promised Land*. John Murray: London, 1992.
Brittain, Vera. *England's Hour*. Akadine: London, 1941.
Bush, Geoffrey. *An Unsentimental Education*. Thames Publishing: London, 1990.
Cadoux, Cecil. J. *The Congregational Way*. Blackwell's: Oxford, 1945.
Camroux, Martin. *Ecumenism in Retreat*. Wife & Stock: Eugene OR, 2016.
Carpenter, Humphrey. *The Seven Lives of John Murray*. John Murray: London, 2005.
Companion to Rejoice and Sing. The United Reformed Church: London, 1999.
Como, James T., ed. *C. S. Lewis at the Breakfast Table*. Macmillan: New York, 1979.
Cornick, David. *Under God's Good Hand*. URC: London, 1998.
Cornick, David, and Robert Pope, eds. *Traditions and Transitions: Studies in the History and Theology of the URC*. United Reformed Church: London, 2022.
Cranston, Ian. *I've Seen Worse*. Ian Cranston: 2011.
Downing, Crystal. *Subversive: Christ, Culture, and the Shocking Dorothy Sayers*. Broadleaf Books: Minneapolis, MN, 2020.

Duba, Arlo. *Presbyterian Worship in the Twentieth Century.* Westminster John Knox Press: Louisville, KY 2014.

Eskew, Harry and Hugh McElrath. *Sing with Understanding.* Broadman Press: Nashville, 1980.

Fraser, Ian. *Ecumenical Adventure: A Dunblane Initiative.* ACIS Publication: Glasgow, 2003.

———. "The Beginnings at Dunblane." *Duty and Delight: Routley Remembered.* Robin A. Leaver and James Litton, eds. Hope Publishing: Carol Stream, 1985, 171–90.

• Frazier, Claude. *What Faith Has Meant to Me.* Westminster Press: Philadelphia, 1975.

Galbraith, Douglas. *Square Dance in Heaven.* George Outram & Co: Glasgow, 1966.

———. *Assist Our Song.* St. Andrew Press: Edinburgh, 2021.

———. "Dunblane Praises." CDH.

———. "Scotland in the Sixties and Seventies." *Landmarks in Scottish Church Music,* part 6. https://www.resourcingmission.org.uk/music/general-classical/landmarks-scottish-church-music-scotland-sixties-and-seventies-part-6.

Hackwood, F. W., and Bev Parker. *Wednesbury Faces, Places and Industries.* Ryder & Son: Wednesbury, 1897.

Hageman, Howard. *Our Reformed Church.* Half Moon Press: New York, 1952.

Hanford, Basil. *Lancing College: A History and Memoir.* Philmore Publishing: Bognor Regis, 1986.

Hawn, C. Michael. *Gather into One: Praying and Singing Globally.* Wm. B. Eerdmans: Grand Rapids, MI, 2003.

Hopkins, Michael. *Spires and Meeting Houses: A History of the Origins, Growth and Development of Congregationalism in and around Oxford.* John Owen Press: Farnham, 2011.

Horowitz, Anthony. *The Sentence Is Death.* Harper: New York, 2019.

Huxley, Aldous. *The Genius and the Goddess.* Harper Collins: New York, 1955.

Huxtable, John, John Marsh, E. R. Micklem, James Todd, eds. *A Book of Public Worship.* OUP: London, 1956.

Jackson, Thomas, ed. *The Works of John Wesley*, vol. 13. Wesleyan Conference Office: London, 1865.

Jacques, Reginald, and David Willcocks. *Carols for Choirs,* vol. 1. OUP: London, 1968.

James, Eric. *A Life of Bishop John A.T. Robinson.* Wm. B. Eerdmans: London, 1987.

James, P. D. *Talking about Detective Fiction.* Knopf: New York, 2009.

Karunaratne, S. D. *Hymns and Verse.* Colombo Printers: Ceylon, 1949.

Kaye, Elaine. *Mansfield College Oxford: Its Origin, History and Significance.* Oxford University Press: Oxford, 1997.

Leaver, Robin A. *A Hymnbook Survey: 1962–1980.* Grove Worship Series, no. 71. Grove Books: Bramcote, Nottinghamshire, 1979.

———. *Hymnals, Hymnal Companions, and Collection Development.* Notes. Music Library Association, December 1990.

Leaver, Robin A., and James Litton, eds. Carlton Young, exec. ed. *Duty and Delight: Routley Remembered.* HPC: Carol Stream, IL, 1985.

Lewis, C. S. *The Pilgrim's Regress*. Wm. B. Eerdmans: London, 1933.
———. *Christian Reflections*. Wm. B. Eerdmans: London, 1967.
———. *Letters of C. S. Lewis*. Walter Hooper, ed. Harcourt Brace: New York, 1966.
———. *Weight of Glory*. HarperOne: New York, 2001.
———. *An Experiment in Criticism*. Cambridge University Press: London, 1961.
MacKenzie, Ian. *I Was Invited*. ICS Books: Glasgow, 2003.
———. *Tunes of Glory*. Handsel Press: Carberry, Scotland, 1993.
Mencken, H. L. *On Music*. Alfred Knopf: New York. Renewal, 1961.
Micklem, T. Caryl, and Alison Micklem. *Looking for a Voice: A Hymnological Autobiography*. Alison Micklem, 2017.
Micklem, Nathaniel. *Christian Worship*. Oxford University Press: Oxford, 1936.
———. *The Box and the Puppets*. Geoffrey Bles: London, 1957.
———. *National Socialism and the Roman Catholic Church*. OUP: New York, 1939.
Mitchell, Robert H. *I Don't Like That Music*. HPC: Carol Stream, IL, 1993.
———. *Ministry and Music*. Westminster Press: Philadelphia, 1978.
Moulton, Mo. *The Mutual Admiration Society*. Basic Books: New York, 2019.
Overy, Richard. *1939: Countdown to War*. Viking: New York, 2009.
———. *The Oxford Illustrated History of World War II*. Oxford University Press: Oxford, 2014.
Parnaby, Mary C. *The History of Augustine Church, 1877–1941*. Augustine United Church: Edinburgh, 2011.
———. *The History of Augustine-Bristo Church, 1941–1977*. Augustine United Church: Edinburgh, 2011.
Phillips, C. S. *Hymnody Past and Present*. SPCK: London, 1937.
Pottie, Charles S. *A More Profound Alleluia: Gelineau and Routley on Music in Worship*. Pastoral Press: Washington, DC, 1984.
Prothero, Rowland. *Psalms in the Human Life*. J. J. Murray: London, 1903.
Rees, Ivor Thomas. *Saintly Enigmas: A Biography of Pennar Davies*. Y Lolfa Cyf Ceredigion, Wales, 2011.
Robinson, John A. T. *Honest to God*. Westminster Press: Philadelphia, 1963.
Runyon, Damon. *Runyon from First to Last*. Constable Press: London, 1968.
Sayers, Dorothy L. *Gaudy Night*. Harper & Row: New York, 1936.
———. *The Man Born to Be King*. Classical Academic Press: Peabody, MA, 2014.
Self, Peter. *Through a Glass Brightly*. Unfinished autobiographical manuscript, The British Library.
Smith, Mark, ed. *British Evangelical Identities*, vol. 1. Authentic Media: Milton Keynes, UK, 2008.
Tindall, Adrienne. *Encounter with Erik Routley*. Darcey Press: Vermont Hills, IL, 1997.
Tomkins, Stephen. *That They All May Be One*. URC: London, 2022.
Tucker, Anthony, ed. *Mansfield's Ministry: A Celebration of Ordination Training at Mansfield College, Oxford, 1886–2009*. URC Historical Society: London, 2009.
Wain, John. *Sprightly Running*. MacMillan: London, 1965.
Watson, J. R. *An Annotated Anthology of Hymns*. Oxford University Press: London, 2002.

Westermeyer, Paul. *Let the People Sing: Hymns Tunes in Perspective.* GIA: Chicago, 2005.
———. *With Tongues of Fire: Profiles in 20th Century Hymn Writing.* Concordia Publishing House: St Louis, 1995.
Warson, Gillian R. *Healing the Nations: Fred Kaan, the Man and His Hymns.* Stainer Bell: London, 2006.
Williams, Charles. *He Came Down from Heaven.* Wm. B. Eerdmans: London, 1938.
Wooten, Janet. *This Is Our Song: Women's Hymn-writing.* WPF Stock: Eugene, OR, 2010.
Wren, Brian. *Praying Twice.* John Knox Press: Louisville, KY, 2000.
———. *Barefoot in the Dust: A Hymn-poet's Memoir.* Cascade Books: Eugene, OR, 2017.
Young, Carlton R. *I'll Sing On: My First 96 Years.* GIA: Chicago, 2022.
———. *Our Lives Be Praise: The Hymn Tunes, Carols and Texts of Erik Routley.* HPC: Carol Stream, IL, 1990.

HYMNALS AND SUPPLEMENTS

100 Hymns for Today. A & M Supplement. William Clowes & Sons, 1969.
Book of Worship for the United States Armed Forces. US Government Printing Office, 1974.
Cantate Domino 1975; 1980, music edition. World Council of Churches. Oxford University Press: London.
Church Hymnary. Church of Scotland. Canterbury Press: 1973, 2005.
Communion Hymns and Motets for Choirs. Erik Routley, ed. Worldwide Music Publishing: New York, 1964.
Congregational Praise. Independent Press: London, 1951.
Dunblane Praises, No. 1 & No. 2. Dunblane Consultations on Music, 1964, 1965.
Ecumenical Praise, Carlton Young, exec. ed. Lovelace, Routley, Wyton, eds. Agape: Nashville, 1977.
Eternal Light. Erik Routley, ed. Carl Fischer: New York, 1971.
Glory to God. Louisville, KY: Presbyterian Publishing Co., 2013.
Hymns Ancient and Modern. William Clowes: London, 1940.
Hymns A &M, Revised. Canterbury Press: London, 1950, 1981.
Hymns and Songs. Methodist Publishing House: London, 1969.
Hymns for Celebration. Erik Routley and John W. Wilson, eds. RSCM: London, 1974.
Hymns for Church and School. Novello: London, 1964.
Hymnal 1982. The Episcopal Church. Church Hymnal Corporation: 1985.
The Mennonite Hymnal. Herald Press: Scottdale, PA, 1969.
Methodist Hymnal, 1966. Carlton Young, ed. The Methodist Publishing House: Nashville, 1966.
New Church Praise. URC. St Andrew Press: Edinburgh, 1975.
New Songs of the Church. No. 1 and No. 2. Reginald Barrett-Ayres and Erik Routley, eds. Scottish Churches House: 1969.

Presbyterian Hymnbook. David Hugh Jones, ed. Presbyterian Church in the US: Richmond, VA, 1955.
Rejoice and Sing. Oxford University Press: London, 1991.
Rejoice in the Lord. Erik Routley, ed. Wm. B. Eerdmans: Grand Rapids, MI, 1985.
Rejoice O People: *Hymns and Poetry of Albert Bayly.* HSGBI, 1949.
St. James's Church Newcastle Supplementary Hymns, 1973.
Scottish Students Song Book. Millar Patrick, ed. Bayley & Ferguson: Glasgow: 1897.
Selection of Hymns for Public Worship in Christian Churches. William L. Alexander, ed. Hugh Paton, Adam Square: Edinburgh, 1849.
Sing Sociability Songs. Rodeheaver: Winona Lake, IN, 1928.
Sixteen Hymns of Today for Use as Simple Anthems. John W. Wilson and Fred Pratt Green, eds. RSCM. Halstan: Amersham, England, 1978.
Songs of Syon. George R. Woodward, ed. Schott: London, 1904.
Supplement '96. HPC: Carol Stream, IL,1996.
The Cambridge Hymnal. David Holbrook and Elizabeth Poston, eds. CUP: Cambridge, 1967.
The Clarendon Hymn Book. Oxford University Press, 1936.
The Church Hymnary. David Evans, ed. OUP: London, 1927.
The Public School Hymnbook. Headmasters Conference. Novello: London, 1959.
The Summit Choir Book. Dominican Nuns of Summit. Monastery of Our Lady of the Rosary: Summit, NJ, 1983.
The Worshipbook. Westminster John Knox Press: Louisville, KY, 1972.
Westminster Praise. Erik Routley, ed. Hinshaw, 1977.
Worship Song. W. Garrett Horder, ed. Novello: London, 1905.

THESES

Elias, Hannah (2016). "Radio Religion: War, Faith, and the BBC 1937–1948." McMaster University, Hamilton, ON.
Gay, Douglas C. (2006). "A Practical Theology of Church and World." University of Edinburgh, UK.
Hopkins, Michael (2010). "Congregationalism in Oxford." University of Birmingham, Birmingham, UK.
Leask, Margaret Anne (2000). "The Development of English-language Hymnody: 1960–1995." University of Durham, Durham, UK.

JOURNALS AND PUBLICATIONS

Bulletin. HSGBI. www.hymnsocietygbi.org.uk.
Congregational Monthly. Archived. CCEW: London, 1951. www.worldcat.org/title/6060690.

Lancing College Magazine. www.lancingcollege.co.uk/lancing-college/news-and-events/publications.
Mansfield College Magazine. www.mansfield.ox.ac.uk/news-publications.
News of Hymnody. Archived. Palace Green Library, FPG Collection, Durham University.
Oxford Daily Mail. www.oxfordmail.co.uk.
Reform. www.reform-magazine.co.uk.
Reformed Liturgy and Music. Archived. Presbyterian Board of Publications, Louisville, KY.
RSCM News. www.rscm.org.uk.
Scottish Church History Society. https://www.scottishchurchhistory.org.
The *British Weekly.* Archived. Redbridge Heritage Center. www.visionrcl.org.uk.
The *Church Times.* www.churchtimes.co.uk/.
The Guardian. www.theguardian.com.
The Hymn. HSUSC. www.thehymnsociety.org.
The Independent. www.independent.co.uk.
The Journal. URC Historical Society. www.urchistory.wordpress.com/the-journal.
The Scotsman. www.scotsman.com.
The Times. www.thetimes.co.uk.
Town Topics. www.towntopics.com.
Worship. www.journalworship.org.

REFERENCE SOURCES

Ancestry.com (www.ancestry.com)
Choral Public Domain Library (www.cpdl.org)
Dictionary of Nineteenth-Century Journalism in Great Britain and Ireland. Gent: Academia Press, 2009.
Hymnary.org (www.hymnary.org)
The Canterbury Dictionary of Hymnology (www.hymnology.hymnsam.co.uk)
The Oxford Dictionary of National Biography (www.oxforddnb.com)
Who They Were in the Reformed Churches of England and Wales, 1901–2000. (URC). Binefield, Clyde and John Taylor, eds. Shaun Tyas: Donnington, 2007.
Wikipedia (www.en.wikipedia.org)

ARCHIVES

Magdalen College Library. Oxford, UK.
Mansfield College Library. Oxford, UK.
Reformed Church of America Archives, Sage Library. New Brunswick Theological Seminary. New Brunswick, NJ.

The Fred Pratt Green Collection. Palace Green Library, Durham University, Durham, UK.
The Routley Collection. Talbott Music Library. Rider University, Lawrenceville, NJ.
The Speer Library. Princeton Theological Seminary, Princeton, NJ.

VIDEOS

Sayers, Dorothy L. *The Man Born to Be King.* www.youtube.com/results?search_query=dorothy+sayers+man+born+to+be+king.
URC St. James's Newcastle Hymns. *Inaugural Recital, Copeman-Hart Organ, 1973.* Lionel Dakers. www.youtube.com/watch?v=9mcK02-qrU4&list=PLieAW-noRArDxHs2Hr7fAe0QBoYJ_AXgI.

Index

Albright, William, 152
Alexander, William L., 79–80. *See also* Augustine-Bristo
"All who love and serve your city," 91–92. *See also* Dunblane
Allen, Hugh P., 41–42
AUGUSTINE, 85–86, 173
Augustine-Bristo Church, 70–71, 79–80, 105, 114, 102n78; Augustine Church, 80, 99n6; Augustine United Church, 80, 92; boiler, 82; Bristo Congregational Church, 80–82; Church family night, 97–98; Duthrie, Charles, 70; Harley, Elspeth, 99, 105n117; Hayes Conference Center, Swanwick, 82, 100n23; Martin, William B., 78n140; Ministry, 82–83; music tradition, 80; North College St. Congregational Church, 79–80; Somerville, Robert, 84

Baker, Robert S., 127. *See also* Union Theological Seminary
Baptist Theological Seminary: Drexel Lectures, 128. *See also* Mitchell
Barker, Thomas, 32. *See also* Mansfield (1880s)
Barrett-Ayres, Reginald, 87–89, 101n55. *See also* Dunblane

Bayley, Albert, 69–70, 77n125, n129
BBC. *See* British Broadcasting Company
Beck, Geoffrey, xii, 46, 52, 68–69, 70–71, 77nn116–117, 82, 109, 116, 121n3, 151–52; Coventry Cathedral, 68–69; Summertown, 68; Von Trott, Adam, 164n6
Bell, Ralph, 182
Benson, Edward, 100n31. *See also* Willcocks
Berry, G. W., 19n89
Biser, Larry G., 150. *See also* Westminster Choir College
Book of Public Worship, 81. *See also* Congregationalism
Bower, John Dykes, 69–70, 77n132
Brent Smith, Alexander, 5, 7–11, 17n40, 18n54, 140, 172. *See also* Lancing College
Brighton, 1–15; Queen Square (Union) Congregational Church, 2–3. *See also* Langridge
Bristol Chapel, 154, 162, 174n5; office 140, 154, 174n10; funeral ix, xiv, 171–72. *See also* Chapel (WCC)
Bristol, Lee Hastings, 121n8, 128, 131, 134, 139, 143–44, 162, 165n10, 167n82

207

British Broadcasting Company, 22–23, 36n14, 57, 75, 77n125, 83–84, 101n56, 115. *See also* Lewis; Sayers; World War II
British Weekly, 65–66, 76n105, 85, 108; Nichol, William, 66; Stoddart, Jane, 76n101
Britten, Benjamin, 107
Brock, Carolyn, 108, 121n15, 125n84
Brombaugh, Mark, 145. *See also* Westminster Choir College
Brumm, James, 163, 179. *See also* Westminster Choir College
Bulletin, 58–59, 79; editors, 74n61; Patrick, Millar 58, 74n61. *See also* HSGBI; Massey; Wilson
Bush, Geoffrey, 2, 5–6, 8, 10, 17n31, 28–29. *See also* Lancing College

Cadman, William, 79, 99n2, 181
Cadoux, Cecil J., 34, 35n97, 50–51, 72n8
Caird, George, 30n104, 45, 66, 68, 70, 77n114, n116, 99n2, 123n44, 175n16; Caird, Mollie, 78, 137, 81
Cambridge University, 12, 31–32, 39n79, 59, 80–81, 108, 133, 146, 156; Caius College, 84; Emmanuel College, 97; St. John's College, 97. *See also* Willcocks
Cantate Domino, 107, 109–11, 129, 131, 140, 191
Carter, Sydney, 90, 103n102. *See also* Dunblane
Chapel (WCC), 137–39, 141, 143, 145, 150, 152, 154, 156–58, 161, 163; Director, 154; Student Chapel Committee 137, 139, 148, 157, 166n57, 174n5. *See also* Westminster Praise
The Christian Century, 185
Christian Congregational Music, 179
Christie, Agatha: Crime Writers' Association, 116; Detection Club, 116, 124n65; Inspector Poirot, 115. *See also Puritan Pleasures*
The Church and Music, 62
Church Music and the Christian Faith, 27, 115
The Church of England, xii, 24, 29, 31–32, 111; *Book of Common Prayer*, 30–31; Elizabethan religious settlement, 30, 38n75; Oxford preachers, 24; schools, 3–5, 7; *Toleration Act* (1689), 42; *Universities Tests Act*, 82
The Church of Scotland, 86, 97, 101n49, 103n111
The Church Times, 193
Coggins, Donald, 75n73
Colvin, Tom, 165n21. *See also* Dunblane
composing, ix, xi, 3–4, 9–10, 29–30, 45–46, 69–70, 86, 98, 128, 149
Conder, Josiah, 63
The Congregational Church of England and Wales (CCEW), 96, 117–18, 124n71
Congregationalism, 30, 32–34, 42, 120; academies, 31, 39n79; church meeting, 84; church names, 99n6
The Congregational Monthly, 66, 70, 76n103
The Congregational Organists' Guild, 54, 69, 77n121, 124n71
Congregational Praise, 4, 45–47, 54, 57, 64–66, 76n93, 77n121, 81, 110, 115, 119, 159; *Companion*, 66, 75n65
The Congregational Society, 54–57, 74n45; choir, 57; Horton, Robert F., 55; The Lake District, 56–57. *See also* Mansfield College (1948–1959); Runyon
The Congregational Union of England and Wales (CUEW), 45, 55, 70, 73n41, 96, 117
Cornick, David, 109

Courtney, Robert, 54, 73n33, 74n45. *See also* Congregational Society
Cowper, William, 63
Cutts, Peter, 92, 102n71, 132, 140, 143, 164n5, 165n30. *See also* Dunblane

Dakers, Lionel, 114–15, 123n60, 157. *See also* RSCM
Dartford Congregational Church, 46–47, 52, 120
Davies, Horton, 40n104, 53, 67. 73n25, 77n114, 149, 168n108, 181
Davies, William Thomas (Pennar), 51, 72n15, 72n16
Dirksen, Richard E., 143; VINEYARD HAVEN, 143, 144
dissertation, 64, 76n91
Dodd, Charles, 72n5
Doddridge, Philip, 63
Dominican Monastery of Our Lady of the Rosary, 111–13.
Duba, Arlo, 131, 134–36, 165n27. *See also* PTS
Dudley-Smith, Timothy, 151
Dunblane Music Consultations, 86–93, 96–97, 110, 122n37, 172, 178; "All who love and serve your city," 91–92; Gay, Douglas, 87, 101n32; Scottish Churches Ecumenical Council, 86, 97; Scottish Churches House, 86, 101n65; skiffle, 90, 101n49; Wilson, Jock, 89, 101n58
Duty and Delight, ix, xi, 30, 175nn17–18, n21; "In praise of God meet duty and delight," 46, 174. *See also* Leaver, Robin
Dykes, John Bacchus, 44, 77n132

Ecumenical Praise, 129, 141, 144, 148, 151–52, 191; editors, 129, 151, 191
ecumenism, 50, 68, 71, 76, 77n116, 85, 103n111, 105, 109–11, 114, 117, 167n83. *See also* Dunblane; *Ecumenical Praise*; Vatican II; World Council of Churches

Edinburgh, 61, 85, 98, 106, 127–28, 161, 179; Christian Aid, 85, 100n40; Cranley School for Girls, 80, 106; festival, 93–94; George IV Bridge, 79; George Heriot's School, 89; Greyfriars Kirk, 83, 85; Heriot Watt College, 85; Jubilee Scotland, 85, 100n41; New College, 97; Penney tenement, 85, 100n27; St. Columba-by-the-Castle, 85; Scottish Congregational College, 70
Emmanuel College, Toronto, 66–67
An English-Speaking Hymnal Guide, 142–43. *See also* Cutts; Westminster Choir College
Eskew, Harry, 61, 74n55. *See also* HSUSC

Fairbairn, Andrew Martin, 33, 39nn92–93, 66. *See also* Mansfield College (1880s–1943)
Faustini, João, 123n40. *See also* *Ecumenical Praise*
financial issues, 60, 116, 128–29; salary, 165n15
Fischer, Robert Harley, 127. *See also* Princeton (1975)
Flummerfelt, Joseph, 144, 150, 154, 171, 174n5
Fonthill Preparatory Academy, 3–4, 12, 115; McWilliams, Margaret, 124n62, 140; Wrightson, Winifred Barbara, 6. *See also* Brighton
Fox, Douglas G. A., 41, 47n3
Fraser, Ian, 87–93. *See also* Dunblane
Frère, Bartle, 5. *See also* Lancing
Funfgeld, Greg, 139, 167n66, n93
Fyfe, Lois and Peter, 168n105

Galbraith, Douglas, 86, 101n51, 102n71, 177. *See also* Dunblane
GIA Publications, 142–43
Goodall, David, 52–53, 70, 73n22, 125n88, 132

Goshen College, 94, 96, 102n92, 128. *See also* Oyer
Gould, Peter J., 10. *See also* Lancing
Graham, Andrew, 80. *See also* Augustine-Bristo
Gray, Nancy Wicklund, ix, xi, 177; Gray, Raymond, 177; Scott, Susan, 177

Hageman, Howard, 134, 139, 150. *See also* Liturgical Studies Institute; NBTS; RIL
Hall, Gwen, 124n77. *See also* URC
Hall, Raymond, 107–9, 114, 121n10. *See also* St. James's
Hampton, Calvin, 144. *See also* Ecumenical Praise
Harvard University, 66; Harvard Memorial Chapel 66
Hawn, C. Michael, 169n144
health, 116, 128, 165n12
Henry VIII, 24, 30, 38n76. *See also* Church of England
Herbert, George, 85–86, 101nn44–45. *See also* AUGUSTINE
Hinshaw Music, Inc., 91, 140, 146, 148. *See also* Westminster Praise
Hope, Leslie Townes, 146
Hope Publishing Company, 77, 91, 102n73, 129, 144, 148, 173, 191
Hopkins, Michael, 39n96, 177; United Reformed Church History Society, 179
Hopson, Hal, 161, 163. *See also* Nashville
Horder, John, 5–8; Horder, William Garrett, 17n27. *See also* Lancing
Horton, Robert H., 55, 73n39; New College, (Oxford) 55
housing, 2, 29, 44, 46, 67, 72, 80, 98, 121n5, 106, 130, 133, 135, 138, 147
Howells, Herbert, 107, 187
Howitt, William M., 7, 10–12, 18n67. *See also* Lancing

Hughes, Carys, 115. *See also* St. James's
Hugill, John C., 5. *See also* Lancing
Huxley, Aldous, 100n24
Huxtable, John, 119, 124n83, 149. *See also* URC
hymnals: *Cantate Domino*, 107, 109–111, 128n39, 129, 131, 140, 191; *The Church Hymnary*, 81, 119; *Common Praise*, 46; *Congregational Church Hymnary*, 43; *Congregational Praise*, 4, 45–47, 54, 57, 64–66, 77n121, 81, 110, 115, 119, 159; *Dunblane Praises*, 92; *Ecumenical Praise*, 129, 141, 144, 148, 151–52, 191; *The English Hymnal*, 4, 11; *Hymns Ancient and Modern*, 4, 11, 69, 80; *Hymns for Celebration*, 153; *The Mennonite Hymnary*, 96; *The Mennonite Hymnal*, 96; *New Songs for the Church*, 107; *The Pilgrim Hymnal*, 139–40; *The Presbyterian Hymnal* (1955), 158; *Rejoice and Sing*, 119, 125n84; *Rejoice in the Lord*, xiv, 158–60, 162, 178; *Songs of Syon*, 113; *The Summit Choirbook*, 111–13; *Westminster Praise*, 91, 139, 144, 146, 148, 167n70; *The Worshipbook*, 130, 158; *Worship Song*, 4, 29. *See also* Wilson
hymn explosion, xiii, 69, 112. *See also* Dunblane
Hymns and Human Life, 64–65, 181
Hymns for Today and Tomorrow, 164n7
Hymns of the Faith, 65
Hymn Society of Great Britain and Ireland (HSGBI), 58, 61, 69, 75n74, 131–32, 174; leaving, 131–32; Lewis, C. S., 27
Hymn Society of the United States and Canada (HSUSC), 96, 143, 179

I'll Praise My Maker, 63

immigration, 131, 165n25, 168n121; green cards 151. *See also* PTS; Westminster Choir College
Iona Community, 87, 92. *See also* Dunblane
Jacobs, Sr. Mary Martin, OP, 178. *See also* Dominican Monastery
Jenkins, Daniel, 40n104, 66, 76n108, 120, 172, 186
John Murray, Ltd., 64–65
Johnson, Sir Ronald, 103n111, 182, 187–88. *See also* Edinburgh
Jones, David Hugh, 130, 165n24. *See also* hymnals; PTS
Junior Commons Room (JCR), 22, 29, 32, 35, 53, 68, 70, 73n25, 97, 168n108, 168n110. *See also* Mansfield (1940–1943)

Kaan, Fred, 122n38, 123n21. *See also Cantate Domino*
Kansfield, Norman, 159, 163, 171, 178. *See also* RIL
Karunaratne, S. D., 69
Kaye, Elaine, 34, 54, 78n137, 164n4
Kelly, Thomas, 99n6
Kemp, Helen, 154, 156–57, 161, 167, 171, 174n5. *See also* Westminster Choir College
Kemp, John, 137, 151, 154, 156–57, 161, 171, 174n5. *See also* Westminster Choir College

Lancing College, 4–13, 34, 151, 172; Officer Training Corps, 6–7; Olds, 5, 17n31, n40; Woodard Corporation, 4
Langridge, Douglas W., 14–15, 34, 43
Leaver, Robin A., xiii, 59, 160, 173, 178. *See also* Westminster Abbey
lessons and carols, 100n31; Mansfield 57; Westminster Choir College, 148, 152. *See also* Willcocks
Let the People Sing: Hymn Tunes in Perspective, 143. *See also* Westermeyer

Lewis, Clive S., 24–28, 30, 41, 68, 124n64, 185; BBC, 25–26, 37n34; first sermon, 24–25; KILNS, 28; "On Church Music," 27; *The Pilgrim's Regress*, 30, 124n64, 185; Routley correspondence, 27; Socratic Club, 26. *See also* BBC
Lippincott, Joan H., 150, 154, 168n115, 179. *See also* Westminster Choir College
Litton, James, 134, 150, 154, 165n26, 166n41, 168n106, 170n161. *See also* PTS
Liturgical Studies Institute, 149, 158, 168n112
Loh, I-to, 123n40. *See also Ecumenical Praise*
Lovelace, Austin P., 127, 129, 144, 164n5, 191. *See also Ecumenical Praise*
Luff, Alan, xii, 91, 124n63, 172–73. *See also* Dunblane; Bristol Chapel; Westminster Abbey
Lumsden, Joanna and John, 74n47, 179. *See also* Congregational Society; St. James's
Lutheran School of Theology, 127

Macarthur, Arthur, 118. *See also* Newcastle; URC
Mackennal, Alexander, 39, 50–51, 53, 72n9
Mackenzie, Ian, 88, 101n56, 182; Student Christian Movement, 88. Dunblane
Magdalen College, Oxford, 21–30; Classical Exhibition and State Scholarship, 21; *Hunsdon House*, 30; Oxford Bach Choir, 28, 41. *See also* World War II
Manning, Bernard Lord, 63, 72n13, 185
Mansfield College, 66, 70, 127, 163, 164n4, 172–73. *See also* World War II

Mansfield College (1880s–1943), 30, 34, 45, 48n25, 162; Dale, William T., 33; foundations, 30–34; liberal theology, 31; Mansfield family 31; Old Testament scholars, 50, 39n96, 72n5; Paton, John Brown, 33. *See also* World War II

Mansfield College (1948–1959), 52, 71; chaplaincy, 53, 70; finances, 49; Permanent Private Hall, 49, 70, 71n2; postwar, 49–50; thesis, 41, 62; tutorship, 52–53; women, 49–50, 72n3

Massey, Bernard, 59, 74n61, 132, 166n32. *See also* HSGBI

Matthews, Arnold Gwynne, 63

McCord, James T., 128, 130–32, 134–35, 137; McCord, Hazel, 136, 138. *See also* PTS

McGill University, 66

McPhee, George, 88, 102n71, 144, 156, 167n85. *See also* Dunblane

Micklem, E. Romilly, 34, 44–45, 54, 63, 73n29, 86, 101n47, 181–82

Micklem, Nathaniel, 34–35, 43, 45, 50–53, 60, 70n1, 72n13, 73n29, 183

Micklem, Ruth (Margaret Ruth Monroe), 55–56, 57, 175n12

Micklem, T. Caryl, xii, 6, 30, 34, 44–46, 57, 64, 67, 102n71, 125n84, 263n132, 149, 163, 172–74, 175n12, 181–82, 187

Miller, Darryl Ray, 163–64. *See also* Nashville

Mitchell, Robert, 93–94, 182; American Baptist Seminary, 93, 102n81–82

Montgomery, James, 63

Moore, A. B., 67

Moore, Gerald, 107, 121n12. *See also* St. James's

Morrell, Clark, 164. *See also* Nashville

Music and Theology, 27

The Music of Christian Hymns, xi, 142–43, 149. *See also* Westermeyer; Westminster Choir College

Music Leadership in the Church, 164n7

The Musical Wesleys, 187

Nafziger, Ken, 96. *See also* Oyer

Nashville, 162–163

National Churches Trust, 80

New Brunswick Theological Seminary (NBTS), 65, 149, 158, 163; Poppen-Young Fellowship, 179; Reformed Church Center, 178; Second Reformed Church of New Brunswick, 163, 170n158

Newcastle, 105; City Central Churches Council, 114; postwar, 105; Tyne Tees Television, 115. *See also* World War II

New Church Praise, 48n28, 119–20. *See also* URC

New College (Edinburgh), 97

New English Bible, 89, 101n62

New Genevans, 50, 72n13. *See also* Micklem, Nathaniel

Newton, John, 63

Nuttall, Geoffrey, 51, 72n17. *See also* Wednesbury

organ builders: A. E. Ingram, 80; Banton, Hugh, 179; Compton Organs of London, 108; Copeman Hart, 109, 114; D. & T. Hamilton, 80; Miller Organs of Norwich, 108; J.W. Walker and Sons, 31. *See also* St. James's

Our Lives Be Praise, xiv

Oxford Organists' Association, 108, 121n14

Oyer, Mary, 13, 94–96, 102n93, 128, 143; University of Michigan, 95.

Page, Sue Ellen, 161, 174n5. *See also* Westminster Choir College

Paisley Abbey, 144, 161, 177. *See also* McPhee; Routley, Priscilla

A Panorama of Christian Hymnody, xii, 62, 142–49, 167, 173, 191. *See*

also Richardson; Westminster
  Choir College
Parry, Kenneth L., 84–85, 181. *See also*
  Congregational Praise
Perkins School of Theology, 16n15,
  78n140, 130, 168n104
Perrin, Ronald, 115. *See also* St. James's
Pfautsch, Lloyd, 151–52, 157, 183;
  A Day for Dancing, 157. *See also*
  immigration
Philips, C. S., 64–65, 76n88
Pilling, Robert Makin, 109–9, 122n23,
  122n26. *See also* organ builders
Pratt Green, Fred, xii, 115, 123n40,
  139–40, 148, 152–54, 165n21. *See*
  also Wilson
The Presbyterian Church of
  England, 96, 118
Presbyterian conference
  centers: Massanetta Springs, 138,
  164n9; Mo Ranch, 130, 164n9;
  Montreat, 130, 164n9
Princeton, ix, xi, xiv, 66–67, 112,
  133–34, 138, 141, 152, 157, 162,
  166n37, 171–79, 189; invitation,
  130–31; travel plans, 132, 189; first
  year, 140–41
Princeton Theological Seminary, xi,
  xiv, 132–34, 138, 141, 158–59, 189;
  chapel services, 135, 189; early
  days, 133; Holy Week (1975), 136,
  166n49; Student Chapel Committee,
  134–35; summer sessions,
  164n9, 165n30

The Puritan Pleasures of the Detective
  Story: authors, 115; James, P. D.,
  116. *See also* Christie, Agatha

Regent's Park College, 53. *See also*
  Davies, Horton
Rejoice in the Lord (RIL), xiv, 158–60,
  162, 178; inclusive language,
  161. *See also* Hageman; NBTS
retirement, xiii, 130, 152, 161

Richardson, Paul A., 67, 142–43,
  167n79, 177. *See also A Panorama*
  of Christian Hymnody
Rimmer, Frank, 93, 102n84. *See*
  also Edinburgh
Roan, L. Eugene, 150. *See also*
  Westminster Choir College
Robinson, John A. T., 119, 124n79;
  Honest to God, 119
Robinson, Ray, 131, 134, 139, 148,
  154, 157, 171, 175n18. *See also*
  Westminster Choir College
Romoff, Todd T., 178. *See*
  also composing
Rooper, Jasper, 6, 8–10. *See*
  also Lancing
Routley, Eleanor Clark, 2–3, 9, 16n5,
  46–47, 74n48
Routley, John, 1–3, 9, 16n5,
  46–47, 74n48
Routley, Margaret (Scott), 44–47, 52,
  55, 92n21, 106, 113, 117, 123n55,
  166, 191–92; Erik's work schedule,
  140; gardening, 138, 153; getting to
  know Princeton, 133–34; Gibbons,
  145, 154; studios, 67–68, 80, 156,
  161; travel to England, 144–45,
  148, 151, 155; US travel, 137–38,
  146–47, 155, 160–61
Routley, Nicholas, 47, 67, 81, 84, 96,
  106, 177, 190. *See also* Cambridge
Routley, Patrick, 67, 81, 84–85, 106,
  115, 173, 177, 182, 190; Routley,
  Angela, 177. *See also* AUGUSTINE;
  Cambridge; *Puritan Pleasures*
Routley, Priscilla, 67, 81, 106, 177, 190
The Routley Collection, xii, 178. *See*
  also Sussmeier, Stephanie
Rowland, Prothero, 64, 76n87
Royal College of Music, 9, 59
Royal School of Church Music, xi, 62,
  84,107, 121nn8–9, 151, 157, 165n10
Runyon, Damon, 55–56, 74n48;
  Hammer, Ambrose 56–57. *See also*
  Congregational Society

Rutter, John, 161

San Francisco Theological Seminary, 146–47
Sankey, Ira D., 123n56, 142
Sayers, Dorothy L, 26; Lord Peter Wimsey, 26; *The Man Born to be King,* 26, 37n42, 47. *See also* Puritan Pleasures
Scarritt Graduate School, xiv, 163–64; Fyfe, Lois and Peter, 168n105; Miller, Darryl Ray, 163–64; Morrell, Clark, 164; Warren, James I., 164. *See also* Nashville
Schall, Stephen, 174n10. *See also* Bristol Chapel
Schisler, Charles, 137, 154, 157, 161–62, 166n55, 171, 174n5. *See also* Westminster Choir College
Scott, Nathan A., 94. *See also* Oyer
Scott, Peter, 29–30, 35, 43, 77n114, 117, 124n70, 148, 161; Scott, Anne Renwick, 37n45, 148, 161; Scott, Dorothy Brodgen, 67, 144, 148, 155, 158, 190. *See also* Magdalen; Mansfield (1880s–1943)
Selbie, William B., 50, 66. *See also* Wednesbury
Shannon, James, 135; *Book of Worship for the US Armed Forces,* 66n47. *See also* PTS
Shorney, George, 129, 151, 174, 191. *See also* HPC
singing, 138, 172; *Benediction,* Peter C. Lutkin 171; hymn sing, 44, 155; Westminster Symphonic Choir, 148, 155, 168n107. *See also* Flummerfelt; lessons and carols
Sleeth, Natalie, 162
Somerset, 1–2. *See also* Routley, John
Somerville, Charles, 81, 84, 98–99, 156. *See also* Augustine-Bristo
Sosa, Pablo, 123n40. *See also* Ecumenical Praise

St. James's Congregational Church, 85, 97–98, 105–9, 118; becoming the URC, 115–24; ministry, 114–15; music, 106; organ, 107–8, 114. *See also* URC
The Stone Lectures, 128, 164nn8–9. *See also* PTS
The Summit Choirbook, 111–13. *See also* Dominican Monastery
Sussmeier, Stephanie, 178. *See also* Routley Collection
Swann, Donald, 149; Flanders & Swann, 98, 103n109

Taylor, Cyril, 67, 182
Thiman, Eric, 45, 191
Tranchell, Peter, 84, 100n35. *See also* Cambridge
Trautman, Mark, 142, 179. *See also* Westminster Choir College
Trinity Congregational Church (Wednesbury), 42–43; Eggington, Edward, 42–43; ordination, 43. *See also* Wesley, John
Trinity Episcopal Church (Princeton), 137, 148, 153, 166n41; Bertalot, John, 168n105; funeral, xiv, 171
Tucker, Anthony, 51, 55
Twentieth Century Church Music, 92

Union Theological Seminary, 66, 127
United Reformed Church, xi, 77n121, 80, 116–21, 128, 176, 179; *Bill of Establishment,* 118; Congregational Federation, 120; Doctrine & Worship Committee, 118–19; hymnals, 119; International Consultation for English Translation, 120, 125n89; *Order of Worship for the Lord's Supper,* 119–20; *Rejoice and Sing,* 119, 124n84. *See also* CCEW; CUEW
University of Chicago, 66, 78n140, 94; Rockefeller Chapel, 127

University of Durham, 178; Palace Green Library, xii, 178

Vatican II, 89, 101, 111–12; John XXIII, 111. *See also* Dominican Monastery; Dunblane
• Vaughan Williams, Ralph, 9, 59, 99n3
Vine, Aubrey, 51, 72n17. *See also* Wednesbury

Wain, John, 24
Walz, L. Humphrey, 67, 76n109
Watson, J.R., 90, 101n65, 103n102. *See also* Carter
Wednesbury, 41, 47n6. *See also* Trinity Church (Wednesbury)
Welch, James W., 25. *See also* BBC
Wesley, Charles, 42
Wesley, John, 42–43. *See also* Wednesbury
West, William Moore S., 53. *See also* Davies, Horton
Westermeyer, Paul, 143, 167n180; *Let the People Sing*, 143
Westminster Abbey, xiv, 173–74
Westminster Choir College, xi, xiv, 123, 137, 139–64; academics, 137, 139, 141–42, 145, 161; accreditation, 145–46; Bicentennial, 143–44; Pi Kappa Lambda, 154.
Westminster Praise, 91, 139, 144, 146, 148, 167n70; Lorah, Theodore R., 140; Parker, Alice, 140; York, David S. 140. *See also* Westminster Choir College
Whale, J. S., 72n13
Whitley, Henry C., 93, 102n85. *See also* Augustine-Bristo
Willcocks, David, 83–84, 100n29; *Carols for Choirs*, 83–34; musical joke, 83–94, 100n35; "O come all ye faithful," 83
Williams, Charles, 16, 185; concept of co-inherence, 26, 37n44; *He Came Down from Heaven*, 27, 185. *See also* Scott, Anne
Wilson, John W., 59–62, 90, 113, 116, 125n84, 132, 140, 142, 151–53, 191; barrel organs, 153; "Come and Sing," 84, 143, 165n10, 167n92; *The Public School Hymnal*, 59–61, 75n65; *Sixteen Hymns of Today for Use as Simple Anthems*, 153; Wilson, Mary, 152, 157, 169n127
World Council of Churches, 86, 109; Amsterdam Assembly (1948), 86. *See also* Cantate Domino; Dunblane
World War II: air raid precautions, 24; bombing, 35n9, 36n11, 36n20; civilian evacuees, 22; draft and exemptions 25, 28; government conscription, 24–25, 35n4; lasting effects, 22; "O God, our help in ages past," 23; postwar, 49; September 1939, 22–23
Wren, Brian, 123n40, 125n84, 165n21, 175n16
Wright, Peter, 137, 166n55. *See also* Westminster Choir College
Wyton, Alec, 129, 144, 191. *See also* Ecumenical Praise

Young, Carlton R., v, xiii–xiv, 92, 102n76, 127, 144, 168n104, 178. *See also Ecumenical Praise*; Westminster Choir College; Westminster Abbey

Zimmerman, Heinz Werner, 151–52. *See also Ecumenical Praise*

About the Author

Nancy L. Graham is a hymnologist, lecturer, and church musician. She has a PhD and doctor of sacred music degree from the Graduate Theological Foundation, Foundation House in Oxford, as well as a master of music from Westminster Choir College. Dr. Graham's publications include *They Bear Acquaintance,* a study of African American spirituals and camp meeting songs; *African American Spirituals and the Revised Common Lectionary*; and "Spirituality By Heart" in the *Music and Spirituality Series*, June Boyce-Tillman, editor; as well as entries in *The Canterbury Dictionary of Hymnology*. Dr. Graham resides and works in Mobile, Alabama, and has served other congregations in Maryland, New Jersey, Tennessee, and Scotland.